As Happy as I Can Stand

3rd Edition of Hatching Charlie

Charles C McCormack

ISBN 13: 9781654589912

Library of Congress Control Number: XXXXX (If applicable)

LCCN Imprint Name: City and State (If applicable)

DEDICATION

To Ron Zuskin

An old friend from the moment we met

Table of Contents

Acknowledgments

What a journey this has been, far different from the one traveled when writing my first book: *Treating Borderline States in Marriage*. That was a lonely endeavor, given its subject matter, technical nature, and that I wrote it during a dark time in my life. *As Happy As I Can Stand*, the 3rd edition of *Hatching Charlie*, is also about the human condition, but this time with the layperson in mind and using my life as the illustrative example.

Some read part of the early manuscript and others the whole of it; some provided feedback while others did not. I thank them all: Even silence tells a story. Then there was The Golden Few, who resonated with the work and rose to meet it. My daughter, Keeley, a psychotherapist herself, responded enthusiastically and provided the cover photo of me carrying my grandson Cormac. Conversely, daughter Caitlin, an accountant, was unabashedly uninterested in psychological teachings but challenged me to create a good read.

There were Mark and Carol Ann, my youngest brother and sister-in-law, who bubbled with excitement. At one point, Mark, sensing my discouragement with some tepid feedback, wrote, "Don't let the bastards get you down. It's good. I never lost interest." In truth, there were no bastards, and it wasn't all that good, only the first of countless revisions to come in the ensuing three years. But intuitively, Mark and Carol Ann affirmed what I was trying to do when I needed it most.

Then there was my sister, Michelle, who, in a moving letter, made me aware of how my memories had rekindled her own and re-enveloped her in mourning. Writing from her memories as a fifteen-year-old girl, Michelle provided a glimpse into the human underbelly of my parents, resurrecting those times in a way that only a young girl can. Her letter inspired me to rewrite several chapters.

There was also Patricia Alfin, LCSW-C, a former supervisee, and a life-long supporter. She brought my first published work to the attention of the Washington School of Psychiatry, thereby altering the course of my life. Quickly reading the manuscript of Hatching Charlie, she saw where the book was going before it had arrived and offered valuable suggestions.

Jason Thomas, my African American son-in-law, brought greater racial sensitivity to my writing, while Wayne "Killer" Kirgel, who plays a significant role in the book, dove in and edited it without my having to ask.

During the writing of my first book, I leaned heavily on my friend, Ron Zuskin (The Z-Man): psychotherapist, raconteur, social work educator, musician, and gifted songwriter, Ron shines with intelligence and driving creativity. We first met professionally and immediately bonded. Over the ensuing thirty years, we have been through good times and bad, standing ever true by each other's side. With my first book, we created a synergy that powered me through the arduous process. But this time, Ron was ill and unavailable. I could only marvel at the miracle of how, when I lost one support, another, in Wayne Kirgel, arrived.

And then, Ron rose from his sickbed and with his usual generosity of time, talent, and grace, edited a later version of the manuscript, humoring, cajoling, and haranguing me to make the book more alive. Ron penned the title, *Hatching Charlie*.

Then there's Jane, my first wife of eighteen years and the mother of our three children. Initially, I refused to write about our relationship. Jane had suffered a psychiatric illness, and I feared rekindling those difficult times. Still, my editor, Margaret Diehl, insisted that the tale would be sorely lacking and depersonalized with my tepid handling of my relationship with Jane, rather than brought to life with a breath and heartbeat of its own. She pressed me to speak with Jane. Finally, after much wrestling with myself, I wrote the chapter on our relationship and then emailed it to Jane along with a message confessing my unease and giving her complete veto power over that section of the manuscript. After several days of skittering angst and nights of troubled sleep, Jane responded that not only did she approve of the chapter, but asked that I not change a word, feeling that it was "beautifully written" and that "Your care for me shines through." I had never anticipated such a bountifully affirming outcome, and my heart swelled with gratitude as tears coursed my face.

Then there is Janet, my third wife, who provided enormous amounts of uninterrupted time for writing and gave unalloyed honest feedback on a moment's notice.

And finally, there is a man I have never met by the name of Frank Parker. A fellow author on Goodreads who reviewed As Happy As I Can Stand and offered a valuable critique. I asked for suggestions and he graciously offered some on how to improve the read. His insights so resonated with me that I immediately incorporated his suggestions into the book.

What do you call such people? Oh. I know. Friends. Not to say that others are not, for they are, but these were The Golden Few.

Love and kisses to them all,

Charlie.

Prologue

*A*s I stand here, nearer life's end than its beginning, looking out upon the Bush River, bejeweled in the rust, copper, and gold leaves of fall, I wonder what you will think, for this book reveals the soft underbelly of this writer, often in ways that are less than appealing. But, if I am to stay true to my goal, writing honestly about the human condition with myself as the illustrative example, I must not only talk the talk but walk the walk, from shadow worlds to sunlit landscapes.

My daughter Keeley, my son Chandler, and my patients inspired this book. Years ago, Keeley gave me a book of questions for grandparents to express who they were for posterity. The idea appealed, the structure did not. Separately, my son, Chandler, asked what I thought it [life] was about. His work and home life were going well, and he wondered, "Is this it?" On the spur of the moment, I answered: "It's about the pursuit of happiness."

Chandler didn't seem convinced. My reflexive answer was not well-articulated nor compelling. Nonetheless, it was true. From that moment on, I felt a growing need to build the case and, as a psychotherapist, to provide some ideas about the often-tortuous path of getting from *here* to *there*.

Finally, through the years, many of my patients have suggested I write a book of the stories I tell in my practice of psychotherapy, which they found helpful in enhancing their understanding of themselves.

Hatching Charlie is written in response to the following two challenges: "Who am I?" and "What's it all about?" However, along the way, the writing became something more. As I described my journey from the Gathering Darkness of my early years, through the directionless acting out of my teen years, onto beginning to find myself in my twenties, to arrive at a state of partial fulfillment today, I recognized that although my story was unique to me, the struggle was not. Subsequently, my goal evolved: Now, I wanted to write on the shaping power of the difficult times in our lives and the importance of confronting their impact upon us if we wish to pursue a meaningful life and the fulfillment it provides.

Such a story requires I tell-all, exposing the uncertainty, shame, low self-esteem, egotism, mistakes made and then repeated, the lessons learned and then forgotten, the failures and successes, the joys and heartbreaks, and the wisdom and folly that have informed my life. Of special significance is the importance of striving for integrity in all that we do, of confronting ourselves in the mirror as objectively as possible, and of reconciling with *all* our thoughts, feelings, and behaviors—the *good,* the *bad,* and especially the *ugly.*

Within the word integrity lies the word integrate, not the word eliminate. To develop a personally meaningful life, we must resist the tendency to deny our unsavory aspects, rather bringing them into dialogue with the other parts of ourselves in service of self-understanding and, with that, compassion.

Reconciling with ourselves is not easy. We naturally recoil from psychological pain and emotional discomfort. However, the price of avoidance is high for the psyche is not a surgical instrument but a nuclear one; it does not curtail single undesired thoughts or feelings but rather the capacity to think and feel in general. When we deny our ugliest feelings and behaviors, we limit our capacity to feel and consequently hinder our ability to feel, to drink in the colors of a beautiful sunset or the exquisite joy of a tender kiss. The curse and the beauty of psychological health are that it entails feeling *more of everything,* not less.

Yet, the cost of denial does not end here. The edited memories, although pushed from consciousness, are not gone. Instead, what begins as gathering darkness in the creosote recesses of our minds, becomes an ever-growing disquiet as we relegate more and more to their number. Here, the darkness festers, feeding upon itself, growing ever more virulent, increasingly pushing against the walls of denial. Inevitably, the banished begins leaking out, in disguised and twisted form, such as in inexplicable anger, hostility, depression, anxiety, dread, emptiness, isolation, and somatic complaints. These symptoms, we carry with us wherever we go, at first in a general unease, but then-growing into alarm bells tolling in the night.

Feeling *all* our feelings and thinking *all* our thoughts is not always a happy business. Life and relationships *can* be scary and embarrassing and confronting our less than socially acceptable thoughts and behaviors does not always support the semblance of a neat and tidy life. But, grappling with our issues does offer the opportunity to become more fully self-and-other accepting human beings. Indeed, regardless of how tarnished we humans can be, I would propose that the sometimes-tortuous path of feeling the good and the bad of our imperfect state *is* the path to a happier and meaningful life.

Awareness of the dark side of the human condition is ancient. In Cherokee lore, the Chieftain tells his grandson the story of the two wolves. He says, "Within me, two wolves are constantly at war with one another. One, the Evil Wolf, feeds on anger, envy, sorrow, greed, arrogance, self-pity, resentment, inferiority, false pride, superiority, and ego. The other, the Good Wolf, feeds on joy, love, serenity, humility, kindness, benevolence, empathy, generosity, truth, compassion, and faith." Tenderly looking into his grandson's eyes, the Chieftain says, "You have these two wolves in you as well. Everyone has them." The grandson, face furrowed by thought, considers this, then, eyes wide in suspense, asks his grandfather, "Which one wins?" Laughing, the grandfather leans forward and whispers, "Whichever one you feed."

Cherokee Indians are not alone in speaking of the dark side of man. The psychoanalyst, Carl Jung, called it the Shadow and warned that one either digests his shadow or is digested by it. Melanie Klein, who pioneered the analysis of children, asserted that the feelings of love, hate, jealousy, greed, lust, and envy are all part of being human and warns that denying rather than understanding these feelings is self-destructive. Freud spoke of the Id, as that part of the psyche that houses primitive impulses and posited that it is these that fuel creativity, as well as destructiveness, and observed that these impulses must be integrated to live successfully in society. The Scottish psychoanalyst, Fairbairn, posited the existence of a dynamic unconscious including an anti-libidinal ego, housing all repressed negative experiences in relation to our others, and a libidinal-ego, holding the unfulfilled primitive and intense yearnings of childhood. Peopled by rejecting relationships, the anti-libidinal ego causes us to fear our dependency needs, such as the need for love and attachment, as Trojan horses trying to penetrate our defenses. He advised bringing the contents of both egos to consciousness where they could be thought about and put into perspective. One everyday example of this dynamic in play would be the fear of asking someone out on a date for fear of rejection.

Whatever the theory, the point is that from the earliest age, while the human brain is in the nascence of its development, there is a Gathering Darkness, a distillation of painful experiences, from which none of us are free. Whatever we choose to call it, the Evil Wolf, the Shadow, the Id, the anti-libidinal ego, or even original sin, it is real, and, if we deny its existence, it only clamors ever more loudly to be heard.

It is important to realize that these dire predictions prove true no matter how successful one is in the external world. We all know or have heard of many famous and wildly successful people who have succumbed to depression, drug addiction, or suicide, thus confirming that fame nor fortune protects no man from his demons: The Evil Wolf ignored bites ever harder.

William Faulkner said, "The past is never dead. It's not even past," thereby referencing a characteristic of the unconscious: Its timelessness. In the unconscious, there is no past or future, just what I call *The Interminable Now*. Fortunately, in consciousness, there is awareness of the past, the present, and the future. Thus, in bringing our conflicts to awareness, we can reconcile with that which troubles us and put it behind, never forgotten but shorn of the tendency to cling like English Ivy strangles a tree.

None of this is to suggest that intellectual insight is the be-all and end-all: thinking and feeling must inter-relate; true understanding is a cogni-affective experience. Also, to fully enjoy our successes in life, other strategies must be employed for the brain, a habituated organ, is both friend and foe. Foundationally oriented toward survival, it is constantly on the alert for *the bad thing happening* and continually reverts to ways of perceiving and relating that undermine happiness. In other words, its embedded concerns with survival support feeding the Evil Wolf at the expense of the Good one. Yoga, meditation, dance, martial arts, and mindfulness are all useful techniques in helping to break this habit or at least soften it. By disrupting the feeding of the Bad Wolf and consciously choosing to feed the Good one, we impede the tendency of the shadow world to overshadow the present and foreshadow the future. Much more will be said of this later.

The title, *Hatching Charlie*, represents my ongoing struggle toward a meaningful and happy life. It recounts my attempts to reconcile with the dark side of my being. In so doing, I ever so slowly break out of the self-limiting *lessons* of my childhood that, like a Russian Nesting Doll, only limited who I could become.

Everyone has an interesting story to tell but often don't realize it. Here, the story of the three fish helps to illustrate. Two fish are swimming one way as a third swims the other. In passing, the single fish calls out, "Hello. How's the water today?" Once past, the pair of fish look at each other, and one puts his puzzlement to words, "What's water?"

I've spent a lifetime trying to discover the unseen waters of my life and helping others do the same with theirs. Interestingly, research suggests that the ability to remember our history effects our capacity to imagine alternative futures. Without history, we do not know where we come from or where we are going. In this directionless state, our yesterdays become our tomorrows, creating a world in which one can only be born, live, and die.

Fortunately, once we begin remembering, other memories tumble out, deepening our understanding of how we came to be the way we are and offering the choice of changing our lives or not. The decision is ours, and only ours, to make. The important thing is to symbolize our experience, to represent it in some way — such as words, dance, or art— for thinking is a symbolic process, and without thought, we are deaf and dumb to ourselves.

Please be aware that I do not mean to suggest that biology does not play a part in our capacity for happiness. Many people suffer from biologically driven mental disorders, including anxiety and depression. Nonetheless, while I have seen many people become stabilized with the help of medication or psychotherapy, I have never seen anyone develop a personally fulfilling life who did not assume responsibility for it.

Finally, please understand that this is my version of events. Perception and memory are notoriously malleable. Parts of my story will meet with agreement from those who have lived alongside me while other parts will not. I have no qualms with this. We can each have our *truth,* as long as we leave room for the truths of others. Play along with me. You are the therapist, and I am the patient. This book is the case presentation. With mischievous glee, I ask, "What could be better than that?

Part 1

A GATHERING DARKNESS

The psyche is like a tree trunk, early experience forever imprinted on the tender flesh of the inner rings. It is the inner rings upon which all else rests, confirming William Wordsworth's assertion that "The child is the father of the man." Amazing—ssuch a critical time of life, yet both before and beyond words.

Chapter 1

The Family Vortex: Violence and Belittling

I grew up in two families: One when my father, John McCormack, an artillery officer of Irish descent, was there, the other when he was not. The family of my father's teachings was tyrannical and sadistic, interspersed with hypo-manic moments of humor, fueled by the tensions and anxieties that had preceded it.

Born to a prominent Memphis, Tennessee family, boasting black servants and field hands, and distinguished history of military service, Dad was of devoutly Southern traditions and beliefs. His father was an aid to General Black Jack Pershing and his mother, a socialite. With this ballyhooed heritage, Dad touted military values of honor and bravery, yet his day-to-day actions were those of a spoiled child.

What Dad valued were not the human capacities to think or feel, to be curious, or to question, but the machine-like ability to "Do what you're told, when you're told." Any questioning was equated with "back talk" and easily earned a slap.

Dad fancied himself another General Douglas MacArthur. He loved to line us kids up like soldiers at parade rest, hands clasped behind our backs whenever he was upset with something we had or had not done and harangue us with our inadequacies. But, in that he was a terrible stutterer, it was difficult for him to pull the whole thing off: Afterall, it is hard to sell a commanding role when strangling on your words.

His lectures were interminable; their approaching end usually heralded with slaps to the face. I welcomed these for the slaps signaled a nearing of the end of his rantings and of the ghastly experience of having to watch his face contort and turn red as he strained mightily to push his words up his throat and out his mouth. Occasionally, unable to bear the gruesome sight a second longer, I would blurt out a word upon which he was foundering. All was well if I guessed correctly, but if wrong, my unfortunate impulse to speak only added to the growing *volcano* of his frustrations and the feeling of chaos and *d—d—d—dread*. The one thing I learned: If there is no avoiding a slap, get it over with.

Dad idolized courage in fighting, telling heroic tales of his ancestors and of his battlefield accomplishments that rivaled the Legends of Daniel Boone, Jim Bowie, and Davy Crockett. Sometimes, he would tell a story of me as a child, swarmed in a scrum of kids, to rise pugnaciously undaunted out of the melee. I do not recall this event, but the story drove home the point: If you wanted Dad to be proud of you, never give up.

Such an attitude sounds admirable, but it is problematic. Sometimes it is wise to give up, particularly if you, like me, are *not* a good fighter. I can honestly say I have never won a fight. I have, however, taken a severe beating due to my continuing to get back up until my opponent quit for fear of killing me.

I was not alone in this unintelligent relationship to physical pain and violence. Mark, my youngest brother, once ran for 250 yards in a high school football game. Dad touted this achievement, so much so that one might have thought it was his own. Curiously, what he never mentioned, indeed, it seemed to reside outside his notice, was that the pounding Mark took permanently damaged the nerves in his face—an injury that forever impaired his ability to smile. From that time on, Mark's smile looked more like a sneer, a cool sneer, but a sneer, nonetheless.

The cloud of my father's sadism also cast itself upon my brother, Ed, who was kicked off the high school football team for battering the coach's face with his helmet. The coach made the mistake of unknowingly impersonating Dad. During practice, Ed had been pushing a blocking sled in the Virginia heat far beyond when the whistle had blown; he had not heard it. The coach then mocked him, "Great, Ed! You kept pushing that sled for two minutes after the exercise was over. Way to go!" He was not laughing after that.

Perhaps the worst thing about my dad was that he had a callous over his heart—a large callous, a small heart. Once, he shoved puppies into a bag and tossed them into the lake, proudly proclaiming that he was preserving the bloodlines of his hunting dogs. His lack of empathy for them was mind-bending. How hard is it to imagine the pain and terror those puppies felt, stuffed into the claustrophobic confines of a burlap bag, becoming weightless as they were tossed into the air, then scrabbling to escape, as they splashed into the lake, and cold water flooded in to steal their breath away.

Another of my father's dubious achievements occurred when we had been hunting. More accurately, Dad had been hunting, the kids along, as was his need, only to keep him company. Nestled in bushes from morning to early afternoon as the pulsating heat of the day reached full stride, Dad mercifully announced he was ready to leave. Parched and pummeled by the sun, that is all I wanted. So, I groaned aloud when, at the last minute, Dad spotted a hawk silhouetted majestically on a treetop on a distant hill. Having found a distraction, particularly a glorious one he could destroy, he had to take the shot. I hated him for that. My heart opened to the hawk, who, though fully present to its moment, was oblivious to the coming danger. I understood what it did not: This was his last moment. I railed in my mind, *What's the point?* But I had no say.

The report of the rifle startled me. But surprisingly, the hawk remained perched upon its tree and then to my delight, took flight. A happy yelp, charged with the joy of the bird's escape and my father's loss of his ill-imagined glory, escaped my lips, when, shockingly, the bird crumpled in on itself, and fell to the ground, like an old work glove. That is when I realized; the bird had not taken flight. It had been lifted in the air by a bullet that had taken a couple of heartbeats longer than I had expected to traverse its course. Bile filled my heart where joy had been, and a mist of melancholy settled upon me.

The truly appalling aspect of this was that Dad had inflicted the hawk's death as easily as the snapping of one's fingers and with as little concern. The bald-faced shamelessness of this act was only compounded when Dad cautioned us not to say a thing, explaining that hawks were on the protected species list. There was no suggestion of moral or ethical conflict; the only concern was with getting caught.

A voracious reader, Dad knew a lot about a lot. He headed his division at the Foreign Science and Technology Center in Charlottesville, VA, an acknowledged expert on Russian armaments. Unfortunately, his was the classic case of having a head without a heart. Absent empathy and compassion, Dad was unusually short on wisdom.

I do not want to suggest that it was always unhappy when Dad was around. When he was in a good mood, we all breathed more easily and rode the coattails of his gregariousness. I always looked forward to Sundays, when he traditionally cooked enormous breakfasts, suffusing the house with aromas of corn beef hash, grits, fried eggs, bacon, and French toast.

And he could surprise me, unexpectedly exhibiting talents I had not known he possessed. One sunny afternoon, he took us to a farm. In the yard was a stallion, a prancing beast who hummed with raw power as corded muscles moved like writhing snakes beneath his glistening black coat. Alongside him, Dad, dressed in riding garb, riding crop in hand, dark hair slicked back from his high forehead, and spit-shined riding boots reflecting the sun cut a dashing figure. I stood in frightened awe as Dad mounted the beast. To my amazement, Dad, unperturbed, controlled the horse with ease, then, without a word, spurred the stallion into a breakaway run, rider and horse melding together as they disappeared across the meadow. Until that moment, I had no idea he could ride.

What made it all so confusing was that despite Dad's intellect, he was obtuse when it came to anything requiring emotional sensitivity. My sister, Michelle, tells two stories dating from when she was fifteen and the only child still at home. In the first story, Dad called her onto the back patio. Michelle knew something was up for Dad did not usually seek time with her. Oddly, he started talking about the University of Virginia basketball team, then about the upcoming ACC Championships. Michelle writes, "God bless him, but even at fifteen, I knew he was floundering. He finally blurted out that Mom had cancer, and her chances of survival were less than ten percent. He went on to note that the UVA basketball team's chances of winning the ACC tournament were also less than ten percent. From this, I worked out that UVA had to win the ACC championship…oh, and Mom had to survive."

Michelle's second story tells of the day he took her to the doctor and asked questions about nodules, breasts, menstrual cycles, and so on. I could readily imagine this; it would be the approach he would take interviewing a veterinarian about the best practices for maintaining the health of a bitch dog. Understandably, Michelle found the whole experience humiliating and confronted Dad. She writes, "He just didn't get it. To him, it was just information, and I was *too sensitive*."

Michelle loved Dad. To be sure, all the kids did, each in their way. For my part, I felt that if love was slow in being returned, it must be because of me. Years later, I wanted to test my ability to

make him happy. I bought him a special Christmas gift that year
that outshone the one I had gotten mother—a turning upside
down of the usual course of things. I bought him a gold golf tee,
a golf hat bedecked with ornaments sure to garner humorous
attention on the links, and a new pair of golf shoes. I was not
with them that Christmas, but Mother phoned, laughing, saying,
"Charlie, you've created a monster. Your dad is walking around
the house in his golf shoes." I was pleased to have been able to
make him happy. However, he never acknowledged the gift or
thanked me. I would later come to understand that generosity of
spirit and the capacity for heartfelt gratitude are two sides of the
same coin, a coin Dad did not possess.

Sadly, at the final tally, my father, for me, was more a model
of what not to be as a man or as a father. Near the end of his
days, I remember him at the beach on the Delaware Bay.
Suffering dementia, he sat hunched on the screened-in porch,
hollowed out and shorn by age, stick-like legs protruding from
his swimsuit like toothpicks from a withered olive. Facing the
beauty of the bay, watching freighters making their way across,
he repeatedly intoned in an awe-filled voice, "Is this for real? Is
this for real?" In an aside, Mark expressed how sad it was that
Dad had come to this. Perplexed, I asked, "What are you talking
about? Dad is a perfect example of addition by subtraction. He's
a much nicer guy now than he's ever been." Mark considered this
then, with that sneer of a smile, said, "You know what? You're
right!"

Happily, when Dad was not around, we were in the family of Madeleine Turgeon McCormack, later nicknamed Mutti (German for mother). Mutti created a warm and happy environment. We were secure in her love and the knowledge she would never do us harm—or so I believed. In Mutti's family, it was not all about her, it was about the kids, and I transformed from a worthless cog to the valued second born of four brothers and one sister: Jacques, me, Edward, Mark, and Michelle.

Mom was French Canadian, born and raised in Quebec to a wealthy lumber family; English was her second language. Her cousin, Roger Lemelin, authored four novels, and wrote, and produced a TV series in Canada. He won the Legion d'Honneur for his contribution to Canadian culture, and a Prix David for a book entitled *The Town Below,* partly based on his observations of my mother's family, who lived in the celebrated Upper Town.

Mother's brother, George, a Kennedy-esque figure, was a millionaire. He founded, then sold, a frozen meat pie company, and spent his time skiing or sailing in the South of France.

But not all had been well in Mutti's family: One brother accidentally hung himself at the age of six while playing cowboys and Indians. Her mother, Matilde, was repeatedly hospitalized for depression, and her father, a lumber baron, and an alcoholic went bankrupt and missed her wedding due to a hangover. The last child living at home, Guy, was taken away by social services.

Despite or perhaps because of all this, Mom was an incredibly strong and determined individual. In her middle years, when she first contracted cancer, it was only with Michelle that she would allow a glimpse of her despair. Suffering third-degree burns from the primitive radiation treatment of that era, Mutti, would occasionally break down, weep bitterly, and lash out in anger. But, most often, she sat stoically, gin and tonic, and a cigarette in hand, her face obscured by the coiling smoke, as her buttermilk skin, hideously red and swollen, peeled.

Mutti was strong. She had to be, raising five kids, while my father was away during the Korean War, on maneuvers, or transferred from one posting to the next. As he went ahead, she followed behind, tasked with closing the old house and transitioning to the new. Her job was homemaker, and my father's was to be an army officer. He never helped around the house and was, in fact, more burden than blessing, repeatedly calling my mother or one of the kids to wait on him in petty ways. I still hear his voice grating on my ears, "Charlie! Bring me a martini," or, "Charlie! Come here. Turn on that light," the lamp infuriatingly well within his reach. The curious thing was that he thought nothing of this kingly behavior, nor did Mutti. To them, his maddening sense of entitlement was the most natural thing in the world. In this, they were like pieces of broken glass fitting perfectly together.

Mom and Dad met at a gala at the Belgium embassy, where she worked. He tells the story of seeing her coming down a staircase and telling his mother, "That's the woman I'm going to marry." Their early marriage seemed satisfactory, but as the years passed and the children grew older, so did the parental conflict. Sometimes, Mutti, out of a mother's love and to divert him from an excessively abusive episode with the kids, would speak to him in castrating tones, seeming to hunger for a fight, egging him on far beyond cautions call. Then, she would be the one to receive the hit and still refuse to back away, playing her part in the ever repeating cycle of abuse. Although the lyrics might change, the strident melody remained the same.

As upsetting and divisive as this behavior was, there was another facet of my parents that joined them together: They loved to entertain. Christmas and Thanksgiving were always sparkling events, the house alive with well-dressed people and the buzz of animated conversation, as wine-filled crystal glasses splashed their ruby light, and music frolicked out of the top-of-the-line sound system—all serving to create the song of people having a genuinely good time.

Upon such occasions, I felt pride in my parents as each moved around the room with grace and refinement. Dad, prominent forehead, trim build, and brown eyes flecked with gold that glimmered with his love of social interaction and Mutti, willowy, with buttermilk skin, ears, and neck adorned with pearls highlighting her sapphire eyes, captivating everyone with the warmth of her attention, and the sound of her voice in its honey-dipped French accent.

My mother and I shared a mental play space. At age eleven, sitting in the kitchen of our apartment in Heidelberg, Germany, I told her that I wanted to be either a farmer or a priest. She laughed, blue eyes twinkling, asking what those different callings might have in common. I had no answer, but it does strike me as oddly foretelling, given that I have spent much of my life hearing peoples' confessions in the privileged relationship of psychotherapy while working to help them grow.

A devout Catholic, Mutti prayed nightly, dressed in her cotton nightgown, hands clasped together, head bent as she knelt beside her bed. Seeing her like this, through the open door to her bedroom, always reminded me of a child. Indeed, this ritual dated from her earliest days and ran like a beaded thread throughout her life.

Determined and imaginative, Mutti possessed a vision of the future my father lacked. As they neared retirement, it was she who set about buying a property at Lake Monticello, a gated community outside of Charlottesville. There, they built a split-level gray aluminum sided home that featured an open floor plan, a fireplace in the wood-ceilinged A-framed great room, and a large deck upon which to sit and observe the tranquil beauty of the tree-lined lake.

Mom and Dad were opposites. Mutti was genuinely interested in people and concerned about them. While Dad focused on himself, she focused on others. Many years later, as she was losing her second fight with cancer, she was still all about others, especially Dad. Fighting nausea and fatigue, she ramrodded a move to Aiken, SC, so that Dad would be near Mark and Carol Ann, devout people themselves, when she passed.

Yet, despite all the good things about Mutti, there are two thorns of memory that have stuck with me over the decades. In the first, I am age eight, playing in the honeysuckle-scented backyard in Montgomery, Alabama, when I feel an unexpected urge to connect with her. I clamber up the worn wooden steps to the kitchen, enter through the screen door, and find her cooking at the stove, her back to me. I reach out to touch the hem of her skirt when apprehension stills my hand. Unaccountably, I feel vulnerable and fearful of rebuke. Hesitating, I struggle to understand these feelings, pulled in one direction by desire, and pushed the other by unease. I break the mounting tension of my impasse by silently leaving the kitchen; Mutti never knew I was there.

This experience suggests that I felt unsafe to be vulnerable or needy with my mother, but I could not put the why of it into words. I had cried or shared troubled feelings with her in the past and been comforted. But this was different. I was feeling fine, just wanting tenderness for tenderness' sake, and yet fearing rejection. I think I sensed a distinction between my mother's being responsive to my anguish versus being sensitive to me. I feared a rebuke if I diverted her from her chores without a pressing need, an outcome I was unwilling to risk, given the tenderness of my feelings.

In turning away from my mother, I fed the Evil Wolf, succumbing to my fear-ridden imaginings rather than allowing my mother to respond in whatever way she would. In so doing, I remained safe but forfeited any possibility of fulfillment. In such ways, I was to learn that the pursuit of happiness and fulfillment takes courage, not because it is risk-free, but because it is not. Years later, as I realized my mother couldn't relate to my feeling of profound loneliness during my separation and divorce from Jane, and after I had learned more about her painful upbringing (of which she never spoke), I suspected that the apprehension I felt all those years earlier had not been entirely misplaced. I wondered what lessons she had drawn from her troubled childhood to protect herself that interfered with her ability to relate to my loneliness.

However, my apprehension may have also been fueled by the nature of the second memory, which demonstrates a characteristic of my mother that contributed to both her enormous strength and her greatest weakness: her tendency to compartmentalize. In her early years, once she held a belief, it was unshakeable, evidenced not only in the way she loved but also in the way she hated.

Compartmentalizing was especially evident in her relationship to my stepbrother, Cris, five years older than me and the product of my father's first marriage. As the story goes, my dad's first wife was a party girl and unfaithful, leading to divorce. She rejected custody of Cris, so my paternal grandmother, Dee, stepped in to raise him.

Cris was a *Mad Magazine* (a comic book of the day) caricature of my father. Not only did he try to emulate Dad's behavior, but he also looked like him, albeit in a strangely asymmetrical way: Skinny as a blade of grass, bird-eyed, shrunken-chested, and sporting a large head with a receding hairline mirroring Dad's own.

Mother hated him; there is no more gentle way to put it. Perhaps some of it had to do with his being from Dad's previous marriage, but also, as a child, he went around the neighborhood begging for food, complaining of hunger, and was constantly misbehaving in attention-seeking ways to the embarrassment of my mother.

The thorn of memory I wish to speak of occurred on another sunny summer day in Montgomery, Alabama. A kiddy pool was in the backyard, directly under a tree. Cris, thirteen, bare-chested, ribs sticking out, and shorts hanging limply from his non-existent hips had stepped in the pool and muddied the water. Mutti noticed from the kitchen window and shouted furiously, "Get out of the pool and stay out. You are not a child." Driven by his need for attention, Cris then opted to climb the tree and literally out on a limb. At first, it was a slapstick moment as the law of gravity showed no mercy, and the limb began to bend, tilting Cris upside-down. Eyes bulging, head dangling ludicrously below his legs, and just above the surface of the pool, we were all laughing when, with a sharp crack, the branch broke, and it and Cris fell as one into the pool.

Drawn by the electric excitement of our laughter, Mutti looked out the window. She was apoplectic. When Dad arrived home, he received the full brunt of her wrath as she confronted him with the misdeeds of *his* son. She was unhinged and seeking blood. To appease her, Dad took Cris upstairs to the master bedroom with its four-poster bed. I snuck along behind to see what was happening.

Peeking through the door, I watched Dad order Cris to strip to his underwear and grip the bedpost on high, thus fully exposing his bony torso. Ominously, Dad took off his belt and, without saying a word, began whipping Cris from head to toe, striping his body with the belt again and again. Aside from Dad grunting with effort, there was no sound other than the whooshing of the belt and the sickening slap of leather against flesh.

Cris, ever desperate for my father's approval, strove to be the brave soldier. He refused to cry out as eyes squeezed shut, face knotted in agony, silent tears fell upon his concave chest. Unfortunately, Dad's approval was always in short supply. But for Cris, it was worse: The rest of us had Mutti; Cris, confused, proud, mismatched boy, had no one. That was the unseen water of his life.

In the following years, Cris was exiled from our house and our lives. He turned to drugs and worked a variety of jobs, finally settling into road work. Cris married, had two kids, and divorced. Occasionally, he would visit my dad, once showing up on a motorcycle, wearing gang colors, with a friend named Spike. In the driveway, he brandished a long-barreled 45-caliber revolver that he extolled as a collector's piece. My mother hissed, "John, get rid of him!" Dad, with only ice in his voice, told Cris never to return.

In the years to follow, perhaps sensing my empathy, Cris would visit me upon rare occasions. But these meetings were always awkward, as he continued to be a parody of my father, engaging in self-aggrandizing stories and acts of social inappropriateness that only made me sorry to be with him. But I never told him to go away, and I never told him not to return. I just could not.

Cris died, like our paternal grandfather, in his early fifties from a heart attack. I had not seen him for years. His ex-wife (whom I met only once) and children have no relationship with the rest of the McCormack clan.

As you can see, Mother had her low-light reels. By all accounts, a religious and loving woman, she was still the one who triggered this merciless assault upon Cris; Dad had only done her dirty work. I took in the brutality of that beating and all that led up to it: Cris's desperate need of attention, the unforeseen breaking of the tree limb, my mother's murderous rage, and my father's subservient going along with it. But most importantly, I took the lesson that when such behaviors are perpetuated by those who are supposed to keep us safe, no one is ever safe.

These experiences taught me that we are all flawed and that the most dangerous of people are those who refuse to see the flaws within themselves. Such denial hinders emotional growth and promotes the tendency to externalize onto others the very characteristics that we are blind to within ourselves. In this way, denial inhibits the development of compassion and empathy for to the extent we reject the feelings within ourselves, we are unable to identify with those feelings in others.

An emotionally chaotic and violent environment promotes feelings of insecurity, mistrust, shame, and doubt. Maybe this explains why I developed the self-soothing behaviors of headbanging and nail-biting as a child. Of course, when you are living through it, you are not aware of the causes of such things, or that there is even any such thing as a cause. To the child, everything within the family is "normal"—just the way things are, becoming the unseen water of our lives.

As the saying goes, "When you grow up in a blue world, you don't know the color blue." I can tell you with certainty that when you grow up in gathering darkness, there are few colors at all.

Chapter 2

The Cultural Vortex: Prejudice and Discrimination

My memory is far from a continuous thing. It does not lend itself to the weaving of a seamless story with a beginning, middle, and end. Rather, it consists of snippets of my life that arise unbidden, like shards of glass, and are often equally cutting.

The memory that I am about to relate is of that nature, speaking to an abiding potential for violence that mirrored in the outside world what was occurring within my family. The outside threat, under the glaze of social veneer, was often less visible but served to intimidate anyone unwise enough to think about stepping outside the cultural norm. This threat is even more potent because a code of silence usually surrounds it, and though felt, its source because of its ubiquity, is difficult to find.

I was eight years old on that summer day in 1957, laboring under the searing heat of the Alabama sun, as I trudged along a dirt track through what was known then as the colored shantytown. The shacks, ramshackle hovels of gray, aging wood, buckling tin roofs and tilting wooden porches, seemed ready to be swept away in the first crackling winds of a thunderstorm. Though only a few hundred yards from my home, on the other side of the highway, the shantytown was a world apart.

Curiosity had brought me here, like a tourist visiting the spellbinding unfamiliarity of a Third World country. As I moved deeper into this new world, mine receded. Thus, untethered, I slogged along breathing in the reddish clay dust from the path that coated my mouth as the aroma of fried chicken and collard greens, cooking in the shadow-worlds beyond torn screen doors, ignited hunger in my belly. Muscular black men in sweat-stained wifebeater t-shirts talked together in twos and threes as the discordant sounds of angry shouts and laughter punctuated the soupy afternoon air. Strangely, these men stared coldly at me or turned away—none spoke or otherwise acknowledged my presence.

I did not understand the undercurrent of hostility. Had I done something? Or was I misreading the situation? Driven by curiosity, I returned several days later, thinking *Maybe I got it wrong*; inexplicably, it felt important to know. Now, like seeing a movie or reading a book for the second time, I was able to discern more and realized the hostility was real, and underneath it lurked fear. I did not know what was going on. All I knew was that I somehow represented a danger to these people, and never intruded into their world again.

The first time I went to the movies in Montgomery, I noticed that the "coloreds" got to sit on the balcony while the whites sat on the ground floor. I was annoyed: *Why do they get the best seats?* To me, sitting up high was a lot more fun than sitting below. Only dimly did I recognize that the whites and coloreds sat apart; something I later learned was called "segregation."

After the movie, I looked for a water fountain, spotted one, and walked toward it, until warned off by a sign that said: "Colored." I was puzzled; I did not know why the sign was there. The realization started slowly, then arrived—only black people could use this fountain. I was indignant; it was unfair. I was thirsty. Why were they the only ones allowed to drink from the fountain?

Baffled, I looked around and spotted a second fountain, this one boasting a sign that read, "Whites." I realized I was being told to drink from this fountain. Thirst sated, I looked back and forth between the fountains, trying to discern the difference. The fountain labeled "Whites" was newer and cleaner. The one labeled "Colored" was old and rusty. That was when it struck me: it was not the whites getting the short end of the deal, it was the blacks.

Innately, I felt the wrongness of this situation. *Why should people of color have to drink from the rusty fountain while the whites enjoy a clean one? Why should anyone be able to tell anyone else where they can drink water?* The injustice of it roiled through me, giving birth to a defiant impulse to drink out of the fountain reserved for Coloreds as if doing so would alchemically change wrong to right.

As I took a step toward the fountain reserved for Coloreds, I considered for the first-time the clusters of white teenage boys scattered around the lobby of the theater and out on the sidewalk. All looked like James Dean wannabes: packs of cigarettes rolled up in the sleeves of their tight-fitting t-shirts as lit cigarettes drooped loosely from their mouths. They were a loud bunch, radiating sinewy strength and aggression, like roosters displaying in a barnyard. That is when a glistening fear coiled within me. I knew, without knowing how I knew, that a white boy drinking out of the Colored fountain would bring dangerous attention. I imagined being yelled at or beaten up, the angry challenges so loud in my mind that they could have been shouted, "Who the fuck are you? What the fuck are you doing?"

Within seconds, my urge to drink from the Colored fountain, to change wrong to right, evaporated as fear overwhelmed courage, and shame grew in place of pride. Just that quickly, I was wrenched from my strong, upholder-of-the-right feeling to a craven, slinking, cowardly me. This transformation, so pitilessly wrung from within, occurred without a word spoken or anyone noticing a thing.

Troubled, that afternoon, I asked my parents about the two fountains. To my surprise, they were not discomfited by their existence, but by my questioning the *rightness* of it. As they groped for a response, I sensed fear stemming from my mother, then shockingly realized her concern was for me. It was as if she were saying, "Harm will come to you if you persist in questioning such things?" At this point, Dad donned his mantle as the head-of-the-family and essentially explained there was a caste system, and that "Negroes" were lesser than whites. That they were lazy and untrustworthy and not only needed but wanted someone to tell them what to do. With this pronouncement, my parents rested easier, having satisfied themselves, if not me.

Over the ensuing months, whenever I went to the movies, I glanced at the fountains and chided myself for continuing to be bothered by the situation. I would tell myself, *Accept that they just are, they always have been and always will be. By what arrogance do I, a child, dare question their rightness? What is wrong with me that I cannot accept what everyone else, older, far more experienced and wiser than me, considers self-evident?*

Several months later, I made a far-reaching discovery. While bending down for a sip of water from the "Whites" fountain, I sensed something different. I looked around, but the two fountains were still there, and the "coloreds" still sat in the balcony. As I brooded on this, I had an epiphany: What had changed was not something outside of me but something within. I was having a visceral reaction, not only to the Colored water fountain as dirty and repellent but now to the blacks themselves. Where once their bigger lips and wider noses had merely appeared different, they now leaned toward repulsive.

With this realization, I felt diminished, changed materially in a way that had been outside my awareness and outside of conscious choosing. Then, I understood: *Oh! This is how you catch racism. It creeps up on you through hidden threats and explicit statements.*

Later in life, I would learn that the child's boundaries between self and others are not well formed, leaving the child susceptible to the implicit and explicit messages from the world around him. In this way, prejudice arises from sensing and feeling, not from reason. What passes for thinking follows unhurriedly behind, solely in service of self-justification.

For me, the ever-present peer and cultural pressure to fit in, combined with my parents' endorsement, was eroding my allegiance to the disquieting weight of the wrongness of the situation. The acquisition of racist feelings was moving me from the isolation and disquiet of my solitary position in southern society toward the rewards of belonging with the group. I only wondered, *Why aren't I happy about it?*

In looking back, I may not have recognized or questioned the rightness of this situation had I always lived in that Southern town, exposed to segregation and prejudice with no perspective rendering countervailing experiences. Perhaps, it was only the fact that I had moved five times in my first eight years and been exposed to different cultures and social norms that provided me with the contrast necessary to recognize the evil that was afoot in Montgomery, Alabama.

Now I better understand the anger and fear emanating from the black people of that shantytown some sixty years ago. Aside from whatever I represented to them, what would have happened if some accident had befallen me through no fault of their own? Would they be subjected to an unreasoning "punish first and ask questions later" reaction from the white community? Why not? That is the way my dad functioned.

The other thing I had observed during my visit to that shantytown was that no one acknowledged my presence. What had not registered at the time was that this had subliminally conveyed to me a sense of power and superiority: Although resenting my presence, none of those people dared challenge me. Why would this be? I could well imagine white adults confronting me if I were someplace they felt I did not belong. But now, I understand or at least think I do. They did not dare risk challenging somebody from the white community, any more than I would dare to challenge my dad or the existence of two water fountains in the movie theater. In such ways, the violence of racism makes itself known even when hidden from view.

In part, I share this memory to describe a dynamic that occurs in all family and societal life. It is in just the way described that our unconscious assumptions and prejudices develop in the supposedly protective confines of our families regardless of social prominence or level of education. These assumptions are taken in as *just the way things are* and typically go unnoticed and unquestioned, contributing to the unseen waters of his life. Thus, it is not uncommon for a patient to describe a "perfectly happy childhood," never thinking to mention that neither parent ever held him or told him he was loved.

Similarly, despite all evidence to the contrary, I felt I had grown up in a "normal family," even an exemplary one until I began examining my family relationships in psychotherapy. There, I moved from an initial reaction of insult that my parents' behaviors would be questioned to seeing the previously unseen waters of my life, all the while feeling irrationally disloyal for presuming to do so. I came to appreciate that normal does not always mean healthy and certainly does not mean right.

Of course, there will always be people who are aware of something wrong. But, such considerations erode under the relentless cultural chorus as the unexamined beliefs come to feel increasingly normal, even if the feeling of normalcy never fully arrives. They begin to feel a part of us, making them all the harder to notice, much less question or change.

The critical thing to realize is that thinking is foundational to the privilege of living our lives. However, it takes courage to have a mind of one's own, to stand outside the crowd, and to question the governing norm. Of course, none of this is easily done in childhood, a time of extraordinary vulnerability and marginality. The role of a child, romanticized in fantasy, yet demonstrated as one of weakness and ignorance in many interactions with the adult world, induces the child to defensively internalize the situation so that it becomes felt like a part of himself as if it were second—or first nature. Thus, accumulates the unseen waters of our live

S.

Chapter 3

Road Warriors: An Exercise in Rootlessness

By age eight, I had lived in Tennessee, Oklahoma, California, and two towns in Alabama, and those are just the places I recall. Here, of course, I am merely reciting facts. What these facts do not convey is the disruption and upheaval created in the fabric of my existence: the rending of relationships, leaving one school and entering another, leaving behind a place called home to slowly turn a new house into another place called home before leaving it as well. There is also an impact on extended family relationships: grandparents, aunts, uncles, and cousins. These people, the ground of my origins, I barely knew. And there was no such thing as a hometown: I was not from any place nor was there any place to which I would return—life was a wandering, rootless journey, with no destination in mind.

The power of early experience to imprint itself in our hearts and minds is remarkable. I suspect that my life-long difficulty in remembering peoples' names may be an unconscious strategy to minimize the impact of the radical temporariness of my early relationships. Perhaps my motivation was, *If I do not say hello, I do not have to say goodbye: That way, it is less painful.* What I do know is that despite having lived in Baltimore, Maryland, for nearly fifty years, I feel ready to move at a moment's notice, suggesting that I have never fully arrived.

Given my experience, I wasn't surprised when my brother, Jacques, following the passing of Christine, his wife of fifty years, felt no sense of rootedness. All the places he considered living were overseas. He finally settled in Lisbon, Portugal. In his decision-making process, he gave little importance to the idea of a support group. Indeed, he dismissed such concerns, noting he could make friends anywhere, and he did. In pondering Jacques's decision, I wondered if he was returning *home, home* being the nomadic life, and making your way alone as a stranger in a strange land.

Aside from the continued threat of emotional and physical violence in my family, and of racial violence around me, other facets of my life in Montgomery were comparatively secure and happy. I felt a growing sense of routine and order to my world: a rhythm that lent structure and stability and hope for the future.

For the first time, I had a best-buddy, Greg Cook, and a sense of belonging. The wonder of that time is captured in my memory of Greg and me flitting like shadows through the Alabama woods and coming upon a dilapidated shack. On the rickety porch sat an old, wizened black woman, head crowned with steel-wool hair and a mouth of tattered yellow teeth framed by spittle-laden lips. Dark eyes gleaming in the dim light, she called out, "Dayawantyafortunered." Neither Greg nor I had any idea what she was saying but not wanting to be rude, I kept trying to clarify, "What?" She repeated, "Dayawantyafortunered." After several concentrated tries, I managed to decipher the stream of syllables, "Do you want your fortune read?" At that instant, electricity coursed through my body; magic was at hand.

Greg and I approached cautiously, ready to flee if anything threatening stirred the air. The woman asked for a coin, and I fished a nickel out of my pocket. Using a cane, she heaved her bowed body out of her squeaky rocking chair and scuttled through the open door, tattered dress loosely swinging from her bony shoulders and flapping around her stick-figure legs.

The impenetrable gloom of the inner recesses of her shack promised countless mysteries and excited my imagination. Warily, my eyes struggling to acclimate to the dim interior, I followed her in. Within this shadow world stood a worn wooden table in a single room, upon which lay a thick, tattered paperback book with a large needle resting on it. The Witch waited for us to gather round, then with astonishing speed, grabbed the needle and drove it forcefully into the book. Startled, we jumped back, on the brink of flight as The Witch cackled in delight. She then opened the book to the page the needle pointed to, promising that therein lay a verse proclaiming our fortune. Regrettably, our fortune was to remain a mystery; we could not understand a word she read. But what was important was the aliveness of the supercharged moment sparking through my body as the worlds of fantasy and reality coalesced into one.

That Christmas, a sparkling red bicycle waited under the tree. To my astonishment, it was for me. I had never imagined receiving such a gift; my heart swelled with love. Ten days later, I was hit by a car while riding my bike. Of this accident, I have fragments of memory: a motorcycle police officer's helmeted face staring down at me and waking in the hospital suffering from amnesia and damaged knees. Bizarrely, I also vividly remember arriving safely home, my mother on the front porch, smiling, and waving in greeting, as the warmth of her love swells within my chest. But this did not happen; my mind created it. My psyche was defending itself from the calamity that had befallen me, telling me, "You're safe. Everything is okay. Life is good." As I examine this memory, I realize it ends before I reach my mother.

Despite the accident, those summer days in Montgomery were some of the happiest of my life. I was waking to myself. My adventures with Greg and the hours spent playing red light, green light with all the children in the neighborhood until dusk turned to night, and walking to the A & W Root Beer stand in the asphalt bubbling heat of the day, the frosty mug of root beer sure to give me a headache remain some of the happiest moments in my life. For the first time, I belonged.

And then, one night at dinner, my parents announced, "We're moving to Hanau, Germany." Several weeks later, I was cleaved by grief as it was all taken away. Like magic, poof! All gone. School, Greg, Montgomery, home, all gone. My life, like a beach, had been swept clean of footprints by the tide. My first lesson that life, like the tide, brings things in and takes things away and that nothing is guaranteed but the tide and I would discover that the tide is unrelenting.

Chapter 4

Disruption and Confusion—Within and Without

Seventeen hours on a propeller-driven plane, sleep-starved, and vomiting during the landing, I arrive in Hanau, Germany. Collapsing onto the hotel bed without undressing, I'm awoken, seemingly seconds later, by Dad announcing, "Get up. It's time to eat." Fortunately, hunger soon supplants the nausea of fatigue as the tantalizing smells of stuffed cabbage and quartered potatoes waft through the air.

Situated on the T of the forested road that pointed like an arrow to the Army Fort where Dad was a battalion commander, the hotel provided a front-row seat from our second-story window to observe the early morning maneuvers. These entailed the deploying of tanks and 8" howitzers, weighing 60,000 pounds each to the border with communist Germany, in the practice of war.

The predawn maneuvers always began with a forewarning: A sound, like the sonorous growl of lions on the prowl, that grew ever louder and more menacing as the behemoths neared yet remained veiled by the morning fog. As the floor begins to tremble beneath my feet, the machines of war finally emerge like wraiths, eerily materializing, and dematerializing in the mist that swirled around them. At last, fully revealed, the tanks and cannon stand as grand as tall ships sailing across a leaden sea.

Their sound is a living thing, thrumming through my body, as these mammoths slow to make the turn below my window perch. There, one by one, gray as the mist that surrounds them, they hesitate, as if sniffing for danger, before making the turn and again gather speed, disappearing ghostlike back into the murk. Preternaturally, a primeval silence is all that is left in their wake.

Nine weeks later, we move to a two-story stone and slate-roofed house attached to a burnt-out factory. A narrow river was situated just yards away, having run a paddle wheel for the factory in decades past. In winter, the river froze over, its crystalline surface beckoning my brothers and me to skate, our ankles buckling under the weight of our bodies. In the spring, flooded by melting snows, the river electrified the air as it roared its approval to the change in seasons.

Under gray skies, with an occasionally magnificent sunny day thrown in, my brothers and I spun our fantasies into life within the factory walls, running like cheetahs through the sodden light of cavernous rooms, while gargoyle stubs of burnt beams peered down from above.

The custodian, an unkempt man, dressed in stained overalls, and boasting a scruffy gray beard, kept a cow and a pig. Each morning, he milked the cow into a metal bucket, creating a pissing-like sound that only added to the pungent odor of straw and dung, that hung thick in the air. With solemnity, the man would offer us the bucket for a sip of the thick milk, as it steamed in the frigid morning cold, its surface speckled with dark fallings from the cow's hide. When we hurried to decline, the custodian let out a good-natured guffaw.

One morning, I entered the cobblestone courtyard and spied the custodian with another man in the doorway of the shed, the pig at his feet. There was a sharp pop, and the pig collapsed as if a marionette whose strings had been cut. After several thrumming heartbeats, I realized the custodian had shot the pig in the head. In horrid fascination, I watch as the two men grasp a rusty chain from a pulley above their heads, wrap it around the pig's hind legs, and grunting with effort, pull it jerkily into the air. There, the custodian stilled the pig's swaying motion with one hand, while deftly cutting it from pelvis to chest with a knife in the other, intestines spilling like boiled spaghetti into a steaming pile on the frosted cobblestones.

Much was good at this time in my life, replete with raw experiences and new adventures and discoveries, but unknown to me, that was not the case for my Dad. The soldiers, tight strung from the incessant maneuvers, were unruly. One night, a riot broke out at a bar, and the commander of the fort arrived to restore order. While inside, soldiers escaped from the rear and turned his car over with his wife inside. Shortly after, my father assumed command of the fort.

Years later, I learned that Dad suffered several "nervous breakdowns" during this time. Given his frequently being away from home, his absence was not outside the usual rhythms of family life, and his hospitalizations went unnoticed by the kids. After years of treating narcissists, I could well imagine the cause of his breakdown. He lacked the psychological infrastructure necessary for coping with less than heroic results. To his shame, he discovered he was not the mythical hero showcased in his stories. In the harsh light of a brutal reality, Jim Bowie and Davey Crockett were nowhere to be found.

Dad was transferred to Heidelberg, Germany. In the past, it was customary for the family to follow behind. But, this time, I was told to accompany him. I was not happy about the idea of leaving my mother and siblings behind and being forced into sole proximity to Dad. But I had no choice. For the next six months, I lived with him in a single room in the BOQ (Bachelor Officers' Quarters), sleeping on a cot and eating at the officers' club. On warm days, I washed the cars of the other officers for pocket money and played by myself. The main negative was Dad; always conscious of appearance, continually barking at me to "straighten up, head up, back straight!" On the positive side, there was a kind of intimacy in sharing dinner and evening snacks. I grew to love smoked oysters and crackers with cheese.

When fall came, my family still had not arrived, but that did not stop the surprises from coming. Instead of attending the American elementary school within walking distance, I would make the daily bus trip to the school for children of the French military located in Spire, Germany. There, I was forbidden to speak English, and initiated into the confusion and fear of not being able to understand what the teachers were saying and thereby sort out how to please them. Rulers striking hands, ears pulled, and saliva spewed by teachers yelling like drill instructors became the rule of the day. In this shock and awe fashion, I learned the vital importance of being able to make sense of things and the danger that arises when one does not.

One disgraceful deed remains fresh in my mind from this time. A little girl peed her pants while being shouted at by the teachers, and, despite her begging me not to, I told everyone on the bus. I still think about her and her shame ridden face, tears falling silently. It was a terrible thing to do and brought me no joy. Indeed, in the very instance of my telling, I felt only contempt for myself—an experience of me seeing how ugly I could be. In thinking about this incident years later, I realized I had been scrabbling blindly for any opportunity that would give me some illusion of command and control and thrust from me, no matter how briefly, the helplessness of my existence. Chronically upset, I was unaware that I was looking for someone, anyone, upon whom I could safely discharge my ire. Yet, in that instant, like being struck by a lightning bolt, I knew my action for what it was: the shabbiest and most pathetic of victories.

Eventually, housing became available, and the rest of the family arrived. It was then, as we were beginning to get back to a semblance of normal family life, that my parents made another announcement: Jacques, Edward, and I were going to a boarding school in France. Mutti couched it as a Great Adventure and fantastic opportunity to expand our cultural horizons.

We could not believe it. Couldn't things ever settle down? Disruption, dislocation, and upset had become constant companions. I was learning that not only does bad follow good, but bad also follows bad. My parents were impervious to our mewling that even to my ears, sounded like the bleating of lambs. Overwhelmed by the intensity of our angst, Mutti sent us to Dad. Literally, on our knees, we begged to be allowed to stay home. In a tone, laden with disgust, he responded, "Stop crying like babies. You're going."

Some things you cannot change; some things you must endure. What I did not fully appreciate was that the tide was going out—way, way out—forewarning a coming tsunami.

1 The Etienne Boys: Jacques, Charles, Edward

Chapter 5

The Abyss: Free Fall

Our Great Adventure began on a frigid, sunny, bright day. I felt like the world smiling, mocking me and gloating over my misery.

Always, the station wagon had been an extension of my home, taking us safely throughout Europe. But today, it hummed along, impervious to my despair as I sat stiff with apprehension, slotted alongside my brothers in the backseat.

To be fair, the car was only following the lead of my parents; its indifferent attitude mirrored theirs as they chattered mindlessly in the front seat, refusing to acknowledge our misery. I felt utterly alone. Worn down mentally and emotionally and sought refuge in the only warmth I had: the blanket of my despair.

After traveling many miles, a burgeoning sense of urgency emanating from the front seat pulled me from my dark cocoon. I soon understood that Dad felt a recurring jolt through the steering wheel and was concerned about car trouble. As a look of apprehension crossed my mother's face, hope flared in mine. Wishfully, I thought, *The car hasn't betrayed me, it has only been biding its time.* As I waited to see what would unfold, I became aware of rhythmically thumping my head against the back seat. Suddenly, I understood. I was the source of the jolting that so concerned my father. Fearing his anger and belittling, I willed myself to be still; It was not easy.

The car powered onward, carrying us along two-lane roads that wound through postcard German towns and villages, across stone bridges spanning turbulent streams, and alongside dung-scented fields upon which farmers labored in the distance. On we went, ever farther from home, toward a town that, for me, despite its inherent beauty, would always be cold and gray as burnt coal—Strasbourg, France.

As Dad parked the car on the cobble-stone street, I had my first glimpse of Collège St. Etienne. It was three stories of a slate-roofed stone building in the shape of an H; one end was closed off by a fifteen-foot-high wall capped with incisors of jagged green and brown broken bottle glass. As we approached the maw of the entrance, I wondered, *Are the walls to keep people in or to keep people out?*

Inside the belly of the courtyard stood an old stone church under reconstruction, surrounded by mounds of dirt from which bones protruded like the spikes of a sea urchin: the remains of an ancient cemetery uprooted by the digging. Adding to this phantasmagoric scene was the jabber of French parents and children excitedly bidding their farewells, a festive mood in jarring contrast to my own. Panic-stricken, heart thumping, I turned to my parents, another appeal to stop this madness scrabbling up my throat, only to encounter the actors playing their roles.

Recognizing the futility, resignation set in, as did my self-questioning: *What's wrong with me? My brothers don't seem to be feeling this way, though they are unusually quiet. Am I the only one? Why can't I, too, see it as a Great Adventure? My parents wouldn't leave us in a dangerous place, would they? Why don't I trust them?*

This self-questioning only subsided when the long-dreaded moment arrived and then passed with shocking indifference. My mother hugged me. I held tight, burying my face in the scratchy wool of her stylish gray coat. Then, as she pulled away, cold air slapped my cheeks where warmth had just been. With dead eyes, I watched her follow my father out of that courtyard and, out of my life. I stood in silent shock with my brothers: Jacques, thirteen, a Clark Kent look-alike, with his dark hair and fair skin, and Ed, only age seven, small and vulnerable yet with a brave smile on his face.

I was wondering, *What are we supposed to do?* when a movement caught my eye. A priest, about forty, average build, with pale corpse skin, ice-blue eyes above cold-reddened cheeks, and dark hair pomaded back from a high forehead, was striding determinedly toward us, his black cape fluttering behind. This vampiric figure began roughly pushing my brothers and me in different directions and into different lines of students that, I would soon discover, went to different places. That quickly, I was shorn of my entire family and felt more alone than I knew alone could be.

Dazed, I followed the line into a large hall filled with worn wooden tables set with plates and utensils. Mimicking the other kids, I stood behind my chair, waiting for what I did not know when there was a sharp tap on my shoulder. Turning, I looked up into the phlegmatic eyes of a young man. He spoke, the sounds a garble to me, his tone as indifferent as his appearance. Wishfully hoping he was asking if I was okay, I smiled wistfully and said, "Wee."

That is when, without warning, he kicks my legs from under me. As I fall to the floor, his thumping feet begin herding me in a circle until I arrive back at the chair. Stunned, heart thundering in my chest, I struggle to comply when he motions for me to stand. Dizzily rising on unsteady legs, I grasp the back of the chair for support. Angrily, he jabs his finger at my arms. Overwhelmed, nauseous, I desperately look around, trying to sort out what he wants. That is when I notice the other children have their arms crossed. Reluctantly, fearful of falling, I give up my grip on the chair and quickly cross my arms, hoping that this is the desired response. Begrudgingly, he moves on down the line.

Deprived of my steadying hold on the chair, I begin to wobble. I then stare at the back of the chair, for its scratched surface provides a point of focus and balance. That's when I make an important discovery: In the dimmest of hours, something as small and meaningless as the scratched back of a chair can become the most precious thing in the world. As insignificant and lifeless as it was, the back of that chair provided something known and stable, a world in which I could take refuge from the one that had gone completely mad beyond its borders.

Several minutes later, The Priest, leading a procession of faculty, self-importantly ambles into the hall and onto the dais that holds the faculty dining table. After a short prayer, the faculty takes their seats, and we are now permitted to take ours. On cue, kitchen staff flood into the room, placing large metal bowls on the tables. One, nearest me, is filled with pieces of meat, each boasting the severed end of a white artery sticking out like a rubber tube. I had never seen such meat before and scurried to name it, stumbling upon the likeliest answer given its shape: tongue. Another bowl contains white mush, drowning beneath a layer of filmy water; I guess mashed potatoes. I do not eat that night, except for a piece of bread and two squares of chocolate that pass for dessert.

Following dinner, The Priest, his black cape once again billowing behind, shepherds us up shadowed marble stairs and along high-ceilinged hallways echoing with the footsteps of our passage. We arrive at a large rectangular room with an uneven wood-planked floor holding three rows of beds, maybe thirty in all. One long wall holds windows overlooking a canal with a fountain. A shorter wall, nearest the entrance, features a metal trough running its length; a row of faucets, like the beaks of blackbirds, poke their heads out from above. The short wall at the opposite end of the rectangle contains a cubicle for the surveillants—those creatures charged with keeping us in line, one of whom had introduced himself to me earlier with kicks.

I am assigned a bed next to a window overlooking the fountain, insanely grateful for the view, but more so for the tiniest illusion of privacy afforded by not being hemmed in on all sides by strangers. Standing at the window in the months to come, I would discover that the fountain had a life of its own as it danced to the tunes of the changing seasons and stopped dancing all-together in Winter's cold embrace.

The bed is covered with an enormous pillow serving as a duvet and, at its foot, sits a locker, washrag perched on top, my meager belongings on the floor next to it. Taking my cue from the others, I store my things and, braving the cold, strip to my underwear, grab the washrag and shivering, wait in line for my turn at the trough: my first French bath. There, I discover that each faucet boasts one handle—there is no hot water. In the winter months to come, the faucets freeze, icicles hanging like the fangs of saber-tooth tigers from their gullets; then, we cannot bath at all, except for weekly trips to an indoor swimming pool. Later, when we visit home, our parents marvel at our smell, and we leave a quarter-inch thick coat of grime on the sides of the tub when we bath.

At the close of that first day, surrounded by darkness and thirty strangers with whom I could not speak, my despair catches up with me. Sobbing, I struggle to remain silent, fearing unwanted attention. Hurtling into this first night away from home, I catch myself thumping my head against the pillow. My last thought before sleep captures me: *Please let this be a nightmare from which I will soon awake.*

Morning comes in a cacophony of light and sound as ceiling lights blaze on, and the faucets angrily spew water into the metal trough with a reverberating roar. This sensory assault is joined by the sound of sharply clapping hands, as the surveillants run up and down the aisles, maniacally shouting, "Allez vous! Allez vous!" My heart quiets as I realize that this is no life-threatening emergency, but only the surveillants taking sadistic delight in rocketing us into the pre-dawn of a new day. The first full day of my Great Adventure has begun.

I was a victim of Collège St. Etienne but could not afford to know it at the time. My feelings, unnamed, scampered about like feral children, their dark eyes darting wildly. If I had known their names, they would have shared two things in common: fear and eviscerating loneliness. Regardless, I had one family rule to hang on to—never give up. I fought back, I rebelled.

On the first day of class, I wore earbuds to listen to my transistor radio. The teacher discovered it and confiscated the radio. On another occasion, an accomplice and I crept out of the dorm and snuck into the church in the middle of the night. In the light of the moon streaming through the windows, I discovered a hole behind the altar filled with bones. Selecting a large one, I threw it out the narrow archers-window into the public street beyond; yells of shocked surprise echoed in return. My accomplice and I laughed, enjoying our journey into the spare joys of sadistic delight.

My signature moment of revolutionary zeal occurred when I brought a large bag of marbles back from a visit home. I had noticed that the floor of the dorm canted toward the cubicle in which my nemesis, the surveillants, slept. An hour after lights out, I slipped from my bed and crept to the top of the room near the trough. There, kneeling, I eased the marbles onto the floor and, with gentle pushes, sent them on their way before swiftly returning to bed. The marbles click-clacked their way over the ancient floorboards toward the doorway to the surveillants' cubicle. My anticipation grew: Would this work? Soon, I had my answer. A surveillant came out to investigate the noise and stepped upon the marbles in his bare feet. Repeatedly cursing and yipping in pain and surprise as he hopped from one to another. Furious, the surveillants rousted the students, made us strip our beds, and empty our lockers, but there was nothing to find and no witnesses at hand.

Even so, I had earned a reputation and was convicted of the crime. As punishment, the surveillants forced me to stand barefoot, in my pajamas, in the dark and cold of the cobblestone courtyard. I imagine they thought this punishment would chasten me, but on the ivory chimes of my chattering teeth, my spirit soared. I felt free and alive, no longer an insignificant cog in someone else's universe. I was learning how action could supplant depression, at least for a while.

However, the perversities continued. When I contracted La Grippe (the flu), the staff, noting the severity of my condition, housed me in the infirmary with its working radiator. Late that night, The Priest entered, bathed in the devilish glow cast by a red-light bulb above the door. As I watched him approach through fevered eyes, he exuded false joviality. Sitting on the edge of the bed, he leaned forward and whispered into my ear, "Oh, La Grande American, you're not so grand now, are you?"

Given that I had never felt like the Great American, I realized I was merely a stand-in for despised Americans in general. Despite my fevered state, I felt a twang of pride, knowing that for this fool to take the time to visit an eleven-year-old in a sick ward in the middle of the night to perform such a petty act of malice was proof positive that this Grande American had gotten under his lizard skin.

I do not want to portray everything as being bad at Collège St. Etienne, just most things. After all, I discovered some of the marvels of France: intensely flavored ice creams and pastries;

beautiful city parks; the smell of roasting chestnuts drifting from kiosks along wintry city streets; street lamps twinkling on snowy nights; grand buildings; and steak au poivre (peppered steak) to name a few. I also began smoking Gauloises cigarettes. But these were fleeting pleasures, soon snuffed out by the ongoing vacuum of care and relationship.

It was in these circumstances that I made a profound discovery: One can grow to hate something precisely because it is loved. In this instance, I am thinking of my parents' visits, which occurred about every six to eight weeks. On warm days, they would take us out for a picnic, my mother spreading a blanket and serving her oven-roasted chicken and home-made potatoe salad, which worked to reignite memories of home. I loved the food, I loved my mom, and I hated those visits. They were a cruel tease, exciting both memory and desire, cutting unerringly through the thick wall of my defenses, reminding me of all I had lost and would soon lose again. At first, my grief reignited upon my parents' every departure, but, over time, knowing what was to come, it flared up upon their every arrival. I came to hate these visits knowing the painful end they augured.

After eighteen months at Collège St. Etienne, I returned to civilization. What words and tears had been unable to accomplish, my body had been able to achieve. I was suffering from stomach pain so acute it bent me over and dropped me to the floor.

At first, the Army doctors recommended powdered milk, given the absence of homogenized milk at the school. Unsurprisingly, this did not help. Curiously though, I did find the nightly ritual of preparing and drinking the foul-tasting brew oddly comforting. I marveled at how something so small and inconsequential could become so important simply because it provided a routine and a mooring and, perhaps most importantly: something all my own. This nightly practice buttressed my embattled spirit in the frigid winds of this abysmal existence. The fact that I grew to like the taste tells all.

Finally, the doctors, fearing the development of an ulcer, recommended my return home. Several months later, my brothers followed when Mutti, during a visit, found Jacques's mattress lying in the cavernous hallway—his punishment for some infraction. This debasing act, directly witnessed by my mother, breached the walls of her denial. Furious, she confronted The Priest and, with my brothers in tow, quit the school forever.

You might ask why my parents kept us in this place. I certainly did. My mother's protestations that it was to expand our cultural horizons were far from compelling. In later years, I did not care that my siblings and their spouses groaned whenever I raised the subject. They wanted to sweep the past away without understanding it—as if this was possible. What they did not realize is that I could not; I had to make sense of things to have any hope of trusting again.

I never did get a convincing answer from my parents. However, I did not fail. I pieced together a story from circumstantial evidence that put reason to our ordeal.

Years later, Michelle, when touring Canada with Mutti, discovered that she had attended Catholic boarding schools from age four. I had not known that mom had been separated from her family at such an early age. This information provided context. I could readily imagine four-year-old Mutti in these bastions of structure, stricture, and faith, receiving validation and approval for her other-oriented, self-less behavior, and steadfast devotion. Always her nightly ritual of kneeling at her bedside, dressed in a cotton nightgown, head bent, eyes closed, hands prayerfully clasped in front of her, had reminded me of a little girl. Now, I could see the thread of that ritual weaving its way back to her childhood and forward to the day of her death. She had discovered her routines, ones that held her throughout her life, where her parents' arms would not. Given a depressed, often absent mother, the death of her brother, and an alcoholic father, I could well imagine that for my mom, boarding school might have provided reason and structure that served as a positive alternative to her sad and debilitating home life. Still, I could not imagine the devastating loss any four-year-old would feel in being separated from home, any home.

Another piece of the puzzle was something about my mother that I knew from personal experience: She *was*, in fact, loving and caring, but she could be a lioness when it came to protecting her family. I could well imagine her whisking us off to Catholic boarding school in service of providing my father a quiet place to recover, free from the noise and energies of her three oldest boys. Simultaneously, she would be providing us with what, for her, had been the sanctuary and asylum of boarding school when her parents were sick and disabled. She was strong that way, doing what had to be done, at least as she saw it.

I only wish that if this was the case, she had told me. Then, I could have imbued my losses with meaning and purpose. Looking out for the family is a value to which I intensely subscribe, and it was precisely that value that appeared breached when Jacques, Ed, and I were exiled to that Kafkaesque existence, without convincing explanation or a sympathetic ear. At the same time, I recognize that Dad's narcissistic vulnerability would be triggered by anything that gave the lie to his omnipotent presentation of himself. How ironic that my mother's attempt to look out for the family might have been the cause of our not being looked out for at all.

Chapter 6

Un-Civilization

War is said to be an experience of days, weeks, or months of boredom shattered by seconds of violence. That description loosely fit my life: People were not shooting at me, but I was repeatedly turned inside out and upside down with little warning. The abiding apprehension of an unanticipated slap, a sudden change in living situation, a kick in the back, or exile to a foreign land did the trick. For me, the world was an ever-changing and dangerous place.

But now, aged twelve, I was older and hardened, no longer grief-stricken by the loss of parental care. Where previously I had felt there had been an "us" of the family, now I knew there was just "*me*" and the world with which *I* had to contend. I braced for the worst; indeed, I expected it. I had been in the Abyss and escaped uninjured, or so I thought. I did not understand that on the inside, I had turned into a dark, brooding soul with little respect for authority.

Home represented civilization, and civilization was in Patrick Henry Village, Heidelberg, Germany. My father, for reasons known only to himself, lobbied the school system to admit me to the ninth grade rather than the seventh, which at age twelve, was where I belonged. He argued that French education was superior, and to place me in the seventh grade would hold me back. Given that it was a school for military dependents, and he was an officer, I was thrust into another foreign environment; this one called high school in the middle of the academic year. Not surprisingly, I floundered right away, but I was used to floundering; indeed, it had become a way of life.

I joined the high school soccer team because of my love for the game, learned in the courtyard of Collège St. Etienne, and instantly became its smallest and slowest member. I remember playing a German team comprised of six-footers, begging the coach to put me in. He reluctantly granted my wish with several minutes remaining in a blow-out loss. I ran onto the field, dreaming of saving the day, only then appreciating that I was a dwarf among giants. But that did not deter me: I gritted my teeth and ran even harder. Unfortunately, my mind had written feats of greatness that my body could not cash. The harder I ran, the more my limbs flailed in all directions, slowing me to a crawl. People were laughing, including members of the German team, who, smirking, looked down at me. But that was not the humiliation it once would have been; I had plenty of experience of being scorned.

Ironically, my biggest nemesis academically was English: I was failing. After struggling to learn French, I now spoke and dreamt in it fluently. But I had lost three years of schooling in English grammar between Spire Academy and Collège St. Etienne and then missed the fourth and fifth years when hopscotched into the ninth grade. Understanding the parts of speech and English grammar eluded me. To me, the term "dangling participle" sounded uncomfortably close to male genitalia. But I did not care. As with everything else, I was used to failure; in fact, I was learning I was good at it.

What I did care about, though, was my father's wrath. Accodangly, I set out to steal the English 9th-grade final exam. Unfortunately, amid the deed, another student happened upon me and sulkily insisted on inclusion. Several days later, I was summoned to the principal's office and confronted with my crime. Like any good soldier or thief for that matter, I stoically denied all. That is when a small voice squeaked from behind, "I've told him everything." It was the other student. Bastard, whatever happened to the military edict to give only name, rank, and serial number, not to mention the notion of honor among thieves and not being a rat? Dad did the predictable.

All was not negative in Heidelberg, though nearly so in that I had no friends. The kids in high school were older and bigger, and the kids my age went to a different school. I spent my time alone, sometimes during the summer, visiting the swimming pool, where I pretended not to envy the camaraderie of the kids around me.

Lounging upon the grass, enjoying the warmth of the sun, I looked up at the diving platform that pierced the blue sky. Kids climbed the rungs, rushed to the edge, then flung themselves off, screaming with delight. I thought *I can do that* and soon was making my way up the ladder. It was then I noticed that what did not look high while lying securely on the ground below, became more Mount Everest-like with each rung ascended. Thirty-nine rungs and thirty feet later, white knuckling the ladder, I was, seriously wondering what had possessed me.

Surrounded by open-air, besieged by vertigo, I crawled ignominiously onto the concrete platform, death gripping the security rail and panting with anxiety. There, I screwed up enough courage to pull myself into a crouch, then, grudgingly, hand over hand along the rail, as if fighting against tornadic winds. In this manner, I made my way to the lip of the platform.

There, I had a second revelation: without my glasses, the pool was a blur. I could see its outline, but not the clear water within. *How was I to prepare myself for entry if I could not see it coming?* As I stood there, wrestling with fear, seconds morphed into minutes and minutes into handfuls of minutes. All the while, my embarrassment grew as kid after kid worked their way by me, some throwing questioning looks, before shrugging, then joyously leaping into the void.

Sick to my stomach, I considered exiting the way I had come—back down the ladder. But that way was cut off as I imagined my cowardly descent on display for all to see. So, again, I pulled myself to the edge of the platform, where I envisioned jumping, then cartwheeling out of control, landing face-first on the surface of the water below.

In this way, like a metronome, I tick-tocked between the ladder and the edge, between shame on one side and terror on the other. Finally, so wretched I could stand no more, I moved to the lip of the platform, took a deep breath, and leaped; *my* scream held no glee. I hit the water, the flats of my feet stinging and plunged to the bottom of the pool as clouds of bubbles billowed past me. Soon, I followed, thinking, *That wasn't so bad!*

Angrily, I climbed that platform, again and again, consciously trampling the fear that minutes earlier had been crushing me. I learned three things that day: One, things look different depending on where you stand; two, fantasy is more frightening than reality; and three, point your toes when plunging into water from a height.

Combatting my abiding sense of isolation was an ongoing challenge. I had not yet turned the magic thirteen, the "teen" part of the word holding all the magic. But that did not deter me; I began sneaking into the Teen Club through the back door. There, I discovered I had a natural eye for shooting pool and, after several months, could make difficult shots, albeit not consistently. Nonetheless, some magical days, I would string together a series of shots beating one after another of the older players.

There was only one pool table, and all the testosterone-filled boys lined the walls, impatiently waiting their turn. The winner of each game held the table while the loser made the walk of shame back to the end of the line. The problem was that losing to me tended to be particularly galling to some of my older and bigger opponents.

One such brute, a member of the high school wrestling team, pressed a pool stick across my throat, choking me from behind. Painfully, I pushed against the cue, angrily hissing, "Get off me, you half-breed," thus providing the excuse he needed to challenge me to a fight. I knew I had no chance of winning, but refusing a fight frightened me more than losing one. So, outside we went, and this fellow proceeded to beat me without mercy. However, he's the one who quit. I made him afraid. Not of me—I never laid a hand on him—but of the damage he was inflicting: my face distended; eyelids engorged to the size of golf balls; one eye swollen shut, the other nearly so; an ear torn; lips split, and blood streaming down my face and from my mouth. The damage to my gums was so extensive that fifty years later, a dentist remarked upon it. Regardless, after each knock-down, I got back up and kept getting back up until a look of growing worry traversed the bully's face. At this, he waved me off and nervously scurried away. When I stumbled home, my mother screamed.

During my time in Heidelberg, I hitchhiked, sometimes visiting Heidelberg Castle, which overlooked the Neckar River and the town of Heidelberg on its opposite shore. Skinny enough to squirm through the bars of the security gates, I played within its walls and explored its dungeons, sometimes stopping to take in the stunning view. On another occasion, I rented a rowboat to paddle the Neckar river, almost spilling over a three-foot-high damn that I did not see until I was upon it.

However, the memory most carved into my psyche was what happened after I took myself to lunch in Heidelberg to eat a green lasagna I had become addicted to when visiting the restaurant with my parents. The meal finished, I was hitchhiking home when an African American male, with a Caucasian female in the passenger seat, picked me up. An attractive couple, they were made more so by their warm and kind demeanors, and we passed the time chatting amiably. All was good until the MPs (military police) pulled us over. It soon became apparent that the two helmeted white MPs were angry about a black man daring to be with a white woman and with a white woman who would accept his attention. They were intent on giving this couple a hard time. As I watched their rude treatment from the back seat, anger boiled within me—more bastards abusing power and authority. My fury gave me courage, and I interjected myself into the MPs tirade. "Excuse me. These people are giving me a ride home. My dad, General McCormack (I gave him a battlefield promotion), is waiting for me. He won't be happy if I'm late." The two MPs locked eyes with me, assessing, but as I calmly held their gaze, their uncertainty grew. After some hesitation, they resentfully backed off and drove away.

We drove on, no one mentioning the encounter, but the atmosphere in the car had changed. Where once warm feelings and good cheer had lived, now hollow silence reigned. Minutes later, the couple dropped me off at my apartment building. As I entered the front door, I turned to wave goodbye, only to discover to my dismay that the MPs had returned, their jeep crowding the couple's car from behind.

I wish I had gone back to the couple's car and bore witness in some way. But, nauseous over this turn of events, I crept inside and, just as in that Montgomery, Alabama movie theatre suffered another humbling and gut-wrenching transformation in my sense of self.

My time in Heidelberg did nothing to change my cynical view of the world and my diminishing view of myself; the acts of intimidation somehow holding more power than the turns of kindness.

Several weeks later, another announcement: We were returning to the United States, someplace called Virginia. From my point of view, it did not matter: Every place was the same; they all sucked.

Part II

PUSH BACK—HATCHING 101

I was tired of feeling pushed around, of feeling like a cog in someone else's universe. I wanted to do more than exist. I was yearning for a more robust sense of self without knowing it. In this dumb to myself state, the best I could do was follow my impulses: They were the one thing I knew was mine.

Chapter 7

Adolescence: Lashing Out

*I*n 1963, at age thirteen, my family returned to the United States via the SS United States. It was a fantastic ship, one of the largest of its day, boasting marble stairways and enormous crystal chandeliers, as well as uniformed waiters ready to discern needs before needs arose. The five-day crossing allowed time to appreciate the immensity of the ocean, how tiny we humans are, and from the bow of the ship the wisdom of not spitting into the wind.

Dad bought a house in Annandale, Virginia, and I entered W.T. Woodson H.S. as a repeating freshman. Its size astonished me: three thousand students with over seven hundred and fifty in my graduating class. A city unto itself that even boasted a planetarium. It was here that school prayer had been challenged and ruled unconstitutional by the Supreme Court a year earlier.

After my ordeals in Europe, I was a changed guy. What once seemed a stable and relatively predictable world, real and tangible, as when I lived in Montgomery, Alabama, now felt ephemeral. I shared little in common with the people around me, who manifested optimism and an unfailing belief in an absolute reality. I, on the other hand, knew the world to be unstable, readily capable of turning upside down in the snap of a finger.

Lacking any sort of compass or future direction, I was adrift, carried along by the currents of the moment, hormones raging alongside an abiding loneliness. I did not have a stable sense of who I was, what I wanted, or where I was going. Stupid with anger and loneliness, I assumed this was simply the way I was.

Ironically, by the end of my freshman year, I had unwittingly earned enough credits, when added to those carried over from Heidelberg, to qualify as a junior, again leapfrogging a year ahead through no special achievement of my own.

I hated school. I did not study; I did not want to study, and I did not know how to study. I performed okay in classes that interested me and daydreamed through the rest until the final bell rang. Then, infused with the elixir of freedom, I would spring to life, and embrace the rest of *my* day.

One class stands out: typing. It was hard and boring, and taught me that boring makes hard ten times harder. The noxious part was the teacher. Not she as a person, although a bit stern and perfectly cast given her pinched face and bent bird-like figure. Disquietingly, she pecked at me in ways disconcertingly like my father. "Straighten your back. Don't look at the keyboard. Touch the board lightly. No, that's wrong." Yet, I could forgive her all that. What was insufferable was her gag-worthy halitosis combined with her unfortunate tendency to lean down and speak into my ear when making corrections, thus enveloping me in the nauseating pool of her rancid breath.

Under this aversive conditioning, I began cutting class. First one, then another and another, totaling twenty-one days in a row without that ever having been the plan: It was wishful thinking in all its glory. *Because I got away with it one day, couldn't I get away with it the next, and then the next, and so on?* A tiny voice whispered warnings but went unheeded. None of this became real to me until an acquaintance, a volunteer in the principal's office, alerted me that I was going to be called in and suspended.

Ever fearful of Dad's wrath, I sought a way out. Necessity fueled creativity. I would strike pre-emptively. I would turn myself in and claim an unbearably guilty conscience demanding I confess. I hoped such purity of soul and flagrant self-flogging would help mitigate my punishment. I hurried to the principal's office, and straightaway asked to speak with him. Hat figuratively in hand, head bent, eyes studying the toes of my shoes, tremorous voice infused with the veracity of the angst I was feeling, I put on a world-class performance of Catholic guilt incarnate.

The principal, moved by my performance, compassionately decided not to suspend me but advised me that he still had to tell my parents. Flooded with worry, I girded myself for another interminable lecture and the staccato drumbeat of my father's stuttering and slaps to the face. I also worried about Mom; she would be upset, and I hated disappointing her. My despair must have been writ large, for unsolicited, the principal rushed to assure me that he would speak to them on my behalf—Hope found, lost, and found again.

On this rare occasion, it seemed my parents had spoken about how to handle the situation. Their response was thoughtful rather than reactive. In truth, Dad had no response at all. Mom did all the talking. Briefly, she scolded me for skipping class, then with astonishing alacrity and ill-disguised pride, jumped to praising me for having done "the right thing" in confessing. She was basking in the vice principal's vouching for me. With his words, he transformed me from sinner to saint, and although grounded for two weeks, I avoided the crucifixion of suspension and Dad's percussive lecture.

Please, do not misunderstand. I was not *only* in the business of breaking the rules; my conduct was more complex than that. Some teachers were taken by me, seeing something in me that I could not see in myself. My French-5 teacher, on whom I had a crush at the tender age of thirteen, would sometimes drive me home after school and talk to my mother about how much she liked me. Nonetheless, she sent me to the principal's office when I used a French cuss word in class when challenged to offer a word that the other students were unlikely to know. That was where I was on November 22, 1963, when the phone calls announcing President Kennedy's assassination started coming in.

A different teacher invited me to his home for dinner with his wife and, on another occasion, to join them for a trip to Georgetown bars. I was flattered, but not more than sixteen, and without a fake ID, I could readily imagine the humiliation of being turned away at the bar, and so, I declined.

Outside of school, my brothers and I vented our pent-up aggression by stealing money from cars in the church parking lot on Sundays and engaging in bloody battles amongst ourselves

Jacques and I, born fifteen months apart and wedded together in time and a love-hate relationship, had developed an uncanny capacity to trigger rage in one other. On one occasion, he cut the back of my hand from wrist to small finger with a razor blade, and, on another, I threw a knife at him that stuck in the wall near his leg. There were innumerable instances of brutish behavior, which felt perfectly reasonable in that it modeled our father's chaotic and violent ways.

One memory of combat stands out from the rest. Jacques and I were fighting in the foyer when I landed a kick to his groin, sending him to the floor, writhing in pain. Fearing reprisal, I raced upstairs, stopping at the top to see what he would do. As he continued to lie, whimpering on the floor, my mother entered the foyer and, to my surprise, responded with disgust to Jacques's mewling. She demanded he stop whining and get up. Strangely, as he lay in agony with no compassion found, a wave of empathy washed over me.

I think my mother treated us differently. If it had been me on the floor, I do not believe contempt would have laced her voice. In noting such differences in family interactions, I marvel at how parents shape their children and how the children shape them. I felt that Jacques served as a narcissistic extension for my parents: polished, handsome, and outgoing; he represented them on the public stage. Accordingly, as part of the unconscious training for this role, he was less likely to garner compassion for any perceived weakness, while receiving praise and admiration for every success. I suspect he internalized this experience. After the death of his wife, when I asked how he was doing, he responded, "It's not as if I'm on the floor crying," perhaps unconsciously referencing the event that had brought him shame more than fifty-five years earlier.

Conversely, where Jacques reaped attention in worldly successes, my role was more thoughtful. My natural tendency toward introspection, fueled by the large heaping of isolation that characterized my life, fostered my role as an observer, and fanned the world of my imaginings. Often described by my mother as thinking and feeling too much, I was labeled "too sensitive." My attention and approval were garnered in long philosophical talks with Mutti and serving in the role of advisor. This dynamic was so prevalent that it went unnoticed and unquestioned. In hindsight, I realize it was no accident that I was the one chosen to accompany my father to Heidelberg after his breakdown.

Nor was it an accident that in my seventeenth year, Mutti asked me to meet with my younger brother, Mark's, third-grade teacher, and his school principal. Mark's school requested the meeting to discuss holding Mark back. I do not know why she or my father did not go; I barely gave it a thought. My going seemed natural, and I was proud that Mom entrusted me with this responsibility. So, there I was, a pimply teenager, wearing coke-bottle glasses, meeting with a perplexed teacher, and baffled principal to discuss having Mark repeat the third grade. I could see their genuine concern for Mark and felt confident they had his best interests at heart. Mark was held back.

As you can see, my behaviors fell on both sides of the moral spectrum. I did some bad things, but I was not a bad guy. I had a moral compass. I knew right from wrong. Sometimes I just chose the latter. In this haphazard and undisciplined way, I fought to establish a sense of self in a world in which I felt largely powerless and unseen. Undoubtedly, it was an immature and deficient sense of self, but far better than no sense of self at all.

Throughout this time, my father's hand lay oppressively heavy upon us boys. From the day we moved into our newly built home in Annandale, Virginia, he put us to work as his slaves. He made us spend every weekend in the yard for over a year, including a snowy Christmas day. We removed tree stumps and brush and dug a hole for a rose garden like none other.

The hole was approximately four feet deep, twenty feet wide and thirty feet long. We had to shovel the dirt out of the hole, sift it through chicken wire to remove the rocks and clods, mix the soil with peat moss, lime, and fertilizer, then put it all back. In the summer, we labored through the Virginia heat and humidity, suffering stinging flies and mosquitoes, and then froze through the winter months. Dad, swallowed up by the deep and narrow well of his desires, was impervious to our protests. It is not that he did not care about feelings; it was that only his mattered.

I resented him; we all did. This became apparent one late afternoon as we broke out in sadistic glee when he nearly set himself ablaze. His was an epically stupid moment. The Great Man was smoking a cigarette, drinking one of several extra dry gin martinis, and engaging in another of his endless mind-numbing prattles, as he poured gas on a large area of brush to burn it away. Blathering, on, he fell ever further under the spell of his own voice, pouring gas the entire time. It occurred to me that vapors had to be spreading during his long prattle. A similar thought occurred to everyone else but the Great Man at about the same time. We started making eye contact with one another, then, without a word, slowly began backing up, like synchronized swimmers, one small step at a time.

Dad, eventually realizing that his audience had evaporated, decided it was time to throw a burning match onto the gas-drenched yard. The gas ignited with a percussive whoosh and instantly transformed into a voracious fireball. The look on Dad's face was priceless: surprise mutated into alarm and alarm into a panic. In a split second, he launched himself into full flight, the fire biting at his heels like the hot breath of a yellow beast. We all noted that despite having run for all he was worth, he never spilled a drop of that martini. At this observation, even he laughed.

Countless times, Dad stole whole days from me, insisting I caddy for him as he played golf. On one such occasion, as I was seething with resentment over my lost day, Dad ordered me not to walk on the putting green since I was not wearing golf shoes. I was wearing tennis shoes and did not weigh much, but it was not mine to question, only to serve. So off we went for a day on the links with a couple of his golf buddies.

Mid-way through the day, we came upon an unusually large green. Dad's ball had landed near the hole, at least twenty feet away from the green's edge. Standing next to it, Dad barked in command voice as if addressing a dog, "Charlie! Putter!" not bothering to use sentence structure or the word "Please." Already simmering with resentment over the loss of my day, and now enraged by his debasing treatment, I instantly recognized that the moment for pay-back was at hand.

Let me walk you through it. First, Dad ordered me not to step on the green. Second, he demanded his putter. Third, I was not to ask questions, simply do as instructed. I sang to myself, *Oh me, Oh my! What to do?* There was only one solution, and I loved it. Slowly I pulled the putter from the bag, took careful aim, wound up, and flung it like Zeus slinging a lightning bolt. The putter, spinning end over end, sparkled in the sunlight like a cheerleader's baton, catching the attention of all present before hitting headfirst, and tearing a large divot out of the green, a couple of feet from Dad.

It was beautiful: He and his buddies frozen in a grand tableau, stupefied by shock and surprise. Red-faced with fury, stutter completely forgotten, mouth opened, Dad screamed, voice rising to falsetto, "Charlie! What the hell are you doing?!"

I promptly came to attention, in a parody of a good soldier responding to his commanding officer and dutifully reiterated his orders one by one in my best soldier-reporting-in fashion for all to hear, finishing with a flourish that made me proud, "Sir! Throwing the putter was the only way I could comply. Sir!" He was furious, but with witnesses present and at a loss for words, he had been hoisted on his own petard. Bam!

We all worked hard to avoid Dad for once he got a hold of us he never let go. One task would morph into another and then another, often hijacking the entire day. Consequently, we became proficient listeners, charting his whereabouts within the house, sneaking out one door as he was entering another. We also excelled at deafness, tiptoeing from the house as if we had never been there whenever he called.

As the terrain of my childhood, my development was jagged and uneven, I was mature beyond my years in some ways and immature in others. I was a mishmash. I could not make sense of the world around me or of myself. I did not know what I wanted or who I wanted to become. I had no idea of what form I would finally take. But, like most, guessed it would not turn out well. So, with no other plan in mind, I kept flailing around like a punch-drunk fighter, vaguely hoping that somehow, someday, someway, something would fall into place. I just had to keep fighting.

Chapter 8

College: First Try

I stumbled out of high school much the way I had stumbled in, a year early and an education short. I barely had the grades to graduate. Going to college was not a burning desire. It was just the expected thing to do for a middle-class white kid, the next monotonous step in the long march called schooling. I had no plan B. The main appeal: I would be away from Dad.

I made it into Lynchburg College in Lynchburg, Virginia, home of ChapStick and Jerry Falwell, under academic probation and the requirement I attend summer school. The trouble with Lynchburg was that it was one of those rural towns that rolled up its sidewalks by 6 pm. Boredom lurked around every corner and was driving me crazy. Consequently, over a long weekend, I decided to hitchhike with a friend the 220 miles to Virginia Beach with twenty-five cents in my pocket; my friend had no money at all. Thus, my cleverness shone forth. The compelling need to get away, bolstered by the irrational belief that "Everything works out," overrode any vestige of common sense that might have argued against the plan.

We began our journey, thumbs out, on the outskirts of town. After a few minutes, a police cruiser passed by, the officer giving us the stink eye. I thought, *Hmm, maybe hitchhiking on this highway is illegal,* so we ran and hid behind a small berm, waiting to see if the cop returned. When he did not, we resumed our quest, and soon were picked up by a guy about our age.

Several miles later, a squad car, siren blaring, pulled us over. We were waiting for the cop to run the tags when our driver became agitated. In a tight-strung voice, he urgently whispered, "What did you guys do?" His demeanor baffled me until I turned my head to see the officer, gun drawn, duck-walking toward the car, then begin yelling, "Get your hands up! Get out of the car! Keep your hands in sight! Get out of the car!"

For those of you who have not had the pleasure of performing these instructions, let me assure you, it is no easy trick. For one, how are you supposed to open the door with your hands in the air? But you will genuinely appreciate the epic nature of this challenge, and the yogic skills required to meet it when you understand that I was jammed into the back seat of the infamous two-door hatchback AMC Gremlin—the awful lime-green colored one no less. The challenge was to push the front seat up, squeeze through the narrow opening, and perform a half twist to make it out the door. How was anyone to do that with both hands in the air? I was beginning to wonder if the cop was not a long-lost relative of my dad's; I was looking for a putter to throw. But, inspired by the fervent desire to keep my body free of perforations, I performed these feats to perfection. Grunting and groaning, I squeezed out of the car, as if birthed by a narrow-hipped lizard.

Staggering into the sunlight, I beheld firsthand three of life's fundamental truths. First: The small hole in the bore of a gun becomes the size of a mountain tunnel when pointed at you. Second: When that tunnel is shaking as if its holder bestrides the shifting tectonic plates of an earthquake, the hole grows even larger. Third: The bore becomes a galactic black-hole, exerting its own mesmerizing pull, when the gun is held by a jowly, middle-aged cop, breathing hard, eyes bulging, belly protruding, sweating profusely, and shaking with fright. In short, the precariousness of our situation was not to be pooh-poohed. The possibility of getting shot was real, if only by accident. Given this circumstance, I found myself in the strange position of trying to calm the cop. Hands out, palms down, pressing them again and again toward the ground, I repeatedly uttered the mantra: "Everything's cool. Everything's cool."

Unfortunately, the cop did not seem the least bit reassured, and my apprehension grew as every passing second increased the possibility of the officer having a heart attack and an accidental trigger pull. Finally, unable to sustain such peak levels of stress, the cop gathered himself and settled down. He demanded identification, that we empty our backpacks, and explain who we were, where we were going, and why we had run. Upon this gathering of facts, he, like Inspector Clouseau, came to a decision. Without preamble, he fumbled his pistol back into its holster and transformed into a Chatty Cathy (a doll popular in the sixties that talked when you pulled a string), explaining there had been a robbery and that my friend and I met the description of the culprits. Our run from the side of the highway had only stoked his suspicion. At that, he let us go.

At Virginia Beach, we swam, ogled the girls, and fell asleep on the sand, waking hours later, starving. We bought a loaf of bread with my quarter, and that night took up residence under a tarpaulin-covered stack of chairs on the concrete boardwalk. The next morning the sound of a car passing close to my head woke me. Warily lifting the tarp, I spied the rear tires of a squad car slowly rolling passed.

Hungry and penniless, taunted by the smell of food we could not afford, we swam and slept the day away before deciding to cut our trip short. Without the benefit of foreplaning, it was nightfall, not the best of times to start a 220-mile journey depending upon the goodwill of strangers.

That said, the saying that God loves fools and drunks is true. We were the former and only failed to be the latter due to a lack of finances. Unbelievably, we immediately got a ride from a man in a white Cadillac: The Cadillac Man. In casual conversation, he claimed he was the brother of the great guitarist, Charlie Byrd, and for the next hour, spewed jealous testimony of his brother's success while lamenting his having to grind out a living as a salesman. Luckily, his generosity offset his less than attractive envy. He paid for dinner at a truck stop and gave us money to stay in the Richmond YMCA. The Cadillac Man is forever okay in my book.

The next morning, I awoke with eyes swollen and glued tight with dried mucus—the price of two days on the beach without shelter. After painfully prying my eyes open with the aid of a hot shower, we hitched another ride. This time, an old couple invited us into their world, and soon, we, or at least they, were having a party.

Swilling vodka from a bottle and bickering non-stop, the party went the way of many alcohol-fueled revelries. The bickering grew into a squabble, and the squabble into a squall as the crone took increasing issue with the man for "drivin' too fas and putt'n dem yung boys in back at ris." I became alarmed when, in the middle of her rant, she suddenly disappeared, and seconds later, the old man began screaming. Hurriedly, I leaned forward to investigate. To my horror, the crone was on her hands and knees, bent forward, and biting the man's ankle in a determined effort to get his foot off the accelerator. Yelling, kicking, and screaming, the old man finally relented and pulled to the side of the road; there, they continued to argue while, our survival instincts humming, my friend and I begged off from the ride.

Eventually, we crawled back into Lynchburg safe and sound, if somewhat tattered. Our mini-vacation having been successful in providing adventure and relief from small-town monotony — so successful that I decided never to do anything like that again.

That fall, I was assigned to off-campus housing. My roommate was a talented guitar and harmonica player and singer to boot. He was also a babe magnet in that he had 'the look' — tall, gangly, and long-haired and entertained at the local coffee houses. He introduced me to marijuana and hallucinatory drugs, and a new world exploded open before me — a whole other kind of education began. I was a quick study and, while watching neon-colored dragons scamper playfully, breathing fire in the brightly lit coliseum of my mind, my grades plummeted. Before the end of the semester, we were both expelled.

My father picked me up from Lynchburg for the endless ride home, made longer by his lecturing and customary pokes, smacks, and slaps to the face — I was starting to think my name was Curly. But I had earned this treatment; my parents were rightfully upset. They decided that I would work for a year to get my head on straight before reapplying to college.

That year proved inspirational, albeit tedious. I learned the limitation of job opportunities one faced without a college degree. The jobs were mind-numbing, and one thing I learned with certainty was that I could not tolerate that for long.

I worked in a government warehouse in Springfield, VA, that distributed medical publications. My job entailed walking up and down long aisles collecting books for shipment. I worked alongside African American trustees from Lorton Prison and befriended them, earning the nickname "ABC." When I asked what that stood for, they all laughed and said, "Ace, Boone, Coon."

One fellow, maybe forty-five years old, was nicknamed Rabbit, purportedly for all the children he had sired. Rabbit used lotion to keep his hands soft, explaining as my uninvited mentor in the romance department, "Da lai-dies luv dat." One day, Rabbit asked me to join him for a night in D.C. to celebrate his release from Lorton. I met him a few weeks later, in a part of town that made me feel like a vanilla cone in a sea of chocolate.

Rabbit and I stood outside, drinking cheap whiskey straight out of the bottle, then walked to a nearby house to meet up with a couple of women. Each of these ladies weighed 250 pounds if an ounce and was not over five foot two. We slow danced but try as I might, I could not fan the flames of romance within myself and, thank God, neither could she. My only thought was *How the hell do I get out of this?* It occurred to me that Rabbit's idea of a great night, the stuff of his legend, might be a little different from mine. I left as soon as possible, and I am sure to the relief of all.

By the time the year was over, I was desperate to return to college. My Uncle, Mac, knew the president of Baltimore's Loyola College of Maryland (today Loyola University), Joseph A.

Sellinger, and arranged for me to apply there. I was accepted under both social *and* academic probation.

I well knew that if I had not had this family connection, my life might have gone in a different direction. I felt sorry for those without such ties and guilty for using mine, believing that in a fair world, I should have had to make it on my own. But if there was one thing I knew about life, it was: forget fair.

Chapter 9

Something Called Thinking

What would you do if you were walking down a city street and came upon a drunk passed out in the gutter with one finger on the sidewalk?" This provocative question prompted several responses, ranging from "Help him up" to "Walk around him." But this craggy-faced priest, so different from The Priest of my previous acquaintance, was vexed by such pat answers, impatiently chiding in his Irish brogue, "No, no, no. You step on the finger!" Stunned, I was more than intrigued by his cruel assertion.

It turned out this priest was not cruel at all. As a recovering alcoholic, he explained: "It's a kindness to step on the finger. The drunk will grab any pretext to negate where he is; with his finger on the sidewalk, he will deny that *he's* in the gutter. The drunk needs to accept his reality to have any hope of changing it." Thus, this priest introduced me to the problems created by denial and the critical importance of taking personal responsibility for your life.

The Jesuits taught me to question authority, including the Catholic Church, more thoughtfully. Noting that the Church was the fifth wealthiest organization in the world, they questioned, "Why would the Church hold onto their countless artifacts and near limitless wealth, rather than use them to help the poor? "Years later, while touring the vast treasures of the Vatican, I thought Jesus would have wondered the same. In such ways, the Jesuits were inspiring, modeling the importance and integrity of critical thinking and respectfully challenging the Church rather than echoing dogma.

The Jesuits also introduced me to a variety of religions and philosophies, from Judaism to Hinduism to Buddhism, and from existentialism to nihilism, along with courses in reason and logic. These disciplines stimulated my questioning mind and fostered a desire to learn. Never having applied myself to studying, I began learning how to learn. I started using as many sensory inputs as I could: Reading out loud to take in the sound of the words, writing out key concepts to make a motor memory of them, and underlining sentences to intensify my visual recording of the information. Whenever my grade on an essay or test was disappointing, I borrowed the same from a classmate who had done well and compared them, sometimes discovering that what was at fault was not so much what I had written but how I had written it.

I developed strategies for taking tests. Ironically, this was prompted by my failing a test because I knew too much. I focused so hard on answering the first essay question in-depth that I ran out of time before I could address the remaining four. I learned to budget my time.

In another class, I recognized that the instructor graded by taking points away rather than by adding them. Stumped on question three, I wrote the answer to question two to the bottom of the page, starting the next page with question four. I reasoned that the professor had to grade at least one hundred such tests and suspected that that wearisome activity would dull his wits, and he might not notice an answer was missing. I was correct.

Over my four years at Loyola, I advanced from a low C-minus grade point average to a solid B, missing qualifying for the honor society in economics by a tenth of a point. That first year of learning to learn had cost me.

I had chosen economics as a major because I still had no dream or burning desire lighting my way. Surprisingly, it was Dad who gave me the best advice: "When you don't know what to do, keep moving from minus to plus, keep moving ahead." Following this advice, I came to realize that learning is never a waste; everything relates to everything else.

I also joined the soccer team where, given my lack of speed, I mainly rode the bench. However, I did have one glorious moment. While playing fullback, I trapped the incoming ball out of the air between my torso and my knee. Gazing at it in amazement, I wondered how I had done that, then came to my senses, realizing I could not just stand there. I started running, miraculously bouncing the ball from knee to knee, covering half the distance of the field before it fell to the ground. This feat, worthy of Pelé, brought a roar from the spectators. Little did they know I was as amazed as they.

I lived on campus in the Hammerman House dorm. From the roof, we students watched Baltimore burn during the riots following the assassination of Martin Luther King. Our grief only cutting more profoundly several months later with the murder of Bobby Kennedy. Much like 9/11, the horror of these events unified the country.

Another, equally powerful experience of unification, albeit from an entirely different and far less reaching cause, came from an unexpected source. Having been in constant motion throughout my life, I had never had an allegiance to any city, much less a professional sports team. But as I joined my fellow students to watch the Colts and Orioles, I became entranced by their tribal enthusiasm and unmitigated passion for these teams. This adulation was not confined to students, but was statewide, and knew no gender, age or racial divide. It was the first utterly unifying experience of which I had ever felt apart, providing a palpable sense of belonging I had never experienced before. When the teams won, the whole state was happy, and when they lost, all despaired. Having been the perpetual outsider, I loved the feeling of being a part of something so primal that it cut through all divides.

During the summer, following my first year at Loyola, a friend declined a job at Assateague Island National Seashore as a lifeguard and arranged for me to go in his place. Thus, I became, as far as I know, the first legally blind (eyesight 20/450 with my glasses off) National Park Service Lifeguard. I could say they hired me sight unseen. Of course, this was not a problem unless I had to rescue someone. Then, whipping off my glasses, an optic fog would encompass me. As luck would have it, I never had to save anyone or, to be completely honest, not anyone I saw.

At Assateague, the head lifeguard was Wayne Kirgel. Wayne was six-foot-tall with light-brown hair that turned blond in the sun. He looked like a gay caballero, without the sombrero but with blue eyes. In contrast, I was 5'10" tall, brown-haired, lean, muscled, and deeply tanned, almost black. Where I was garrulous, Wayne was quiet and unassuming.

We drilled daily regardless of the weather. During a storm, the sky stained dark with menacing clouds, the ocean flogged by gusts of wind and the sea running high, I was to 'rescue' Wayne who had swum out about seventy-five yards. Standing atop the lifeguard tower, glasses on, windowpane lenses beaded with rain, I could barely see him as his head bobbed erratically in and out of view amongst the frothing waves.

Upon a signal, I whipped off my glasses, plunged into blindness, and lept to the beach. Grabbing the rescue board, I darted valiantly into the tumultuous sea, where, within

moments, I was swept several hundred feet downstream by the

fierce current and rendered wholly disoriented. Paddling

frantically, I looked for Wayne far and wide, and wider yet, but

to no avail. After a few minutes, panting like an Alaskan Huskie,

tongue lolling, I heard a wavering bellow floating above the din

of wind and crashing waves. "McccccCorrrrrrmackkkkk!...

McccccCcccccormackkkkkk!... YYYYOOoouu

BASSSSTTTTTTARD!" The absurdity of the situation struck me. I

began laughing, and then laughing more, unable to stop. When I

finally found Wayne, guided by his unrelenting invectives, I

dragged his sodden form onto the rescue board between

continuing jags of uncontrollable laughter. From that moment on,

we were fast friends and proceeded to get into lots of trouble

together.

The ocean, particularly on big sea days, taught me

something about dealing with the power of natural forces,

including emotions. On this day, a Nor'easter was passing

through, sky seething with clouds. The 40 mph winds, along with

the mountain size waves crisscrossing crazily and crashing into

one another like locomotives driven by wild men, had swept the

beach clear of people.

Taking in this spectacle, I wanted to join the cacophony that

resonated with my soul. I wanted to surf one of those waves.

After several exhausting attempts, I succeeded in fighting my way through the mountain range of incoming breakers. Sitting astride my surfboard nearly two hundred yards from the beach, just beyond the enormous break, I gathered myself while drinking in the power and tumult surrounding me. As waves pounded like bass drums, and the wind shrieked like cats flung through the air, fear prickled my chest as adrenalin driven excitement causes me to exult in the tumult.

I waited: First to catch my breath and then to catch a moving mountain of water as it swept beneath me before morphing from swell to breaking wave. Each passing surge lifted me and dropped me down like a child on a giant swing. My view of the distant shore blocked, I felt alone in the foaming, crashing bowels of the beast, simultaneously frightened and exhilarated.

It was time. I began to paddle, catching a swell that became a living thing as it shape-shifted into a wave. Tottering, I rose to my feet, begging myself not to fall, and managed to stand just as the wave broke, slinging me down the falling mountainside. I was riding the monster.

I thought, *Holy shit! It's high up here. Whoa! Going so fast, keep your balance.* Soon, this self-conscious patter separated me from my instincts, slowed my response time, and sealed my fate. Down I went into the trough, the crashing wave jack-hammering me into the muffled silence and dimness of the world below, while simultaneously rocketing the surfboard, which I had previously detached from my arm to avoid being dragged along by it, high into the air.

Now I was truly afraid. Afraid of being hit by the board when it returned to earth and of the unrelenting power of the waves that continued to drive me down head over heels to the ocean floor. I worried about breaking my neck.

I knew to give in to panic, to fight the ocean, was to lose, so I ignored the urge to battle to the surface and focused on conserving my breath and protecting my head. Time and space were thus created within which to take in my surroundings.

Wonder soon supplanted fear as I opened my mind to the symphony of sights and sounds that surrounded me. As waves rumbled past like freight trains overhead, a shaft of Cathedral light bore through the turbulent water, revealing the sandy bottom. There, rivers of sand and millions of sparkling bubbles swirled Dervish-like along the ocean floor, glimmering like sequins on a dancer's dress. Held in the ocean's firm embrace, rocked back and forth by the ebb and flow pressures of the waves trundling overhead, awe and an unexpected sense of peace and beauty came over me, not unlike that of a child, securely held in the arms of his mother: Mother Nature.

I questioned, *Is this the bliss of asphyxiation?* but reasoned I had not yet felt starved for air. Reassured, I returned to the glittering spectacle that surrounded me until a lessening of the pressure that was holding me under signaled the passing of the current set of breakers. I kicked hard toward the surface, moving from shadow to light, from muted sound below to the fury above, and fought my way to shore, dragging myself, limp as seaweed, onto the beach.

In later years, I learned to co-exist with powerful emotions rather than try to defeat them. I would sit with them, suffer them, observe them, and appreciate the power of their terrible embrace. I would discover that the fact of observing emotions protects from being completely swallowed up by them and creates the space necessary to think and feel and learn about oneself. I discovered that observing emotion is the difference between having an emotion and being that emotion; between feeling panic and being panicked and that feelings, just like waves, expand and contract, ebb and flow, and, given time, dissipate. The thing one must accept is that it is typically not up to us to say when this will be: Waves must run their course.

Assateague is a desert island, famous for its wild horses, mosquitoes, and carnivorous flies that bite like vampires until killed. One such bite became infected, and the vein near the bite turned dark blue; the blue had been traveling up my arm for days. On a visit home, I showed my arm to my parents. Contrary to expectations, instead of going to the hospital, Dad happily took this opportunity to demonstrate his army First Aid know-how. He soaked my arm in hot water and Epsom salt, then, using a steak knife, cut open the wound, reached in with a pair of tweezers and pulled out a white sack holding the offending pus.

As impressive as this was, the absence of anesthesia impressed me more. Nonetheless, per the mores of my family, I gritted my teeth and endured without complaint. To give Dad his due, my arm quickly healed, aside from the scar that remains with me to this day. In such ways, history inscribes itself upon our bodies.

The National Park Service fired Wayne and me for throwing a party at the lifeguard barracks. Our crime was twofold: bringing females into a male barracks and charging admission to a government building. What the NPS did not know was that Wayne and I had liberated the keg of beer from the Ocean City Police Department's beach party the night before. We had dug a hole just outside the reach of the light of the bonfire, rolled the keg in, and covered it for retrieval the next day.

We then took a job at Phillips Crab House in Ocean City. There, in a dingy, smelly room, I picked shell fragments from cans of crabmeat while sitting alongside Mrs. Phillips, the grandmother of the clan, and a millionaire businesswoman. All I can tell you is that if I had her money, I would not be sitting next to me in a dingy, smelly room picking crab shells. But of course, I am sure some party-killing dullard will point out that that is why she has the money.

Phillips Crab house fired us for skipping out of work. We then gained employment at a gas station featuring bikini-clad beauties at the pumps. Somehow, despite, or perhaps because of our sins, we had landed in heaven, proving that God does indeed work in mysterious ways.

Forever restless, Wayne and I rode his Honda 450 motorcycle to Baltimore and D.C. to party. On one such occasion, during a torrential downpour that stung like bees, Wayne sped up trying to make a yellow light before it turned red. Instantly, I recognized that we would never make it and shouted at him to stop; I had the insane urge to bite his ankle. At last, recognizing his effort was doomed, Wayne slammed on the brakes and propelled us into a 360-degree spin on the wet asphalt. Instinctively, we kicked out against the road with our feet in a frantic effort to stay upright, looking for all the world like men performing a wild Cossack wedding dance. In this frenzied manner, we completed two 360-degree turns before arriving, against all the odds, perfectly situated at the stoplight next to a van, the windows of which were filled with a bug-eyed family staring out at us as Wayne and I slumped with relief.

On another occasion, we were pulled over by police outside of Berlin, Maryland, in a random traffic check. I was driving and had no motorcycle license. Lamely, I protested I could not find it, and the officer, unimpressed, insisted we follow him to the station. The latter was a two-room building. The officer had us wait in the front room before disappearing into the back. To my puzzlement, Wayne immediately began taking off his shirt while urgently whispering, "Charlie, give me your shirt and glasses." In seconds, we exchanged clothing. When the officer returned,

Wayne pronounced, "Sir, I found my driver's license." The officer looked at us suspiciously and carefully examined the license. He looked at the photo, then at each of us, then back at the photo. Perplexed, he went through these deliberations several more times before, in a slow country drawl, begrudgingly said: "I know sump'n goin' on heah; I jus don know wat it is." He puzzled over it a while longer and then, shaking his head in bewilderment, let us go.

When school resumed in the Fall, Wayne visited me and had the opportunity to observe a soccer game. There, I was holding down my usual honored position at the end of the bench several time zones away from the coach. After the game, one of my teammates pulled me aside and asked in a reverent tone, "Is that Killer Kirgel?" *Well,* I thought, *Kirgel was right, but who the hell was Killer?* My teammate, acting like a rock-star groupie, went into breathless detail, describing Wayne's dominance and a national ranking as a champion wrestler on the Old Dominion wrestling team. Indeed, that was why Wayne was in town: He had a match, and I was attending. Wayne asked if there were anything I would like to see during the event. I told him it would be helpful if he waited until the third period to pin his opponent, thus giving me every opportunity to analyze his game and afford him my vaunted insights. He snorted.

That night, during his match, Wayne was repeatedly put into exotic holds by his opponent. Looking like an upside-down pretzel with his head mashed sideways cheek to the mat, his feet dangling incongruously over his head, and his coach screaming, "What are you doing? What are you doing? End this now!" I kept thinking; *It doesn't look like Wayne will be ending anything.*

The third period arrived, and I took solace knowing that soon, the match would be over. I watched as Wayne's head, firmly framed by his opponent's arms, was again bent painfully askew, his appendages impossibly intertwined with those of his opponent. Together, the two formed a bizarre Cubist painting, hinting uncomfortably at a newly discovered position in the Kama Sutra. It was then that Wayne looked directly at me, his one visible eye, as large as a cyclops', peering through a jumble of crisscrossing limbs. His eye bored into mine from this crazy-making upside-down position and then… winked. I could not help but laugh. Within seconds, Wayne was out of his opponent's hold and pinned him.

All things end, and that magical, manic summer was no exception. During the ensuing summers, I worked sixteen to twenty-hour days for a moving company, packing boxes and loading trucks, carrying washing machines on my back, sometimes throwing up from the heat of the day and the physical strain.

One customer stands out, a hatchet-faced woman, about 5'6" tall with lank shoulder-length dark hair, and a face turned roadmap by harsh living. She lived in a moving man's nightmare: a third-floor walk-up apartment. The day was dripping with humidity and well into the sweltering 90s, and I asked if I could have some water. To my astonishment, she looked at me without expression, and flatly responded, "No." Dumbfounded, I exited the apartment and rested in the shade of the truck. She then appeared on the balcony with a pitcher in hand. Waiting until she was sure I was watching, she slowly poured water from the pitcher to the ground below. Wow! There was a lady baking in the acid of her bile. I did not know this woman and, to my knowledge, had done nothing to upset her.

It got me wondering. *Why would this lady do this to a stranger who had given no affront and done no harm?* I concluded that some people, some of the time, feel so small or angry at the world that they take these feelings out on whoever they can. Had I not done the same years earlier when I had tattled on the little girl who peed her pants? But that was typical childhood cruelty, where an adult had done this: That is a league of its own.

Fueled by curiosity and a burning desire to make sense of things, I felt a pressing need to make sense of myself and the people around me. For me, the only way to do this was to find myself in others and others in myself. I needed to be able to identify with what was going on. At this early phase in my development, I had no idea that this compelling inclination would one day guide my life.

Chapter 10

Lottery of Life

Three-one-six, Three-one-six. The number rang in my head like an auctioneer's chant. "Going once, going twice, sold!" I felt like dancing as James Brown's voice rang in my head, "Watch me now!" and I performed several tight spins, before breaking out into Little Eva's version of "The Locomotive," followed by Chubby Checker's "The Twist," finishing the whole thing off with Elvis the Pelvis's signature thrusts. I was a dancing fool— at least, in my mind.

The date: December 1, 1969, one month and twelve days before my twentieth birthday: I had just won the Lottery of Life. The selective service had conducted a lottery to draft men for the Vietnam war; my birthday was the 316th number drawn. Uncle Sam would have to empty America of young men before turning his baleful stare upon me; I had just escaped the Vietnam War.

There was one hitch: I had enrolled in the Reserve Officers Training Course (ROTC). As a single male, I was likely to be drafted and wanted to complete my college education first; I was hoping the war would be over by then. Also, the ROTC had provided a scholarship to help me pay for college, an important consideration given that aside from $1500 my mother had donated, it was up to me to fund the rest. But now, with the number 316, a new calculus was in play. I learned I could void the contract by quitting school.

The Colonel was not happy, but I did not care; he had not paid a cent toward my education. Then there was the Army captain in charge of the ROTC program. Richie Havens singing "Freedom" at Woodstock played in my mind drowning-out the Captain's in-my-face spittle-laden tirade, which concluded with, "You're not officer material anyway!" I knew he had no care of me, just a quota to fill.

I enrolled in night school, where I discovered that it does not matter where you go to school if you hunger to learn. By this time, I was learning so well that the professor of economics asked me to teach the class when he had a schedule conflict. I was surprised for my night school classmates were older, with families and full-time jobs, some having operated in the business world for years and thus, to my mind, more qualified. Fortunately, the professor arrived early enough that night to save me from total humiliation. While trying to expound on various economic concepts, I stumbled upon gaps in my knowledge that paralyzed my capacity to teach. In this painful way, I discovered that if you do not understand something, you cannot explain it, and often, you cannot know what you don't know until you *try* to explain it. I would later learn that this is an important part of how psychotherapy works.

After a semester in night school, I re-enrolled in day school. Despite a growing number of successes, I still felt like I couldn't quite make the grade. In the previous three years, I had barely made it out of high school, gotten myself kicked out of college, been fired from several jobs, rode the bench on the soccer team, tried unsuccessfully to teach a class in economics, and missed membership in the honor society. The dysphoria and anger of my youth, to which I repeatedly returned, as if it were home, continued to act as the quicksand of my adulthood. Although making progress, I was still far from having arrived.

My standard for success was Jacques. Talk about opposites. He was graduating from the University of Virginia as the president of his class and had been wined and dined by prestigious accounting firms, landing a well-paying position with one of the Big Eight in Atlanta. I was proud of him, all the while, knowing I fell far short in comparison.

As I saw it, not only was that the story of his life, but it was also the story of mine. That was just the way things were, the way it had always been, and I feared the way it always would be.

Upon graduation, I searched for work. It did not matter what; I still had no burning desire lighting my way. Meanwhile, Killer Kirgel, in his irritatingly understated way, managed to make news in the *Washington Post* and on National TV. He accomplished the latter on no less a show than that of the iconic

Walter Cronkite. Wayne did it by turkey-nabbing the National Turkey from the National Zoo, leaving behind a note identifying the kidnappers as The Filthy Five, along with a demand for $250,000 on behalf of the American Indian. That evening, Mr. Cronkite, with a bemused expression, noted the turkey-nabbing at the end of his broadcast, followed by his signature sign-off, "And that's the way it is." The following day, Wayne dropped the turkey off at an animal shelter with a note saying it was in the turkey's best interest to be returned. That night, Mr. Cronkite signed off, once again, mentioning this event with wry amusement.

While Wayne was making national news, I visited Atlanta, in quest of employment. I had none of Jacques's polish, nor air of confidence. Feeling every inch 'the country bumpkin,' I came nowhere close to landing a job. Tail between my legs, I returned to the moving company to run their import/export desk, arranging for the shipment of goods around the world.

Several shipping companies vying for cargo invited me to Baltimore. Three sales guys took me to dinner at the Playboy Club, and then to a strip joint on the infamous Block. At the strip club, everyone was solicited for oral sex and accepted. I might have accepted as well, but I did not have any money and feared that my Catholic guilt and discomfort with the whole situation would get in the way. So, I politely declined. The woman responded, "I didn't think so, honey, but I thought I'd ask." I imagined she detected straw poking out of my young ears.

In the car, after leaving the club, someone produced a joint, and shortly after, internal filters down, my driving need to understand things came into play. I tried to make a deeper connection with these guys. In so doing, I managed to suck the air out of the evening. Apparently, asking if they liked their jobs was not the way to go, especially when it turned out, they hated them. I then compounded the problem by wondering aloud how it felt to have oral sex with one woman while married to another. I wasn't judging; I was naïve. I was genuinely curious about how one navigated those rocky shoals. In other words, I was the worst kind of fool, the kind that does not know that he is the idiot in the room.

That night, drunk and stoned, I stayed over at the home of one of the salesmen and awoke the next morning to a family breakfast. I met his classically beautiful and warmly welcoming wife and two delightful, elementary-school-aged daughters. While breakfasting with them, I could not help but think, *Why?* I thought about the secrets we keep and the primitive desires that skulk just below the surface. I was fascinated by the difference between how things look and how things are and wondered if anyone could truly know and trust anyone else.

Similar human dramas were being played out at the moving company. The manager, blustering, fat, and married, loved to show off his Masonic square ring, touting principles of morality and virtue, while flagrantly engaged in an affair with the Hispanic secretary. She, a full-figured woman, relished strutting about the office in stiletto heels, short black skirts and tight white blouses, buttons straining to hold in her considerable charms while lording it over everyone else. I felt for her. She seemed unaware that hers was a moment of fleeting power on this smallest of stages.

All the while, I was being tossed about by my primal impulses. While using my brother, Ed's Honda 450 motorcycle for transportation, I discovered that youth, hormones, and powerful vehicles make a dangerous combination, particularly when combined with attractive women.

One Friday evening, I was leaving work, excited about the weekend off. I got on the 450, turned the ignition, and *Varoom!* The vibration of the Honda tingled my groin, rumbled up my spine, and exploded in my crocodile brain. Revving the engine, I kicked the motorcycle into gear, popped the clutch, and screeched away. Despite the misty day, I was exalting in my freedom from work and singing fragments of *King of the Road* in my off-key, cracking voice that had gotten me kicked out of required choir.

The mist cast an oily sheen atop the asphalt road—the effluvia of countless moving trucks over the decades. Driving along, I spied a car pulling out of an alley some seventy-five yards ahead and reasoned I had plenty of time while the driver sped up. But, amazingly, she did nothing of the kind. Instead, she stopped in the middle of the road. As I strained to see through the mist, I realized she was using her rear-view mirror to adjust her makeup. *Unbelievable.*

I was slow to react. Brakes locked tight, hydroplaning across the oil-slathered tarmac, my first thought was *Oh shit!* which then transformed into the lyric, *"Slip sliding away,"* only to be converted into the *"Going, going — gone!"* of an auctioneer's chant, the *"Gone"* punctuated by the sound of bike meeting car: *Crunch!*

Lying supine on the oil-slick road, airborne droplets of water misting my face, motorcycle between my legs, I struggled to avoid the hot exhaust pipe. As I lay there gasping, a concerned Asian female face framed by long, straight, black hair appeared in disorienting upside-down relationship to my own. Leaning forward to get a better look, face concerned, almond eyes reflecting worry, she spoke in a singsong voice, "Hello. My name Sunshine."

The juxtaposition of her name with the soggy weather and the fact that her thoughtless actions had contributed to me lying crumpled on the cold, wet tarmac was so absurd that laughter bubbled up from within me. I answered, "You're certainly the Sunshine in my life," hoping this clever irony would lead to a date. Unfortunately, I failed to evoke either a smile or her phone number.

The following week, having grieved the loss of my never-was and never-to-be relationship with Sunshine, and of the Honda 450, I stood before the next new-and-true love of my life.

She was perfect: sleek and curvy, skin smooth and glistening, with a throaty voice that rendered me weak-kneed. She embodied power and confidence. I hungered to be inside her, to claim her as my own, all the while wondering: *Am I up to the task? Can I push her limits without exceeding my own?* Well, time to find out. *Varoom!*

She was my Dad's midlife car: A shiny dark blue Pontiac GTO with white racing stripes, hood manifold, front and rear stabilizer bars, roll bar, and a Hurst four-on-the-floor stick shift. Her engine, crowned by three deuce carburetors, generated 360 horsepower. Given my previous week's encounter with Sunshine and the resultant lack of a ride to work, Dad let me borrow her. As I was leaving that morning, he called out, "Ignore the oil gauge. It's broken."

Throughout the day, I looked forward to getting together with another true love of my life that evening. Also built for speed, we had already been around the track several times together. She was sleek, blond, and blue-eyed, pure sex poured into head-turning outfits and entirely out of my league. She was used to dating suits on Capitol Hill, who knew how to order wine. I did not understand why she was hanging with me; I just hoped she would not ask herself that question anytime soon.

That evening, enjoying titillating fantasies as I drove the Washington beltway in light rain on the way to her house, I felt the GTO falter. It was a fleeting sensation, so threatening to my evening's plans that I immediately passed it off as *only my imagination.* All the while, another part of my brain implored, *Oh God! Not now! Not this night.* The engine stuttered again. I prayed more fervently. *Please, God. Be the kind, compassionate, change-water-to-wine, party-down, New Testament God. Let the car hang together long enough to get me there.*

Deciding to cover my bases, I went secular, reasoning: *The oil gauge is bottomed out, but Dad told me it was not working—ergo, it couldn't be the oil.* The car faltered again, basically replying, *"Wrong, Idiot! It's the oil."* I could not bear this thought, fearing it would spell the end of my erotic aspirations. Face scrunched, hands death-gripping the steering wheel, I attempted to hold the car together by sheer force of will. *Bang!* The engine seized. I coasted to the side of the beltway.

Although sick at heart about the car, I quickly reasoned that I could not do anything about it at this hour, but I *could* salvage the evening. I stepped into the rain and stuck my thumb out. Ninety minutes later, nerves frayed, wet and smelly, having basted in a marinade of misty rain and carbon monoxide winds from thousands of passing cars, I arrived at her townhouse. She opened the door, her red lips spread wide in greeting. Her bright smile telling me it had all been worthwhile. Visions of sugarplums danced in my head. *Varoom!*

Tragically, this euphoric state vanished as I looked over her shoulder to spy a guy, seeming very much at home, on the living room couch. *Plop!* What was this? My fevered hopes for the evening, repeatedly splinted and propped up against all the odds, could take no more. I slumped on the couch, accepted a beer, and tried my best to affect nonchalance. My rival pulled out a joint. Soon, eyeglasses slipping askew down my wet nose, I was unable to move or speak, while acutely aware through glazed-over eyes that my true love and my rival were chatting animatedly while entirely ignoring me. Slack-jawed, inwardly suffering a rending agony of humiliation and shame, I watched as she moved on from me without saying a word. My last thought, *I wonder if I am drooling.*

Of course, take this jokey rendering of the tale and turn it upside down, and you will appreciate how eviscerated I truly felt.

Back at work, the manager kept stringing me along with promises of salary increases that, like mirages, remained just out of reach over the next horizon. Eventually wising up to his deception, I quit and accepted a three-month contract as an accounting technician for the Department of Defense (DOD).

My workplace at the DOD was a cavernous room filled with rows of desks. Each morning, I marveled inwardly at the wooden faces of my co-workers that greeted me. Blanched by the unforgiving fluorescent light, lacking any sign of spirit or playfulness, these people were resigned to the drudgery of their jobs as necessary evils. They were so inanimate that I questioned whether they went home at night or remained frozen in place at their desks until someone came along and dusted them off each morning to begin another day, just like yesterday.

Almost certainly, their lack of liveliness was attributable to the work we did. What awaited me every morning at my desk was a two-foot-high ream of computer paper, laden with two columns of long numbers. My mission was to ensure that the figures in the right column matched those in the left. If not, I was to circle the offending digits. I had no idea what these numbers represented.

I became proficient at running a ruler down the pages, looking for any hint of deviance, like a sheriff on the prowl. Finished after a few hours, I would pick up a book, such as D.T. Suzuki's *Zen and Japanese Buddhism*. Some weeks into my job, the supervisor stopped by my desk as I was reading and asked: "What are you doing?" I thought it obvious, so the question confused me. He elaborated, "Why aren't you working?"

"Oh!" I exclaimed, "I've finished." Then helpfully added, "If you have more for me to do, I'll be glad to do it."

Irritated, he said, "I don't have more for you to do, but you can't read a book, you have to look busy."

I thought about this, then responded truthfully, "I'm sorry, I can't do that, that's too hard. If you have more work for me to do, I will gladly do it, but I can't do "'looking busy.'"

He appraised me silently, trying to discern if I was disrespectful and correctly concluded that I was neither rude nor insincere. He grunted and left without another word.

More weeks passed, and my contract neared its end. The supervisor returned to my desk, "We would like you to enter the fast-track management training program." He explained that this entailed intensive management training over six months and then exiting the process as a GS-9. I would get a substantial pay increase and more challenging responsibilities. I was surprised and appreciative, thinking, *This is a great opportunity, the possible beginning of a career. I too can be legitimate. I also can be respectable. Take that, Jacques!* But, as one part of my mind was thinking these thoughts, another was looking around the room, seeing these timeworn people, doing their jobs day in and day out, without fire or joy in their bellies. I then knew that continuing to work for the DOD would bleed me dry and not fit with some ill-defined vision I had of myself. I expressed my appreciation for the offer and declined. Two weeks later, I joined the ranks of the unemployed.

But I was not alone. I had met Jane through a friend. Smart, petite, pretty, quiet, and gentle, I was immediately attracted. We hit it off and moved in together three weeks later. We had been a couple for about six months when I entered the newfound freedom of the unemployed.

Following my usual faultless planning, I decided to do something that virtually everyone was against: go on a camping trip. Not any camping trip but one with no end date or destination in mind. Curiously, although I could appreciate that this would do little in the way of career advancement, I did not feel I had a choice. Something unnamed but powerful was moving me. I knew I was drawing outside the lines and that I had no idea what form, if any, my scribbles would take. I was searching for something without knowing what that something was. All I *knew for certain* was that I needed the freedom to find *it* and would know *it* if I did.

Jane and I cashed out our bank accounts, paid the penalty for breaking the apartment lease, packed up my VW Beetle with tent and supplies, and drove out of town without a backward glance. My plan—yes, by golly, I had one—go until the cash runs out: go for broke.

Chapter 11

Escaping to Find Myself

I carried a gun. Everybody needs a gun. After all, we need to protect ourselves, don't we? There must be hordes of people, some I know personally, who have required a gun for protection. Let me list them: Hmm. In ten years, twenty years, thirty years, a lifetime, I realize I do not personally know anyone who has needed a gun to protect himself—unless you count war.

The whole headline-grabbing news strategy of, "If it bleeds, it leads," unfailingly works angst into our collective hearts, leaving people afraid of the unknown or the unfamiliar, of people that do not look the same or speak a different language.

Everyone had been worried about our safety, including Dad. He insisted I take his .38 revolver. I wondered, *Was he hoping for a gunfight at the OK Corral? Another story he could tell, this time about his brave, now possibly, dead son?*

Jane and I camped on a treeless hillside outside of Atlanta, Ga., only to be awakened in the middle of the night by the arrival of several pickup trucks full of rowdy guys. Anxious about these fellows, my mind went into hyperdrive: *What if they decide to cause trouble? Jane is attractive and the only female around; there is only one of me. Okay, I have the answer: I'll shoot the bastards. But under what circumstances would I do that? Someone telling a risqué joke or engaging in threatening talk or posturing? Or would it have to escalate to the laying on of hands?* Then there were other questions: *Where should I keep the gun so that I could get to it? If I pulled the gun, must I use it, or could I bluff*

I immediately leaped to considering the when and how of using the gun, strangely forgetting that I had other options, such as my wits. In thinking about the weapon, I had gone from one to one hundred in a heartbeat. What had seemed like an easy enough decision in the calm light of day over a cup of coffee was proving difficult to sort out startled from sleep in the dark of night. Here, fear intensified as the sound of trucks racing off-road echoed across the previously peaceful hillside, and shadows, cast long by the bobbing yellow beams of headlights, danced crazily through the night. The raucous comings and goings blurred reality, fueling the boil of anxiety. If a problem arose, the chance of making a life-changing mistake was real.

Fortunately, I never had to answer those questions. Jane and I huddled in the tent until the guys finally departed. But the experience had shaken me. I put the gun out of sight and out of mind. The way of the gun, as much as I had played Wyatt Earp in childhood, was not the way for me; the gun complicated rather than simplified. I decided that in the future, I would only think of using it if I was already in trouble, not in fear of it. With that decision, I hung up my gun forever, and a legend was never born.

The next morning, we drove to New Orleans, where it rained for five days. Tired of trying to wait out the storm, we decided to push on until we hit sunshine. Sunshine met us in Corpus Christi. We poured out of the car and walked the beach, our spirits lifted by the lemony sun, and the warmth of the buffeting wind frothing the Gulf of Mexico. Camping nearby, we befriended a couple from Pennsylvania and decided to cross the border into Mexico together the next morning. They offered to hide the gun inside the body of their van.

That afternoon, I walked the campground and met an old, silver-haired man who, having just returned from fishing, was busy cleaning his catch. As he established a comfortable rhythm scaling the fish, he told his stories, the scrape of the knife pleasantly joining with the dry-leaf rustle of his voice. "Of all the things I've learned in life, the most important is that ninety-eight percent of what I worried about never came to pass." I left the elder behind that day, but never his words.

The following morning, we drove across the border. We had all heard the stories: Tales of corruption, of police planting drugs, and of gun-toting soldiers extorting money. We had heard of drug dealers who would kill you and of locals who would slide under your car, cut your fuel line, and come along later to repair your vehicle for a price. Soon, our new friends facing the barrenness of the land around us became anxiety-ridden and decided to return to the US.

After making plans for retrieving the gun, Jane and I drove on and discovered that the stories were partly true. There were police and rifle-toting soldiers, and armored pillboxes squatting in bank lobbies with gun barrels protruding through the slits as if waiting for the return of Butch Cassidy and the Sundance Kid.

We crossed miles of arid, barren landscapes; the terra-cotta expanses accented by flat-topped plateaus crouching massive in the distance. Even though there was little sign of human habitat, we came across people walking along the side the road, women holding young children and men carrying machetes on their shoulders, causing us to wonder, from where had they come, and where were they going?

Gradually, the landscape changed, the road meandering among conical, treeless hills, jutting into the blue sky, made more breast-like by the single shack resting upon their hilltops like wooden nipples. Jane and I were perpetually intrigued by a landscape foreign to us, and a way of life only hinted at.

Eventually, we came upon a small fishing village on the Gulf of Mexico, near Tuxpan. There, a grove of coconut trees grew fifty feet from a silken white sand beach, as a hacienda-style Inn beckoned from the shade. Camping in the grove, we paid young boys to climb the trees for coconuts, and we swam in the gulf. We slept late into the morning and toured on foot in the afternoon, engaging sun-blackened fishermen in conversations rife with comedic attempts at sign language, causing everyone to laugh. One sinewy middle-aged fellow asserted that shark blood was the fountain of youth and offered a pull of the black-red substance sloshing thickly in a worn, plastic bottle. I could not bring myself to do it. He laughed good-naturedly and guzzled it down.

Following Tuxpan, we came to a larger town and hired a personable guide to show us the sights. One of the highlights was a building full of open coffins displaying naturally mummified bodies, their skin, the yellow of old parchment. One long-dead woman seemed caught in a scream; another held a child. I wondered about their stories.

In yet another small town, the main street a dirt road, we checked into a hotel. That night, as laughter and Mariachi music echoed off the plaster walls, we noticed the comings and goings of couples and realized the hotel doubled as a brothel. It was a noisy, sleepless night, mainly after spying the dark silhouette of a man spying through our bedroom window.

We drove on, forever south toward the Yucatan jungle and the Inca pyramids. That is when trouble found us. In a small town, I turned the wrong way on a narrow, shadowed alley of a street. I had not noticed the faded blue arrow painted on the corner of an aging building pointing the other direction. A young police officer standing on the corner motioned for me to stop. He made known by pointing to the arrow the nature of my mistake.

Then he crouched down and began removing my license plate. It took several moments for me to process what he was doing and only seconds longer for fears fueled by all the stories of extortion, incarceration, ransom, and rape to avalanche through me.

My head spun as fear eroded composure, and terror took hold. I knew I could not let this happen, and the longer I waited to act, the further down the road to helplessness Jane, and I would be.

Panic coloring my voice, I asked, "What are you doing?" But the officer did not understand. I kept repeating, "Stop, leave the license plate alone," my voice rising in volume, along with my growing alarm. But he ignored me. No longer able to contain myself, I pushed him away from the license plate, shouting, "El Capitan! El Capitan!" intent on drawing the attention of passer-byes.

A yell arose from behind me; I turned to see a heavy-set, middle-aged police officer in the distance, a white hat with gold braid crowning his head. The younger cop angrily pointed to the older, gesturing for me to go to him. I asked, "El Capitan?" Irately he responded, "Si. Si."

As I approached El Capitan, the alley opened into a treed town square, dotted with park benches, upon which sat people quietly chatting, the scene brushed by the light of the late morning sun. In this tranquil atmosphere, so different from the claustrophobic feel of that dark alley of a street, my panic began to recede. I could once again breathe and think.

Awareness of the antagonism between Mexico and the United States in mind, I decided that declaring myself a Gringo was not in my best interest. As I neared El Capitan, I called out in my rusty French, "Parlez-vous Francais?" He rewarded me with the beam of his smile. Thankfully, he said, "No," and, in broken English, asked me if I was French. I replied, "Non. Non. Je suis Canadian Francais." To this, he responded warmly, and as we spoke, he happily insisted that the guide I had hired several towns back was his cousin; apparently, this fortunate accident of fate made us friends. I certainly was not going to argue. After several minutes of amicable conversation, El Capitan indicated I was free to go, calmly brushing aside the strident protests of the young officer.

The latter angrily spat words at me as I got in the car. Shaken by the encounter, I willed my rubbery legs to work the clutch well enough to put the car in gear and make our escape. The nightmares of my inner world had penetrated the nightmarish possibilities of the outer one, and far too close for my liking.

As we moved further south, the landscape became increasingly lush, heralding our arrival in the Yucatan. Dripping with sweat in the humid air, we toured the remains of the Inca city and climbed its Pyramids. The bird calls and monkey cries echoing from the jungle, combined with the pyramids and ancient sports arenas, and the historical teachings of the guides all transported us to another time and way of life. After several days, curiosity sated, we turned north once again, this time through the center of the country, on the way to Mexico City.

Throughout our journey, the people we encountered were warm and welcoming, as curious about our culture as we were to theirs. Often, we laughed together, amused by each other's fumbling attempts to communicate, as we took turns trying out words and gesturing like mimes: The fully engrossing experience of adults at play.

Despite the richness of these experiences, the nomadic life was beginning to take a toll. Like any aging relationship, the new and novel were becoming ever less new and novel. I returned to reading more hours of the day and discovered the works of Carlos Castaneda. As he recounted his shamanistic journeys under the hallucinatory influence of mushrooms, I was living mine, moving along the same scorched landscapes and gazing up at the same star-encrusted night skies. I also stumbled upon the works of Joseph Chilton Pierce, who, like Castaneda, challenged the assumed order of reality and the nature of the extraordinary. Imagination stimulated, my eyes imbued my surroundings with color, wonder, and enchantment.

I had begun this journey to sort myself out, and now something that had always been there, but I had barely recognized, began coalescing within me. This trip and these authors were beginning to breathe fresh air into my love of religious theory and philosophy, the power of spirituality, and

the importance of living a creative and perhaps, sometimes—
dare I imagine—even an inspired life.

On the outskirts of Mexico City, our VW broke down.
Stranded on the side of a crumbling road that wound its way up
a barren hill, Jane and I were at a loss as to what to do. As we
talked, a car pulled in behind us, and a lean, Mexican man in his
forties, with short-cropped hair, just beginning to gray, got out.
To our delight, he spoke fluent English.

His name was Juan, and he and I hit it off immediately. Juan
revealed that although a trained psychotherapist, in fact, a Doctor
of Psychology, his work had become too administrative. In
response, he gave up his practice and started a business servicing
Volkswagens at peoples' homes and, despite the loss in income,
was happier than he had ever been.

I was impressed. A gentle soul and thoughtful man, Juan
had the quiet courage to forsake his career to follow the song of
his heart. As importantly, this change was not a blind leap based
on wishful thinking: He had turned his dream into a reality, the
ultimate *realization*.

While we talked, Juan diagnosed the VW's problem: A
broken alternator. He explained he would order parts, but their
arrival would take several days. Then his inherent generosity
shone forth when he invited us to stay at his Ranchero. Both Jane
and I were thrilled. I was especially excited to have the
opportunity to participate from the inside in the workings of a
Mexican family.

Juan's one-story stucco ranchero stood alone in the middle of a vast flat tilled field. A small farming village huddled in the distance. That evening, sitting by myself enjoying a cigarette on the front stoop, I watched as an archetypal sight unfolded before me. In the waning light of the sinking sun, women emerged in ones and twos as small dots on the horizon, slowly making their way home passed Juan's ranchero after a day in the fields. Silhouetted by the faltering sun, they moved as silent shadows, faces creviced by the relentless workings of sun and time, and wrapped in dark shawls that covered their heads, eventually disappearing into the distant village as the last rays of the sun winked out like a guttering candle. This scene could have taken place two hundred years earlier, given there was nothing to indicate modernity. After dinner, Juan and I smoked cigarettes, drank tequila, and shared stories late into the night under the light of a propane lamp.

By the end of the third day, we were ready to leave. Not only was the car repaired, but I could no longer tolerate being in the house when Juan's wife cooked. Her food was delicious, but everything was seasoned with hot peppers fresh from the garden: breakfast, lunch, and dinner. By the third morning, the pepper-infused air was too much for me. I love spicy-hot food, but in Mexico, hot ratcheted up to a whole new galaxy of meaning. We left Juan and his wife that day, but as with so many memories in the making, that chance meeting has remained forever with me. And why wouldn't it? It changed my life.

Upon returning to the US, the border patrol pulled us over for inspection. Ordered to empty our pockets, turn them inside out, and to stand apart on the veranda of the station building, we nervously watched as they searched our car.

The search was exhaustive. One custom's officer completely emptied the car, while another circled it with a drug-sniffing dog. They examined the engine, removed the air filter, and inspected the manifold. Thirty minutes later, grinning triumphantly, the border guard approached holding a single marijuana seed between thumb and forefinger, saying, "I knew there was something," and let us go.

That evening, we became ill, Jane deathly so. She was vomiting, had diarrhea and fever, and alarmingly the slightest touch to her forehead caused pain. I suspected that earlier in the day, we had eaten undercooked chicken at a taco stand and were now paying the price.

This part of the US was indistinguishable from rural Mexico—there was no medical help to be found. So, I drove fifty miles across the desert before finding a clinic where relief was available.

Several days later, we pushed north across New Mexico into Arizona. In Sedona, the cosmic charming of our travels continued. Juniper trees, supposedly twisted by the energy vortexes for which the area is famous, dotted the hills, and the setting sun revealed countless shades of red striping the hardened clay.

Next was the gaping divide of the Grand Canyon where, aboard an eight-seater plane, we dove into its depths, swooping past a towering waterfall pouring out of a-cliff-side and stampeding a herd of wild horses, their manes whipping in the air as they ran before us.

The Painted Desert soon followed, its colors bursting to life with the rise of the morning sun, and then we came upon the fallen tree trunks of the Petrified Forest, scattered like the pillars of Stonehenge across the desert floor.

We drove on to climb the cliff dwellings of Colorado and then into the Rocky Mountains, which spun a magic skein of their own as they stood in stark contrast to the flat plains that had preceded them. The Million Dollar Highway pulled us into hairpin turns through gorges, up mountainsides, and across soaring bridges that spanned vast chasms. Fall was now flirting with winter, and the mountainsides, bewhiskered with evergreens, grew crystalline beards, creating a stunning snow globe effect.

Each night, we made camp and enjoyed the dark skies so ballooned with glittering stars and streaked by meteors that the cosmos had to be celebrating. We camped on the rim of the Black Canyon, its dark recesses, and chiseled cragginess amplified by the knife cut of its narrow divide. The next morning, we awoke to a landscape newly blanketed by falling snow, its muffling quilt lending an eerie silence as its sparkling whiteness vivified the dark and roughhewn danger of the canyon.

Mile after mile, we drove across the unending flatlands of Kansas before they gave way to the rolling hills of Missouri. Then, several days later, the monuments of Washington, D.C., rose with the sun to greet us as we had traveled through the night to return to where our adventure had begun: We had gone for broke and arrived.

By the calendar, we had journeyed for nearly three months, but to us, it had been light-years. Though near penniless, we were happy. We had learned that everything could become routine, even non-routine, and now, wanderlust sated, for the first time in my life, I felt the need for a purpose-driven life.

During this trip, I had come to understand the paradox of freedom: I was free to choose among many options but was free only until I did—once committed, I was on a path. By the same token, if I refused to commit, I was also not free, destined as I would be to a directionless life. At some point, we all commit, whether we want to or not. I felt driven to dedicate myself to something and, for the first time in my life, had an inkling of what that was.

Never knowing what was around the next bend in the road, seeing everything for the first time and the last, had freed me from the muddling impact of the demands of everyday life. In the space provided, I could more easily discern the emergent seedlings of my desires. What I discovered had been in front of me all the time, manifested in the fibers that made up the fabric of my existence. These included the endless curiosities that had pulled at me and the places to which I would naturally go when free to do so.

My need to make sense of things was the key, whether of two water fountains in a movie theater, of being abandoned in a foreign land, or of the experience of that sales guy getting oral sex and then going home to a lovely wife and family, to recall just a few.

With the forbearing of Jane, the inspiration of Juan, Carlos Castaneda, and Joseph Chilton Pierce, as well as D.T. Suzuki and the Jesuits, I had come to understand that I did not need a job. I needed a calling: Something that sang to my heart and indulged my need to wonder about life and relationships.

A shell, almost unseen, had cracked, and I had fallen through to another world, a world I had instinctively sought but never known. I now had a destination in the twisting journey that had been my life. I was looking forward to the straighter path it promised; I did not hear God laughing.

Chapter 12

Waylaid

Night splintered into day. *Something terribly wrong.* Fragments, images, coalescing, then dissolving. I emerge into a nether world, a succubus clinging to my face.

Awareness flares. Jane's voice says something about a car accident. I'm pulled under in a riptide of unease.

Consciousness returns. I'm in an ambulance, an oxygen mask strapped to my face.

Next, I am traveling down a white tunnel, fluorescent lights flickering past overhead, sounds echoing off the walls as the astringent smell of antiseptic burns my nose. I think of Jane: "Is she okay?" I must have spoken. Her worried voice reaches me from behind, "I'm okay. I just have a fractured wrist." I think, *"Just?"*

When next I open my eyes, it is to a circle of guys with ponytails looking down at me, one asking, "Who's going to do it?" I wonder, *What is it?* before noting the long thick needle. Dread swells within me as each guy squeamishly tries to avoid the task. Understanding looms—these guys are interns trying to decide who is going to shove that thing into me. Done in by the never-ending debate, I blurt out, "For God's sake, somebody do it!" Embarrassment paints their faces, then disapproval—soon, the hard, cold quill slides in. Fluid pumps in, then out. Inflated, then deflated, I'm a human balloon, a sack of skin holding fluid and flesh together — the verdict: no internal hemorrhaging.

I surface to yet another debate: "Who's going to hold him up?" Worry writ large on their faces, they are talking about x-rays: They fear radiation poisoning. One guy gruffly commands me to sit up, but my muscles refuse to obey. Another guy, resigned compassion on his face, grudgingly dons a lead-lined jacket.

I awake in a hospital bed, attended by a real doctor. His hair is gray, and he emanates competence and professional demeanor. He says, "We're keeping you overnight for observation." Given that I am incapable of moving, I think this an excellent idea.

It's the middle of the night. *What woke me? Oh…I'm filling up again. Is this my imagination? No. Best mention it to a nurse.*

Minutes later, an aide is shaving my torso and pelvic area, then wheels clickity-clack as fluorescent lights again flicker by overhead. I am being pushed along another corridor, this time by an enormous black man in a bulbous green shower cap. It's been explained; I'm on the way to a major laparotomy, exploratory surgery. Dumbly, I focus on the word "major."

Not wanting to be alone with my thoughts, I look up into the face of the attendant and say, "Wow, this reminds me of a scene from General Hospital." He shows no sign of having heard me, rather like a minion in the realm of Hades, he continues plodding along, staring straight ahead, stone-faced and unreachable. I return to my thoughts. Shortly later, his baritone voice reverberating in the empty hallway like a B-movie rendition of the voice of God says: "Yeah, man. But this is for *real!*" then returns to silently plodding along, pushing me toward my fate. I am alone; I know no one here, and no one here knows *me*. I am in the world of the forsaken.

During these cheerless musings, I have a showstopper of a thought: *I could be dead soon.* Paradoxically, having confronted this realization, my anxiety ebbs. Whatever is about to happen is completely out of my control, just like the ocean, I can fight it, or I can flow with it—flowing seems wiser.

As calmness encompasses me, I realize *I may soon know the answer to The Big Question: What, if anything, follows death?*

October 22, 1972, age twenty-three, I was waylaid on the way to visit my parents in Charlottesville, VA. Napping in the passenger seat of the VW while Jane was white-knuckling the steering wheel, following her Eleventh Commandment: Thou shalt never exceed fifty-five miles per hour. A car pulled out of a side road, and Jane T-boned it, later confessing she had frozen and never used the brakes. From fifty-five mph to zero in a nanosecond—a hard stop in anybody's language. I had not been wearing my seatbelt.

Surgery revealed a fractured spleen. A blood vessel to a kidney was also damaged, but that fact was not discovered until twenty-five years later when x-rays revealed that the kidney had atrophied.

Post-surgery is when all the fun begins. Split open like a frog in high school biology class, the incision held together by nearly two hundred stitches, the outermost layer comprised of thick thread encased in plastic tubing in defense against the sutures cutting into my flesh. Unfortunately, the tubing can't follow the thread where it enters my body. That is where the pain lives, particularly when I laugh, my stomach pulling on the threads, as humor turns to agony, and tears of laughter into beads of blood.

Mucus gathers in my lungs, pneumonia a growing concern. The nurses pummel my back twice daily, trying to clear the phlegm while I protectively clutch a pillow to my stomach trying to hold my innards together. The physical sensation of bursting apart is so acute that one day, I adamantly refuse the treatment.

Pneumonia has its way. With extra morphine coursing through my body, I enter the blissful world of Morpheus, amongst cotton clouds soft and reassuring, until the nurses force a tube down my throat into my pleural cavity. As I gag, choke, and fight for breath, the guitar strings tightly strung across my stomach, shriek their terrible tune.

I live in dread of the nursing staff and their infinitely creative capacity for torture. As I lay in pain on that hospital bed, time takes on new dimensions. Second, after interminable second, transforms into minute after endless minute, then into day after eternal day, stretching to infinity. I wonder, *How long I can endure?* I discover the answer, however long I must.

My family visits: Mom and Dad, Mark, and Michelle. Jacques and Ed fly in from Atlanta, everyone fearing I might die. During one visit, Dad whispers in my ear, "Charlie, I can see you are in a lot of pain. You can't hide it from me. But you never complain. I'm proud of you."

Several days later, Mark and Michelle visit, telling me that Jane, having been berated by Mutti for having extra-marital sex, had left for Baltimore. I was enraged; what a way to treat someone when they are a guest in your home and as gentle and kind a person as Jane.

I called Jane to pick me up. Tentatively scheduled for discharge in a few days, I was not too worried about leaving. All I knew was that I needed to be gone before my parents returned. I left the hospital against medical advice, armed with a prescription for Percodan. Thank God for Percodan.

My parents and I barely talked over the next several years. One of those times was to invite them to our wedding. They gave three hundred dollars as a wedding present—no card. Jane and I bought the cold cuts and beer for the reception at her father's apartment. Unlike Jacques, who eloped to marry but still got a well-laid-on reception, Jane and I got nothing. We were citizens of the second rank, members of that lower caste, and there was not even a balcony in which to sit.

But then, the miracle of miracles, Jane and I were changed from water to wine, from least to most, from last to first—a position of honor to which I was entirely unaccustomed. Our achievement? Jane got pregnant. Nine months later, their first grandchild was born, not any grandchild, but a *Grandson*—Chandler. He was the Messiah, and Jane and I, by extension, held the honored roles of Mary and Joseph in the McCormack family. Now, there was always room at the inn.

Isn't it amazing how values often change in perfect tandem with self-interest? The good news was that the Hatching of Charlie was proceeding. One of my teachers had just arrived, and others would soon follow.

Chapter 13

Childbirth

1975. Age twenty-five.

*J*ane calls out in exasperation from our second-story bedroom window, "Charlie! What are you doing?"

It was a damn good question. What was I doing? I had no clue. It was patently stupid, but I could not help myself. I felt driven to complete the building of a fence to protect my backyard. *What was I thinking? That we were going to come under attack at any moment? And what was this need to plant a tree? I just had to plant a tree as if doing so was imperative, like raising a flag or marking ground I would defend against all comers.* I thought, *Won't it be great that our child can return thirty years from now and see this tree planted on the day he was born. Christ, what the hell is wrong with me? I am out of my mind. Jane's having contractions, and I am here in the backyard. Stop it!* Shoulders hunched, I took myself into the house and Jane's recriminating stare.

Years later, I shared this incident with a child psychologist. She laughed, "You Idiot. You experienced the nesting urge. You were preparing for your child in your Cro-Magnon way—no disrespect meant to the Cro-Magnons." Mercifully, it all made sense. Finally, I could stop castigating myself for what I had assumed was my uncaring ways.

Young and idealistic, Jane and I were going to do everything *right,* certainly much better than our parents had. Jane attended La Leche meetings like a nun attending mass, and we opted for natural childbirth, at home no less, using a midwife. How perfect were we?

Long and arduous, the delivery did not proceed according to plan; we had to go to the hospital. We piled into the midwife's car; she and Jane in the back seat while I drove. Her car was old and kept stalling. Irritably, I asked myself, *What had the midwife been thinking? Why didn't we take my car?* Then, the answer arrived: *Her car's backseat is much bigger; she can deliver the baby there if need be.* I drove faster.

We arrived at the hospital. I dropped Jane and the midwife off at the emergency room entrance. Upon my return from parking the car, I asked the receptionist for directions. She explained I must wait until they called for me. I could not do that—the clarion call of impending birth resounded through my soul, and I did not want to miss it. I explained that to the receptionist as the elevator door was closing. She seemed dazed by my explanation. Maybe she did not know what a clarion call was, or perhaps it was that these words were being delivered by an unshaven man with tousled hair, eyes lolling bug-eyed from a combination of exhaustion and adrenalin. The door to the elevator shuts as she dials security.

I found Jane and the midwife in a supply room; the delivery rooms already occupied. Within minutes, Chandler emerges. Wet, tiny, helpless, and one hundred percent dependent on Jane and *me*. Whoa, *Me!*

As I held him in my arms for the first time, a burning ball of white-hot fierceness surges in my chest, incinerating all the nagging questions and self-doubts. I did not know how I'd take care of this tiny monkey, but I knew one thing with absolute certainty: I would. As Chandler moved from fetus to infant, he pushed me from boy to man.

Four years later, Keeley's born. Guess what? We were doing natural childbirth again. *Why not?* Bemusedly, I ask myself, *Hadn't the first time been swell?* But this time, we were delivering in a hospital. During delivery, I announced to Jane that the baby looked exactly like Chandler, then revamped my pronouncement as Keeley fully exited her mother.

As a proud all-knowing father and training therapist, with at least one course in early childhood development under my belt, I spent months preparing Chandler for the arrival of this little angel. I talked to him, drew pictures, told him what a good big brother he was going to be, and so on and so on—and then some more so ons.

Finally, the momentous day arrives, and Chandler meets Keeley for the first time. I watch over them, a paternal smile on my face. In my finest *Father Knows Best* voice, I ask, "Chan, would you like to hold Keeley?" He assures me he would. Holding her, looking down in what I am certain is an explicitly loving way, I intuit that he is hesitating to speak, shy in the presence of this tiny Goddess. Feeling the bounty of love in this *Golden Moment*, I encourage Chandler, "Is there anything you would like to say to Keeley?" He nods affirmatively, confirming the acuity of my perceptions. In the glow of the moment, I watch Chandler holding Keeley—*maybe a little too tightly*—as he stares intensely into her eyes. He then speaks in an earnest voice that brooks no misinterpretation: "I hate you! I hate you! I hate you!"

I am speechless. In the years to come, I would find that Chandler has a gift for rendering me speechless. Sardonically, I think, *Wow! That went well.* And then, trying to salvage the moment, think, *At least it was real.* The real-ness heightened only moments later when Chandler proceeds to pee on the floor in every room of the house. His message is clear. Where I had once felt driven to nest, Chandler is driven to mark his territory—so much for those classes in early childhood development.

Three years later, Caitlin was born. This time, we were not going the natural route. The first two pregnancies were breech births and very painful. Now, Jane unabashedly wants medications and plenty of them. I could imagine her calling out, "Back the truck of pharmaceuticals up over here." Somewhere along the road, the purity of our birthing drive had bleached away. Unfortunately, someone screwed up, and Jane did not get the medications when needed. Then, the birth was upon us. Once again, Jane gave birth au naturel.

Caitlin emerges, a bounty of dark hair helmets her alabaster face, creating so stunning a contrast that I spontaneously exclaim, "Jane, she's so beautiful!"

Chandler had now grown to the point where he cared little about another intruder into the family. Keeley, on the other hand, felt blessed, having a live doll to play with, and play they did. A fond memory is of Keeley and Cait, with a group of girlfriends, playing hair salon at the picnic table under the shade tree on a summer's afternoon. Keeley chatters away while working on Cait's hair. Cait, now age four or five, chubby face set in a serious rendering of her role, sits patiently as the girls flutter and gab around her, touching her hair here and there. The unselfconscious chatter of females bonding reminds me of the excited chirping of birds. Thrilled by the aliveness of it all, I set up a video camera on a tripod and just let it run. I have no idea where that tape is today, but I do not need it. I see it all in my mind's eye as fresh as the day it happened.

Probably the smartest thing I ever did as a Dad was to build a pool in our backyard. I cut down a sixty-foot-tall tree, scaling it repeatedly to trim its branches, then taking it down eight-foot lengths at a time: Paul Bunyan had nothing on me. A dangerous venture, especially when done alone. Stupid, really, but at that time, life was good, safe, and assured, and I still recoiled from asking for help. I paid a heavy equipment operator to dig a hole and spent weeks shaping it with a shovel into a facsimile of a pool. Then I called a pool installation company to complete the job.

As a family, we spent the best times in and around that pool. I taught Caitlin to swim underwater at age eight months, and we all swam for hours each week. It was magical, the kids, cherubic angels, seeming to fly in the depths of the crystal-clear water, as their long golden hair, strobed by sunbeams, streamed shimmering behind. It was astonishing. Their unblemished delight so filled me with joy, that I *was* joy. Those were the best of times, some of the best of my life. Unfortunately, they were soon to end.

Throughout what was to come, these children were always there: growing, changing, needing me in ways I could not possibly have imagined, and only partially understood, forever pushing me to grow beyond myself.

Chapter 14

Getting Schooled

Before the car accident, I had been following in the footsteps of Juan, pursuing a master's degree in psychology while scraping out a living as a mechanic and an auto-body man. At the speed my education was proceeding, I estimated that I could obtain a doctoral degree in a mere eleven years. In the meantime, these blue-collar jobs taught me an important truth: There are many forms of intelligence, and auto-body restoration and engine repair were nowhere to be found among mine.

Like Juan, I tried servicing Volkswagens at peoples' homes, but unlike him, failed miserably. Then I tried my hand as an auto-body guy, welding the undamaged front and back ends of two wrecks together to form a functioning car for sale to unsuspecting customers. Again, I marveled at the difference between how things appear and how things are. Morals aside, I could not begin to accomplish that task and was fired.

I then found employment at a Toyota dealership. With unnerving perceptiveness, they recognized my innate talents, assigning me the simplest of tasks: changing oil and pasting on racing stripes. They also instructed me to ignore the "change transmission oil" order on the service sheets. No dummy to deviousness, I deduced the dealership was charging for a service they were not performing.

Three days later, the car accident in Virginia. Fortunately, the accident had a silver lining: a twelve-thousand-dollar insurance settlement after attorneys, plastic surgeons, and doctors received their cut. I could now pursue my education full-time and performed well—I had found my form of intelligence.

There was one unusual incident of that time, at least for me. The professor of my abnormal psychology class invited me to dinner at his home. When I knocked on the door at the appointed hour, the tall, middle-aged professor, hair slicked back as if wet from a shower, answered. Oddly, he was in his bathrobe. I greeted him warmly, but he did not respond. Instead, leaving me on the front stoop, he turned and walked back through the living room, disappearing through a door beyond. Left on the front stoop, I wondered, *What the heck? What was I supposed to do?*

Finally, I chose to interpret the open door as an invitation to let myself in.

The first thing I noticed was the absence of cooking smells or any evidence of a dinner party in the making. *Did I have the wrong evening? I don't think so. The professor hadn't seemed surprised to see me, although his welcome left much to be desired.* I thought, *This is weird,* but chased further concerns away before they could begin to scamper disquietingly around my mind. I told myself, *Stop it, he is merely getting dressed, embarrassed for running late and being caught in his bathrobe.* Thus, reassured, I stood patiently.

Minutes passed, and there was no sign of him: the house stood creepily silent. Time dawdled in inverse relationship to my mounting unease, and my thoughts returned, skittering dangerously here and there as I was feeling ever more the fool. Finally, realizing I was in danger of moving from fool to moron, I decided to put a stop to my unease. I walked to the door through which the professor had vanished.

Whoa! It was a bedroom, and the professor was lying on the bed facing me, his face a mask of neutrality. Flashes of Little Red Riding Hood and The Big Bad Wolf came to mind. Thankfully, he was still in his robe. I noticed a bronze bracelet ringing one arm: *Tres chic.* He spoke not, just continued to look at me with round, unblinking eyes. *What was he doing? What the hell was going on?*

Then, the penny dropped. *Oh. Shit! He wants to get it on.* Absurdly, I felt insulted. *Is this his idea of seduction or foreplay? Aren't I worth more than this? Am I merely seen as a sexual object?* Then I moved to other thoughts. *I'm married, and heterosexual; I would not be open to this even if the professor were an attractive woman.* Returning to my senses, I turned and walked out of the house. Driving home, I realized the professor had never uttered a word.

Aside from that experience, I had learned important things about myself since my return to Baltimore. I was an inveterate risk-taker, bull-headed, had a strong work ethic, was tunnel-visioned in my pursuits, and possessed a strong will to persevere. Once I had a plan, I saw it through. Sometimes, I became stuck, not seeing any way forward. Then, I would keep plowing ahead until something unforeseen and unforeseeable came along, allowing me to break through the impasse to whatever was beyond.

As I doggedly pursued the master's degree in psychology, a troubling thought occurred to me: *What if I don't like working with the mentally ill? My love of theory was one thing, but the practice of psychology might be another. Wow! What a time to consider this. What if all the sacrifices Jane and I had made were for naught? What would I do then?* After all we had been through, the thought of failing terrified me. It was one thing to follow my heart but another to cause harm to others in the process. With trepidation, I set out to answer that question. I drove to Sheppard and Enoch Pratt Hospital (SEPH), a renowned psychiatric hospital in Baltimore to volunteer.

Part III

If Only I Had Ears to Listen

I was breaking out of my shell into my vocation. All along, it had been calling to me in the form of my interests and yearnings. My single regret was that I had lost so much time; if only I had had the ears to listen. My ignorance of myself had been profound, and now, as the veil lifted, I could only accept the costs as I also relished the discovery. If there was one thing I was coming to understand, it was that we must each live our lives: There are no shortcuts.

Chapter 15

Asylum

I drove onto the grounds of Sheppard-Pratt Hospital one fateful October morning in 1974, not knowing what to expect. I pass through a stone gatehouse and follow the wooded country lane across a rock bridge spanning a trickling brook. Then, I come upon a pedestrian overpass that leads to a gazebo, both hewn from yellow wood, glowing golden in the morning sun. Slate-roofed stone and brick buildings, designed by architects in the late 1800s, grace the top of a hill, surrounded by expansive lawns adorned with countless species of shrubs and soaring trees through which columns of sunlight stream.

Inside the main building, high-ceilinged rooms replete with over-sized windows, accented with stained glass, infuse the air with color and light. The windows open to a view of staff and patients strolling the grounds and sitting on the Adirondack chairs that are strewn across the lawn, offering a silent invitation to conversation and reflection. The sounds of birds singing and bees buzzing float through the open windows. I imagine well-dressed patients and staff mingling on the lawn enjoying high tea on a Sunday afternoon as had been the tradition decades past.

Grace emanated from this place, hinting at things seen and thought about in ways not common in the world rushing about just beyond its borders. Sheppard-Pratt embodied the best meanings of the words sanctuary and asylum and promised a respite from a harried world. It was clear to me that Sheppard-Pratt had one purpose in mind—the care and healing of the human spirit.

I sat apprehensively before the Director of Volunteers. Describing my assignment, she said, "These are adult psychiatric patients on a short-term locked-door unit. They might stay anywhere from two weeks to three months." As her voice flowed on, the sound of her words receded as I thought about the varied implications of locked doors. *Why were they locked? Were the patients crazy? I mean, really crazy. Violent crazy. And what does crazy look like, and how does it act? Is it as portrayed in the movies? Wild-eyed, raggedy-haired people, dressed in gray sackcloth, who will rise in unison to attack me?* My body hummed with these unasked and unanswered questions; I would not risk being refused a position because I was anxious.

Accompanied to the short-term unit, my escort rang the buzzer. Moments later, a nurse peered out through a small, reinforced glass window set into the door. She smiled kindly and unlocked it. Like a swimmer entering the border of a frigid lake, I hesitantly step inside, the heavy security door clunking shut behind me with a tone of finality.

Alert to signs of danger, I look around these unfamiliar surroundings, noting people sitting quietly alone or chatting together. Some looked depressed, others distressed, some seemed perfectly fine, but nowhere was there evidence of an imminent threat.

The nursing staff welcomes me and explains my duties. I am to talk with patients, escort them off the hall, and otherwise help in any way I am willing. My first task, I will always remember: A geriatric federal judge suffering from dementia and the loss of bowel control. I hold his arm and take him into a bathroom with a showerhead and tub. He dumbly stands next to it, having no idea of what to do, brown-stained pajama bottoms hanging limply from his bony hips. I fight the urge to gag as his stink threatens to chase me from the room. All the while, I think, *How incredible is this? A man of such intellect and accomplishment rendered*

I talk to him softly, telling him what I am going to do before I do it. I gently pull down his pajamas and rinse him off the showerhead, relieved as his feces releases its clammy hold. Then I bath him, all the while speaking quietly, instinctively realizing it does not matter what I say, only how I say it. I shave him, comb his hair, and dress him nicely in slacks and shirt. Later, I watch as his wife and adult children visit, their affection plain to see. I feel rewarded that they had this time together, their father looking more like himself with a vestige of his dignity intact.

I soon discover that most of these patients are like you and me. The difference: They are overcome by psychological issues or deficits, rendering them unable to manage their lives, at least for a while; I could relate to this. I knew something of being alone in the world, of being overwhelmed, confused, and disoriented, of feeling helpless and needing time and space to sort myself out and discover a purpose for living. I also recognized the importance of having someone who cared about you in your life and knew that despite my lack of skills, that was the least I could provide.

I was interested in the patients' stories, how they came to be here, and what kept them from moving on. I could not think of a more interesting way to spend a day. Their tales prompted my thinking about my own life, as I interrelated the personal and the professional, softening the division between them, the patients, and me: I came to see us all as fellow travelers on the obstacle course of life.

Upon occasion, the treatment team invited me to sit in on interviews with patients. I cherished these opportunities. My very first team meeting, the service chief, Meyer Liebman, M.D., interviewed a young man awaiting trial, who had physically abused his girlfriend. Afterward, Dr. Liebman shared his evaluation, noting not only what the patient *had* said but *how* he had said it *and* what he *had not* said. He concluded that the patient, a voluntary admission, was only there to seek favor with the courts *and* one other, less obvious thing: to become more skilled at controlling women.

I had always been a thinker, but these were thinkers' thinkers. I had found a place where nothing was taboo about which to think. The value determined not by social niceties but by whether something might deepen understanding. And, although understanding might be slow to arrive, arrive it usually did.

In those first weeks at Sheppard-Pratt, I had the strangest, yet incredibly palpable, sense of being home. It was as if in recognizing what was going on around me, I was also being recognized. I do not know how else to say it—I was getting myself back from this place. It was not an experience I had

knowingly sought: I had not known of its existence. I had fallen

into it, and it fell into me like a spark laid to dry grass. Something

within me burst into flame, a fire that would only grow.

Chapter 16

Early Days: Becoming a Psychotherapist

In January 1975, age twenty-six, I was offered my first job at Sheppard-Pratt's Comprehensive Drug Abuse Treatment Program (COMDAP). My naiveté and idealism were staggering. On the walls of my office, I hung encouraging posters assuring that by working together with goodwill, we would overcome all problems.

I was functioning like a camp counselor. Picture me, strumming blithely away on a ukulele while staff and patients sit around a crackling campfire, the flickering firelight illuminating upturned hopeful faces as sparks leap toward the stars. Imagine the smell of roasting marshmallows perfuming the air as song and laughter fill the night. In cringe-worthy hindsight, I can imagine shouting, "Kumbaya! Kumbaya! It's great! You're great!

I'm great! Everyone's great! And we're all so special. Don't we all feel better now?"

Now imagine, I come to my senses and realize that the boy and girl scouts are streetwise, hardened heroin addicts, many middle-aged, and having done prison time. Some of the women, if not all, had sold their bodies for drugs. Envision what they must have been thinking about me. I dare wager it was not how lucky they felt that I had arrived to save them.

Looking back on those times, I'm amazed by the grace and compassion those people had for me. They never mocked me, nor made a face. It was not me taking care of them; it was them taking care of me. I had been adopted and didn't know it. Even the medical director, Bill Abramson, M.D., one of the most scornful and scathing individuals to ever walk the planet, largely resisted the opportunity to belittle me. He would enter my office each week to provide supervision, take my chair (he loved those power games), briefly cast a smirk at the posters, but never say a thing. Later, he invited me to his home to bestow upon me his grown children's old toys for Chandler. It was an uncharacteristically warm and tender moment, representing the ending of one era and the beginning of another. With this symbolic passing of a torch, I sensed he was grieving the loss of those sepia-colored times, the aura of which lingered on those well-kept toys.

The following year, there were cutbacks; my counseling position reduced to half-time. Fortunately, the administrator, Carl Thistle, arranged to add a half-time research position. My job: Track down the heroin addicts who participated in a program testing an alternative to methadone. I was to find and interview them to evaluate how they were doing.

The typical interview would go something like this. I knock on the door. A woman answers, her narrow face furrowed by lines of hard living. I ask, "Is Johnny home?"

Suspiciously, she responds, "What do you want him for?"

I do not know who she is, so I cannot say; I would be breaching Johnny's privacy. I tell her, "It's personal."

She looks at me with tired, weary eyes, considering, then shouts over her shoulder, "Johnny, someone here wants you."

A scruffy guy, T-shirt and jeans draped on a skinny frame, comes barefoot to the door, scratching his bed-head hair and rudely demands, "What do you want?"

The woman, who looks twice Johnny's age, has not moved. I guess she is his mother. But I still do not want to breach his privacy. I say, "It's confidential." He pauses a moment, considering, then says to the woman, "Sarah, go get me a beer, will ya?"

She looks resentful but goes on her errand.

I tell Johnny, "I'm here to interview you for the drug-treatment research." Visibly relaxing, he opens the door and invites me in.

Contrary to expectations, the house is neat and clean. We sit in the living room, and Sarah brings Johnny a beer. Johnny offers me one; I decline. Johnny explains to Sarah who I am, and Sarah also relaxes. It is now becoming clear that Sarah is Johnny's girlfriend. Sarah then leaves the room. Johnny assures me he is doing fine, maintaining employment, and has no complaints about the drug l-alpha-acetylmethadol except that he misses the quasi-high obtainable from methadone.

And so, the interviewing goes, typically mundane by the end, but often awash with undercurrents at the beginning. After dozens of interviews, I felt graced by these people allowing me into their homes and their lives. In some way, I was one of them, feeling far more alike than different. Indeed, these addicts were you and me. Many held good jobs; their employers and co-workers never suspecting a thing.

There were exceptions, however. One guy wouldn't allow me into his home, firmly stating, "No man! We talk out here." Of course, this made me wonder what he was hiding. When I told him that his urinalysis proved positive for heroin use and had resulted in his discharge from the program, he raged, "I'm go'in to kill you, you punk. You think you're a big deal, but you're not.

I'm going to take you down to size, and you won't know when it's com'in. I'll find out where you live." It appeared to take every ounce of his self-restraint not to attack me then and there.

Among many memorable moments, another stood out from my two years at COMDAP. It occurred on a snowy Friday evening. A couple, with three children in tow, appeared at the open door of my office. Clinic hours were over, and I was preparing to leave. The mother, an attractive blond with an open face, held a toddler in her arms. The other kids, girls, looked to be four and six. With beseeching eyes, she explained they needed methadone and a place to stay. Her husband, standing behind her, nodded anxiously in agreement.

What could I do? Didn't they know you can't just walk in and get methadone? Nonetheless, I couldn't let these people return to the snowy night. I explained the situation and assured them I would find temporary shelter. Remarkably, they declined. They knew everything about the shelter, far more than me and had no interest in going there. I marveled that they did not seem all that concerned. If it were me, I would be in an absolute panic. Hell, I was in a panic, and it was not me. But they were calmly resolute, promising to return the following Monday, before walking back into the cutting embrace of the winter night. I went home thinking; *I should have done better; I should have done more.*

Monday morning, the family returned, completely unfazed. They had found someone to take them in. What for me would have been a panic-stricken experience of not having a warm place to stay, was for them, part of the norm of a rootless life and nothing about which to get excited. Later, my naiveté and idealism worn down by the grindstone of experience, I considered the possibility that the parents had been playing me to get methadone and had always had a place to stay. Was it unkind of me to think that? Maybe. Or maybe I was growing up.

In 1977, age twenty-eight, I was selected from eighty applicants for the position of Program Coordinator of SEPH'S Evening Treatment Program, a social support program for patients who worked during the day. In truth, it was a dull and lifeless affair; people just sitting around. Worse, it was contagious. Soon enough, I too was sitting around, smiling the smile one has when their shoes are too tight. As I went through the same boring and predictable routine night after tortuous night, I finally had enough. To quote Popeye, "That's all I can stands, cuz I can't stands n'more."

The psychiatrist assigned to the program, Steve Saunders, and I began taking patients into the community to restaurants and exhibits. I successfully made a case to the Outpatient Treatment Committee to allow patients and staff to have one drink, like a glass of wine, at a restaurant. My thought was that these were working adults and should be treated as such. We also invited people of varying talents, such as yoga instructors and art teachers, to share their knowledge with the group. We went on excursions, once watching sculptors make clay rise into vases as the potting wheel turned. The Evening Treatment Program was thus transformed from a resigned march to lifelessness to vibrant adult get-togethers with people interacting and laughing with one another.

There was one problem. From the outset, the program administrator— whom I shall call Ms. Glum, to protect the guilty— and I clashed. I do not know if she did not like me or perceived me as a threat to her position. In any event, she had been crowing at me for months concerning the need to increase the size of the patient population. I did not see this as my responsibility. Mine was a clinical position, not public relations or advertising; she was the administrator.

Ms. Glum did not see it that way and was always at me about it, although sorely lacking any suggestions as to what I could do. One afternoon, I was at the nursing station when the phone rang. It was Ms. Glum calling from her second-floor office. In a sharp, contempt-laden voice, she reamed me out once again about the low census, concluding her demeaning rant by demanding in a belittling tone, "What should I do with you?"

Oops! That was it. She had strummed the chords of my father's denigrating attitude.

At that moment, my McCormack Clan craziness poked out its head as I responded in a deadpan voice, dripping with equal parts challenge and disdain, "I think you should draw and quarter me and feed me to the wolves." At the time, I was reading a work of fiction set in England in the 1300s when this form of punishment was commonplace. My statement met with total silence and, I imagine, bewilderment. Holding the phone to my ear, I pictured Ms. Glum trying to make sense of my words so out of step with anything she could have anticipated. I heard a click: She had hung up on me.

A month later, Ms. Glum called me into her office to impart *sad* news: "Charlie, I'm so sorry to inform you that we have to let you go. Because of the low census, we can no longer afford your position. Please accept this meeting as your two-week notice." Honestly, she did not seem all that sorry. However, she also did not look all that happy. Her look was along the lines of that found on the face of a toreador carefully placing barbs into the bull to weaken him before the final sword thrust. She was not going to celebrate until the bull was dead. Then, I could easily imagine Ms. Glum running naked up and down the halls of the treatment center, well after closing time, laughing maniacally as she danced the Funky Chicken. It is an image I hurried to get out of my mind.

Stunned by this unanticipated turn of events, I left for home feeling a mix of fear and excitement. Fear in that I had a family to support and no job, excitement in that I faced a challenge and an open future. The only clue that I was more discombobulated than I knew occurred when I could not find my car in the small parking lot. I looked everywhere, before discovering it hiding in plain sight directly in front of the entrance.

The next week, I received a call from the Outpatient Committee that oversaw the Day/Evening Hospital. The chair, Dr. Robertson, M.D., invited me to an exit interview. As the tiniest cog in the Sheppard-Pratt machine, I was surprised. *What could they possibly want to know from me?*

When I arrived for the meeting, I learned that we were waiting for a final member: Ms. Glum. *Damn! I didn't know she was on the committee.* After the passage of a few minutes, Dr. Robertson elected to start the meeting without her. "Charlie, we're so sorry to hear that you're leaving us. We invited you in for any thoughts or ideas you might have about the evening program." His phrasing confused me, suggesting that he saw me as choosing to leave rather than being bum-rushed out the door. I probed, "Thank you, Dr. Robertson. I, too, am sorry that budget cuts necessitated the elimination of my position." Now, it was his face that held a puzzled expression, along with those of the other committee members. That is when I knew, "The game was afoot."

Dr. Robertson explained that Ms. Glum had told them I was leaving because of conflicts between my work and school schedules. Wow! My appreciation for Ms. Glum rose ten notches. She had done a Machiavelli—straight-out lied to both the committee and me. She would have pulled it off too, if not for the fortuitous invitation to an exit interview that it was now clear she also had not foreseen. I assured Dr. Robertson that there was no such conflict.

At this point, Ms. Glum arrived, and Dr. Robertson questioned her. She handled the confrontation peculiarly: sitting stiffly, back straight, stone-still, and silent. The silence went on, becoming increasingly awkward and uncomfortable until understanding bloomed for Dr. Robertson: Ms. Glum was not going to speak. Visibly unsettled, Dr. Robertson turned to me, "Charlie, I apologize to you for any anguish that this has caused you or your family. I sincerely hope that you will choose to stay on." I assured him that I would like nothing better and took this as my cue to leave. Ms. Glum never bothered me again.

Pretty crazy, but there is always plenty of crazy on the merry-go-round of life. It is, in fact, a crazy world. And why wouldn't it be? It is full of people, each flaky in their way, inflicting their craziness on others, at least, until they resolve their issues.

Chapter 17

Man Plans, God Laughs

1978. Age twenty-nine.

The night lay like a shroud over the dimly lit streets of the projects, the tinny sound of my moped engine echoing hollowly off its dreary walls as I made my way home from the University of Maryland School of Social Work located in one of the worse parts of Baltimore. Shouts erupted from behind me, immediately answered by yipping noises reminiscent of jackals feverishly tracking their prey. I look over my shoulder, my heart turning to ice as I see a gang of black youths shouting like Zulu warriors, running full-out trying to close with their quarry—*me*. Mesmerized, I can only watch as the Warriors maneuver this way and that, trying to cut off my escape, effortlessly hurdling the obstacles in their path. Excitement writ large on their faces, each vies to be the first to count coup and divest me of my transportation, if not rearrange my facial features. Heart thumping, quickly understanding my role as the hare to their hounds, I break out of my trance. With an immediacy I have rarely felt, I realize I must quickly counter the moves they are making, or my fate will be in their clawing hands. A wildly chaotic game of move and countermove ensues until, finally, I break clear, giving my war cry as I jolt from terror to exhilaration: I had won, at least, this night.

What made this experience exceptionally unnerving can only be understood if you have driven a moped. If so, you know mopeds are deservedly renowned for their lack of get up and go—there is a reason they come with pedals. Indeed, it is not an exaggeration to suggest that they accelerate like sand through an hourglass. There was only one solution: once top-end speed is reached—twenty-five to thirty miles per hour—never, ever, slow down.

So there I was night after night, like a grain of salt in a land of pepper, barrelling through stop signs and stoplights, around and between traffic, and cutting corners to avoid slowing down, all with little regard for what lay ahead, given full knowledge of what followed behind.

Though the Warriors never caught me, there were some close calls. Ironically, the most significant came when I was not being chased at all. That night, I had left the pursuing gang far behind and stopped for a red light, given the better lighting, denser traffic, and random police patrols at the corner of North and Charles. Still, I kept a vigilant eye—this area of town was also infamous for its crime. So, there I sat, waiting patiently for the light to turn green, enjoying the gentle breeze of warm air caressing my skin and the smell of cooking hamburgers wafting over from the White Castle restaurant situated on the corner when out its door stepped a shark.

Immediately, I knew he was a shark. Maybe in his thirties, sporting a garish gold chain and red baseball cap planted askew on his head, he had instantly begun scanning his environment. His eyes passed over me unseeing before they jerked back in an almost comedic double-take. As I quickly recognized him for what he was, he instantly recognized me for what I was: prey. Fear tightened my chest as he swaggered towards me. The sights and sounds of the city faded as I focused on the incoming threat.

The shark said, "Was' dat you ridin'?" as if we were long lost buddies, only his hard, scarred face and dead-fish eyes giving the lie. Time was on my side—a squad car could roll by at any moment—so I did my best to put off the confrontation, going along with the pretense that we were simply shooting the shit.

"It's called a moped. They use them a lot in other parts of the world." He pretended interest as he walked around the bike, head tilted quizzically, and then with brotherly camaraderie said,

"Get off da bike. I tries it out," as if he were going to take it for a spin, then return it to me.

Understanding that any trace of fear or indecision would only encourage him, I dryly responded, "That isn't going to happen." He froze into place, staring at me silently, dead-fish eyes coldly assessing, waiting for me to fold.

He did not know that I could take a beating with the best of them. Several heartbeats more, and he realized I really was not getting off that bike. Sharply, he barked, "What if I jus shoot you in da hed and takes' it?" That strange feeling came over me, rather than anxiety, a sense of acceptance and resolve, and a curiosity as to how this was going to play out. I only knew one thing: I was not getting off that bike. I responded quietly, "You got'ta do what you got'ta do. I got'ta do what I got'ta do."

He stood silently, as surprise and curiosity flickered behind his eyes. After a short time assessing the situation, he broke the stand-off with a bark of a laugh and said, "You aw-rite. I jus kiddin'." He turned and walked away.

Such is life, as capricious as the weather, fickle in ways beyond anyone's ability to foresee or control. Though my life sometimes seemed—and seems—on track, I know things can fall apart in a nanosecond. My tumultuous childhood was reason enough to see the truth of this. Indeed, such things happen to everyone with enough regularity to give rise to the Yiddish saw, "Man plans, and God laughs."

One such event is what landed me on that moped, careening through the projects. I had been pursuing admission to a doctoral program in psychology, confident that I would be a desirable candidate. To ensure this, I had applied to twenty schools and then sat back to wait for the acceptances to start rolling in. However, rejections were all that followed. The worst part was that I did not understand why and fell back on an explanatory concept in keeping with my default insecurities: I deduced that these schools had recognized my underlying inadequacies. Then one day, a letter arrived that gave reason to my plight. It stated that with only six credits in psychology, I did not qualify for admission.

I was dumbstruck. I had a master's degree in psychology. Instantly, I realized that Loyola had sent out partial transcripts. Perhaps my roaming moves from day school to night school and back again, or from part-time to full-time student, had created an archival complexity that invited mistakes. In the end, however, the cause did not matter. Loyola's oversight dealt a fatal blow to my ambition to become a psychologist. Even with my bullheadedness, I could not imagine putting my family's needs on hold for yet another year. I accepted this bitter pill and thought about my options. My ambition to become a psychologist was not to be, but the more bedrock desire to become a psychotherapist was still within reach. At Sheppard-Pratt, I had discovered that unlike the master's degree in psychology, a master's in social work offered the license to practice psychotherapy.

That is how, in 1978, at the age of twenty-eight, I entered the two-year master's program at the University of Maryland School of Social Work. I put in eighty-plus-hour work weeks for the next two years. A hardship for me, but even harder for Jane, burdened with taking care of Chandler in my absence. Nonetheless, I was determined to get my license as quickly as possible, driven by an intense desire to put the hard times behind us.

I graduated with a master's in social work on January 13, 1980, my thirty-first birthday. In several months, I would be a licensed psychotherapist. Life had presented unanticipated obstacles, and, like most people, I had learned to adapt, sometimes moving back to get ahead, but never losing sight of my goal.

Chapter 18

Power???

Master of Social Work degree securely in hand, along with three years as the Program Coordinator of Sheppard-Pratt's Evening Treatment Program, I felt the need to expand my clinical horizons. Fortuitously, a family therapist in the Day Program wanted to make a change. Ta-da: I transformed into a family therapist with the business cards to prove it.

On the first day in my new role, I walked down the hall toward my office, anticipating meeting with the family of a newly admitted patient. As I neared, I observed a group of people milling around my office door. Beaming in the glow of their family support, I greeted them warmly, and we all squeezed uncomfortably into my closet-sized office.

Sitting knee-to-knee, I began the interview. After several minutes, I found myself becoming more, rather than less confused. Nevertheless, I fought even harder to make sense of things. But the more I dug, the deeper the hole: I could not figure out how the patient had two fathers, two mothers, and two wives. Finally, I confessed my confusion. Soon, the problem was made clear: I was meeting with two families, not one—I had double-booked the hour. Thankfully, aside from my red-faced embarrassment, all escaped without harm.

As the weeks passed, I grew into my job as a family therapist. In some ways, it felt familiar, harkening to my role in my family of origin. Still, I was becoming ever more knowledgeable about how little I knew. Daily, I discovered the uncomfortable truth that graduate social work programs cover a wide variety of topics but specialize in none. The nine credit hours I had completed in the theory and practice of family therapy had not prepared me for the shifting complexities presented by a single family, much less many different families, each of whom posed an ever-mutating challenge to my efforts to help.

Feeling my deficits, I signed up for a workshop conducted by Bill Silver, DSW, a faculty member of the famed Philadelphia Child Guidance Clinic, on the practice of Structural Family Therapy (SFT). The workshop was well-attended, and the auditorium was abuzz with conversation as we waited for Dr. Silver's arrival; he was ten minutes late. Finally, rushing, he entered the auditorium disheveled and wrestling with a jumble of files that threatened to spill from his arms with every jagged step. Already the poster child for overwhelmed and disorganized, he tripped on the stairs to the stage, launching the files across the floor. The audience gasped, and nearby attendees jumped to the rescue.

Files clutched anew in his arms, Dr. Silver completed his unceremonious journey to the podium. There, he transformed and proceeded to use his dramatically bumbling entrance, and the assemblies' rescuing response, to illustrate how the group was rewarding dysfunctional behavior. He pointed out that it was his job to be on time, organized and prepared, yet here he was, none of those things, and we were showering him with concern and care.

From there, Bill used storytelling and video clips to illuminate the theory of SFT. His ideas were new and heady stuff. I might even say, *empowering,* given that that was the buzzword of the workshops of that era. He certainly had me excited by the promise of mastery and competence that thus far had eluded me.

Consequently, I implemented a plan to acquire such training. I could ill afford the time or money to travel to Philadelphia, so I decided to bring the program to me. Sheppard-Pratt agreed to provide a meeting room, video recording equipment, and a one-way vision room. The participants would pay Dr. Silver. He was receptive to the idea, and in 1981, eight of us began meeting for three hours every other week, a practice that would continue for the next three years.

It was an exhilarating time: learning theory, applying theory to practice, analyzing videotapes of sessions, receiving live supervision from Bill via phone from behind the one-way vision mirror, and even having Bill join the presenting therapist with the family to demonstrate in real-time how a master therapist works. I learned the importance of observing patterns of interactions that unfolded like a dance within each family and how to create paradoxical interventions to disrupt these sequences so that the family would become more amenable to grasping new, healthier forms of organization. I made use of field theory, that questioned the relationship between cause and effect, and learned about sub-groups, triangulating communications, and shifting family alliances. I also learned of the tendency for family members to exchange roles, thereby providing the illusion of change while maintaining the same dysfunctional family patterns. Such shifting of roles, managed by an unskilled therapist, would result in the focus of attention careening from one family member to another, while the dysfunctional family structure remained untouched. Over time, Bill validated me as a skilled therapist, admiring to the group my willingness to "go where even angels fear to tread," and predicted that I would publish professionally.

But the biggest thing I learned over those three years was this: SFT was not for me. I would tell Bill, "It's manipulative." Bill would argue that all therapy was, equating influence with manipulation. I would respond, "Influence isn't orchestrated or disguised, and no trickery is involved."

In the structural approach, there was little valuing of the importance of understanding someone—his heart, soul, or motivations—nor of an authentic relationship between therapist and patient. The therapist did things strategically to affect the way members of the family related to one another—presumably from his position of superior wisdom. I did not like the feel of that, smacking as it did of presumption and arrogance, two attitudes that seemed to go together with the pursuit of therapeutic "empowerment."

The last problem and the most crucial was: It did not work. Sure, in the short-term, patients and families would change their behaviors, but significant regressions soon followed. I saw two reasons for this. One: The therapist eventually lost credibility because the manipulative nature and lack of authentic connection were felt, even if not named, by the family. And, two: Change was built on something exterior to the person—observable behavior—rather than something interior, i.e., the way people saw, thought, and felt about things. SFT relied on the premise that if you can change a family's behavior, the psyche (if the existence of such an entity was granted) would follow. It sounded good; it just did not work that way. To me, this only made sense: If the pathological needs of people went unaddressed, the likelihood of any change in behavior enduring was minimal, relying as it would on *will* rather than *want*.

Not knowing what else to do, I decided to plunge deeper into the human condition to better plumb its mysteries and applied for a job as a clinical social worker on Unit B-2, a locked-door, long-term adult psychiatric inpatient service. Here, I would be treating the sickest of the sick and introduced to a different treatment approach, one far more complex and thought-provoking. What I did not anticipate is that it would turn *me* inside out in ways that I could never have forecasted or imagined

Chapter 19

The World Gone Crazy

1982. Age thirty-three.

Within days of beginning work on B-2, I was wondering, *What have I gotten myself into?* These patients were suffering from a word-salad of major disorders manifested at their most extreme: depression, bipolar disorder with and without psychotic features, dissociative disorder (at that time known as multiple personality disorder), eating disorder, narcissistic and borderline personality disorders, and schizophrenia.

Many patients were suicidal, some homicidal. One woman, the mother of two, self-enucleated an eyeball, literally interpreting the biblical injunction, "If thine eye offends thee, pluck it out, and cast it from thee." A twenty-year-old girl jumped seven floors from a parking garage and survived. She was now suffering the ongoing anguish of her severely broken body and festering regret. Yet another woman drowned her three children during a psychotic episode to "Save them from the Devil." Imagine that. How does anyone come to grips with the horror of murdering their children once the psychosis lifts?

These are tales of human tragedy with a capital T. Such suffering was not the kind touched by so-called empowered therapists. After all, what therapist would be so arrogant as to assume the all-knowing mantle of power in the face of such grisly life-and-death realities? What reward could entice a fundamental change in a compelling wish to die? What is that extraordinary gift that would allow a therapist to "fix" a person in the devastating aftermath of a psychotic desire to kill?

Sheppard-Pratt was famous for treating the troubled of the troubled, often providing the last hope for patients who had experienced multiple failed inpatient treatments elsewhere. They came from Asia, Europe, and Latin America, as well as across the United States and Canada.

When I arrived on B-2, the staff equated social work with handing out benefit checks and serving as a family liaison/discharge planner, none of which held the slightest appeal to me. Also, B-2 was psychoanalytically oriented, concerning itself with the workings of the human psyche and forces not visible to the naked eye, just the opposite of SFT. I had little knowledge of psychoanalytic theory, and thus, once again, found myself starting over from scratch, learning a new culture and a new language: I feared I had made a colossal mistake.

Attending my first treatment team meeting, I observed Dr. Klement, M.D., B-2's service chief. Austrian, her English heavily accented, her bearing queenly in the best sense of the term. She sat tall and austere, thinning black hair coiffed, back ramrod straight—regal without effort or pretense. I would learn that she was one of those rare people whose poise never faltered come turbulent sea or mutinous crew. In the years ahead, despite the life and death dramas that surrounded us, she remained above the fray, maintaining perspective, never becoming reactive or raising her voice, her hand ever-steady on the rudder of the treatment team.

The chairs surrounding her, forming the necklace to her focal stone, were occupied by gems in their own right. Clarence Schulz, M.D., author and senior training psychoanalyst for the Baltimore/Washington Psychoanalytic Training Program; two psychiatrists, one from Mexico, Dr. David Gonzalez, and one from Wales, Dr. David Cowie; and a psychiatric resident, Dr. Roger Lewin, a graduate of both Harvard and Yale, who would author several books in the coming years. Rounding out the team was a post-doctoral fellow in psychology, Denise Forte, whose husband was the medical director of Chestnut Lodge, a famous psychiatric hospital outside of Washington D.C.

But that was not the end of it. A potpourri of nurses, art therapists, dance therapists, occupational therapists, and mental health staff with decades of experience and hard-earned wisdom augmented the team. Viewed through the eyes of a guy who had barely made it out of high school, was kicked out of college, had a less than stellar career in business, followed by an even more humbling tour as an auto-body man and mechanic, this was heady stuff. With relief, I escaped from that first meeting unscathed by any requirement to participate but intuiting that I was swimming waters far deeper than I knew.

My saving grace was I had experience in persevering alone in foreign places. I knew how to nod my head in a parody of wisdom and to avoid saying "Wee" at all costs. I could manage my fear of figuratively getting kicked to the floor or slapped in the face if I said something wrong. Most importantly, I knew to keep my mouth shut as I dug in to listen, and listen, and listen, in hopes of learning what I sensed these people had to impart.

In the ensuing weeks, I was surprised by something that should not have been surprising at all. Despite the academic accomplishments and worldly successes of the treatment staff, each of them, except the elder statesmen, Doctors Klement and

Schulz, was rendered human by the need to vie for position in the intellectual pecking order.

The psychiatrists had cherished egos and would posture intellectually, theorizing ad nauseum, which would bring them into conflict with the nursing staff who faced the practical day-to-day reality of contending with twenty ever demanding and sometimes combative patients. The nursing staff was not seeking theoretical discussion but concrete directions.

Despite the ensuing vitriol, I would learn that these moments of intra-team hostility fit within a broader tapestry of deep relationships and caring that only accrues among those who have been in battle together. In the months and years to come, I would learn that we were all in the trenches, and no one escaped unbloodied, including me.

Within several months, my frustration was profound. All the treatment team seemed to do was talk, talk, talk, the emphasis on thinking about thoughts, feelings, and underlying motivations rather than on doing anything. The inaction drove me crazy. I wondered, *How are we helping?* I was forever teetering on the cusp of leaving, but couldn't. My curiosity would not let me; I sensed that these people knew something profound, and I wanted it for myself.

I started going to the medical library every free moment, reading psychoanalytic texts over lunch, in my office, between meetings, and at home. For the next five years, I immersed myself in the psychoanalytic literature, paying particular attention to writings on primitive mental states. What I read was often so erudite that it left me cold, but along the way, like sluicing for gold, I would unexpectedly come across a nugget of knowledge that shined a light of understanding on what previously had been in shadow, not only about my patients but about me.

What I came to understand is that primitive mental states are part of healthy development. Indeed, they are childhood ways of feeling, thinking, and relating that comprise the inner rings of the tree trunk of the psyche through which all of us travel on the road toward psychological maturity. The two-year-old's obstinacy or dramatic loss of control exhibited in an adult is only one of countless examples. As such, primitive mental states are not crazy in and of themselves. Indeed, all people move up and down the developmental scales on a near-daily basis. The difference is that the psychologically vulnerable regress more often and more deeply, or even dwell in these early ways of perceiving and relating.

I also learned that people do not regress haphazardly but to former states of mental/emotional functioning that date to the time when their problems first began sending their development awry. Being able to understand and personally relate to the ways of perceiving and relating of my patients helped immeasurably in helping them to understand themselves. I grew to appreciate the central importance of establishing a relationship with the patient, wherein the implicit and explicit, conscious, and unconscious, communications that are a part of every relationship can help promote human connection and stimulate development.

I can imagine some of you taking issue, saying, "I don't regress. I don't enter primitive mental states." But I would respectfully say, "Toro Caca." Have you never been reactive? Have you never yelled out of control at your kids or your spouse, your brother, or your sister? Have you never experienced the breakup of a relationship or loss of a loved one like a blow to the stomach that left you wanting to die? Have you never peeked at a Jerry Springer show, or been to the dark places inside yourself? For that matter, have you never shouted at or imagined inflicting terrible things on the turtle-speed drivers who insist on staying in the passing lane or fail to use their turn signals?

That is what I am talking about, reactivity, absent hesitation, self-observation, or reflection. These are the hallmarks of a primitive mental state. Now, imagine not being able to get out of that mental state. Bingo, you are there.

I could go on with examples from the everyday life of so-called ordinary people—that is, you and me (okay, maybe just you)—who are normal-neurotics. We suffer guilt (unlike the sociopath or the narcissist), generally function well, and yet still run up and down the scale of psychological capacities. Why? Because we are not machines, we are living, sentient entities, cursed and blessed with astounding sensitivities, responding in ways large and small to the moment-to-moment fluctuations of the innumerable happenings in our lives and our minds.

Psychoanalytic thinking helped me make sense of things, not only of *what* people were doing but *why* they were doing it and to inter-relate the way we treat ourselves with the way we treat others. I had lived in such states more times than I care to remember, and they return with all their gothic intensity during times of severe relationship or family difficulty.

What I had not understood was that my learning had started the day I had driven onto the grounds of Sheppard-Pratt Hospital. It had begun as I drank in the sight of the spacious green lawns dotted with majestic trees and the well-spaced groupings of Adirondack chairs. It had continued in the large airy rooms full of light and color, ensconced in the protective battlements of those aging buildings. Sheppard-Pratt had been whispering its secrets all along; I just had not had the ears to listen. What were they saying? History, setting, time, space, light, care, and an environment in which it was safe to consider one's thoughts and feel one's feelings no matter how dark or socially unacceptable they might be in the world beyond its borders.

I came to experience the incalculable importance of having someone to talk to who is honestly interested and thoughtful, someone not frightened or appalled by the muddy side of human experience but willing and able to explore those dark corners with you. When you can do that with someone, you *know* you are not alone. You come to appreciate that you're not even all that unusual.

The self-examination of psychotherapy helps you realize that your thoughts and feelings are valuable in ways beyond your imagining. As the therapist asks about a word you used or a specific idea you uttered, or merely about the way you spoke, you start to consider your thoughts and feelings more seriously.

Think of that, to become the object of your curiosity. It seems simple, right? Self-reflective. Yet, people are almost universally apprehensive about engaging in the process, typically rejecting the idea out of hand. Why do you suppose that is? Is it fear of letting someone in, of exposure, embarrassment, shame, or ridicule? Is it concern with allowing someone else to see that you are not quite how you like to present yourself or of discovering that you are not quite who you think you are?

With these words, please do not think that I am criticizing you. Most of us suffer from these insecurities. Also, be aware that

I am not discounting genetic or constitutional contributors to psychiatric issues. Nonetheless, each of us is responsible for how we deal with our thoughts, feelings, and behaviors. And I will venture that to the degree you are unhappy and engage in a psychotherapeutic process, you will discover that the source of your disquiet does not rest outside of you but within. That is good news; it means *you* can do something about it.

Wrestling with these ideas and my troubled feelings, while also being confronted by growing marital conflict, mental illness in my own family, and the confrontations of challenging patients, I realized it was my turn to go under the analytic spotlight, to sort out from whence I had come, and to where I wanted to go.

Chapter 20

Psycho-Analysis

*A*side from my wish as a therapist to experience therapy from the inside out, I was in touch with a disquiet I could no longer deny and one I had felt most of my life but always explained away: *That's the way it is. It is just the way I am. It is just the way things are.* But now, immersed in examining the issues of others, I was forever in a hall of mirrors reminding me of my own and feeling increasingly disingenuous, encouraging others to confront their unrest while ignoring mine.

Unable to afford regular psychoanalysis, I became a training case at the Baltimore Washington Center for Psychoanalysis and Psychotherapy. I met four times weekly, lying supine on an analytic couch, while the analyst sat behind me, out of sight but certainly not out of mind. I had no real goals, other than to go through the experience so I could see what it was like and, perhaps, deepen my understanding of myself. Still, trepidation lingered. A friend had entered analysis several months earlier and told me how, after just a few short minutes lying on the couch, his feelings became so intense that he shot bolt upright and could not continue.

Just think about that. You are lying on a couch talking with someone sitting behind you, and the experience becomes so overwhelming that you feel compelled to sit up as if you just stuck your toe in an electric socket. One can only ask, "What would cause that?" If we consider my friend's panicked experience, we soon deduce that the only frightening thing in the room was the inner workings of his mind. After all, it was not likely that the analyst was going to pick up a meat cleaver and attack him. So, maybe we need to recalibrate our thinking. Is it possible that confronting the workings of one's mind is one of the most courageous things a person can do?

Now, it was *me* in that circumstance, lying on the analytic couch, my horizons limited to the ceiling of the room and the wall beyond my outstretched feet. The analyst sat behind me. The object of our mutual attention? ...*Me*. The only instruction, "Say whatever comes to mind without editing." From the outset, it was disconcerting. There was no guidance, no questions asked, and no indication of what topics I should discuss. Out of my line of sight, I could not read the analyst's facial expressions or body language. Even garnering cues about what he might be thinking or feeling from his speech was nearly impossible, given he was a man of few words. Even when he did speak, it was not in conversational form, but in pointed questions, observations, or commentary, advanced for my consideration. In a typical session, he might not say more than twenty words. All of this, I found increasingly annoying; after all, *If I knew what to think, why would I need him?*

Left to my own devices, I soon became a blathering idiot. What could I possibly talk about for four hours a week with a person I couldn't see and who rarely responded? I didn't have much to say, or at least, not much that I thought was worth saying (I was immediately editing). What I was rapidly discovering was that it was relatively easy to be in the role of a psychotherapist, listening as the patient supplied the grist for the mill of therapy and quite another level of difficulty being the patient, expected to provide that grist.

Such a lack of structure fosters regression. My thinking blurred as I shadow-boxed with my thoughts, particularly those of my internal board of critics, whose unkind assessments devalued almost anything I might consider saying, often rendering me deaf and dumb. My mind shied away from saying anything that would pin me down and leave me open to possible censure, either in the form of the therapist's private thoughts, upon which I would endlessly speculate, or my scathing self-criticalness honed at the feet of my father. Add to this caustic soup, the sarcastic and competitive quips of my brothers, echoing unbidden in the corridors of my psyche, and the situation became a cocktail for mental paralysis. I could now understand why my friend bolted upright after just a few minutes on this rack of self-recriminations.

Assured of the vapidness of my thoughts, I experimented with different subjects, trying to discern which, if any, would capture my therapist's interest and, hopefully, elevate me in his eyes. Such an outcome would keep me safe, at least momentarily, from the shame or ridicule I so feared. No matter how hard I tried, I could not stop relating to my non-visible therapist as if he were a stand-in for my father or siblings. Increasingly desperate, I attempted to take control of the situation by telling the most inappropriate or repulsive things that came to mind, now simply trying to provoke a reaction, any reaction, from my silent partner around which I could organize myself and not feel alone. My initial pristine goal of self-understanding had quickly become secondary to my need for connection, even if it was a connection to some stand-in for my noxious father. What did I get back? Typically, silence.

Absent the external cues to which I usually moored, I slipped anchor and was adrift in the swirling currents and eddies of my mind. I wished for something, anything, around which to center my world, not unlike the back of that chair in the dining hall of Collège St. Etienne. The security strategies devised in the formative years of my development, that had organized my understanding of life and how to keep safe, strained to wrap themselves around this formless experience.

My thinking fed upon the smoke and mirrors of my imaginings, becoming a wormhole catapulting me back in time to childhood ways of thinking and feeling. I was discovering what people learn in a sensory deprivation tank: There is no place in this world or beyond more frightening than our minds. Or, to paraphrase Freud, "There is nothing so frightening as the return of the repressed."

Worn down by the constant, urgent whisperings of my psyche, I came to recognize that I needed to break free of the labyrinth of my self-flagellating criticalness and the fear of rejection or attack that formed its walls. Exhausted from being kicked about by this self-disparaging, frightened side of myself, I did the unthinkable: I quit. I gave up the futile effort of worrying about what my analyst might be thinking and focused on *my* thoughts and feelings, at last, adhering to the impossibly simple, yet incredibly difficult, analytic injunction to, "Say whatever comes to mind without judgment or censorship." I had fired the critics, recognizing them as at the root of my self-inflicted misery and the first impediment to my recovery and growth. To my dismay, I had found the process of psychoanalysis had amplified my disquiets, not relieved them, but in doing so, had given them a voice. No longer nameless, I could now think about them.

Within this kinetic mental landscape, I discovered that the most productive sessions occurred when I relaxed into my stream of consciousness. In these relatively calm and clearer waters of my psyche, sub-conscious thoughts and feelings would emerge. These denizens of the deep would rise slowly to the surface like manatees and become illuminated in the moonbeams of my awareness or by the analyst's comments, facilitating further discoveries.

I had entered psychoanalysis determined to endure the experience—to see where it and I would take me. As profoundly disturbing as it was, the process was not as bad as I had feared. After all, my bar for isolation and loneliness and for being left with only my thoughts and feelings for company was high. However, inexplicably, I did begin crying that first session and every session after that for the next six months, yet I had no idea why. Only later did I realize that the isolation of psychoanalysis, my seeming inability to connect with my therapist, strummed the taught chords of the terrible emptiness of my childhood. It was

all there, and it was happening all over again in the *right now* of
my regression.

What I learned in four years of psychoanalysis can be
summed up in a few words. But do not misunderstand,
psychoanalysis was not a waste of time. Far from it, it was life-
changing, fostering emotional development, not merely
intellectual insight. This growth required the full four years,
lying supine on that couch that became home as I time-traveled
through my life.

Psychoanalysis can be an intensely absorbing and regressive
experience for those willing to give themselves over to its
undertow and carried down into long-forgotten childhood states
of heart and mind that in quiet but incessant whispers, continue
to profoundly influence our lives. Psychoanalysis helps break the
hypnotic suggestions of childhood, allowing for psychic freedom
and the adult capacity to think for oneself, which is foundational
to owning and creating one's own life.

I will spare you slogging through all the psychological
swamp mud with which I dealt and, instead, jump right over to
the firm ground of what I learned. First, having recognized the
failed strategy of trying to be dependent upon my analyst, I
turned to self-observation and reflection to assess what was and
was not important in my life.

With this painfully won shift in focus, I settled into treatment, studying my thoughts, feelings, and sensations: the mental contents of my psyche. In doing so, I came to appreciate my analyst as someone upon whom I could rely on inserting himself into my musings when he felt he had something to offer. His role was not to lead the way but to follow alongside as a faithful companion lending the staff of his powers of observation and thinking to supplement my own. Independent of me and my upbringing, he was in a better position to identify the unseen waters of my life. He assisted in my evolving from a self-suppressive tyrannically governing psyche, to one of greater psychic freedom, valuing freedom of thought and speech above all else—that liberating process took a year.

That may sound like a long time, but it is not if you consider the nature of it. I was on what the psychoanalyst, Melanie Klein, called *the road toward autonomy*. The word "toward" used because one never fully arrives.

In the second year, I learned the importance of confronting my fears instead of running from them. When I faced my fears, they became manageable and often dissipated altogether. It was a lesson I had learned before: Something seemingly unmanageable in the distance when taken in whole, can be overcome, often easily, up close, a step at a time. Also, I learned that the unbounded imaginings of the internal world of fantasy were almost always more frightening than reality. Consequently, an internal play-space unfolded in which I could consider my thoughts and feelings without fear of becoming them.

Thus, I discovered that psychotherapy is a revolutionary process, helping me break free of the constraining rings of my childhood, and its legacy of self-fettering prejudices and assumptions. Ironically, these I had learned from the *adults* in my life who *did* tell me what to think and feel in childhood and would do so in my adulthood if I let them. I further recognized that my parents, as well as the generations that had preceded them, had imbibed the imparted *truths* of their elders with hardly a hiccup, their ways of being and behaving passing down through the generations without a second thought, or even a first.

I finally understood that to the degree any of us goes unthinkingly along with the familiar and the familial, we are living cookie-cutter lives, just marching in lock-step with earlier generations, only singing new renditions of the same old songs. In my case, this included the underlying assumptions that quitting is always wrong, that one should endure without complaint and be heroic (whatever that meant), and that I should stay on the periphery and support others, but not expect success, much less demand it of myself.

In the third year of psychoanalysis, I was made aware of an underlying assumption that had been at the hub of the way I was living my life and yet, had been almost entirely outside of my awareness. It was not an unusual day; I was telling my analyst something that seemed innocuous, a recently articulable ambition, yet one strangely tinged with regret for it accepted limits on who I could be and what I could accomplish. I'd assumed this acceptance to be a sign of maturity: the wisdom of accepting one's limits.

In the vernacular of the army brat, I exclaimed, "I want to become the top master sergeant at Sheppard-Pratt Hospital." In the medical model, psychiatrists, followed by psychologists, were the officer class, while the best a social worker could hope for was to rise to the top of the non-commissioned ranks. I aspired to become the Senior Social Worker of Adult Long-Term Inpatient Services. This position entailed supervising social work services on seven inpatient units, covering 140 patients with diagnoses ranging from personality disorder to eating disorder to schizophrenia.

After a short silence, my analyst, himself a psychiatrist, responded with a deceptively simple and softly posed question, the five words of which, like a pebble thrown into a pond, rippled outward in ever-widening rings, toward a world of potentials that would forever change my life. "Why just a master

sergeant?"

Part IV

-

The World and I—Co-mingling

Now I was breaking out of my shell into a world I was helping create. Instead of feeling like a leaf swept along in the river of life, I was now actively swimming and choosing my direction. The possibilities were many: I could swim against the current or with it, or I could swim to the shore and hike cross-country. Nothing was fated; I was shaping my world as the world was shaping me. Now, we—the world and I—were co-mingling rather than co-mangling, engaged in an inter-enriching relationship. I could live with that. Hell, I could thrive.

Chapter 21

"Why Just a Master Sergeant?"

Why just a master sergeant?

Those words hung in the air then careened around my brain like ping pong balls in a lottery machine. Numerous glib responses sprang to mind, but I could not push the question away.

It was not only the question but the fact that he, a psychiatrist, had asked it. *He could imagine my being more than a master sergeant, so why couldn't I?* I could not envisage how rising higher in the professional ranks was an option, but clearly, he could. My analyst had given me a gift: an unfolding horizon rife with the possibility of potentials yet to be birthed.

In the prototypic framework of my familial role, I was always the support person or spectator, while Jacques was center stage. To me taking the spotlight had never occurred: It just was *not* the way of things. In the months to follow, I recognized that I had patterned my existence on this habituated role and its implicit, unconscious assumption, even going as far as recreating my familial role as a support person within the treatment team. There the psychiatrists stood center stage, and I played the role of the younger brother.

But what was my alternative? How was I to compare to people from Vienna, Harvard, and Yale and all the medical and doctoral programs the others had attended? How was I to overcome the *medical model* of the hospital where psychiatrists ruled, and social workers were lower on the caste system? In this model, mine had been a role that fit me like an old suit; it felt a part of *me* as if it were *me*.

As I considered the question, "Why just a master sergeant?" I realized I couldn't wholly attribute my life as a spectator to the familial and familiar. I reasoned that for me to sustain such behavior, I must find it rewarding in some way. I soon realized the reward was a defensive one. Being center stage would make me vulnerable to attack, criticism, second-guessing, and getting knocked down.

Conversely, if I kept a low profile, my chances of remaining unscathed were better, unless, of course, I counted the cost of a self-limited life. If I wanted to see who I could become, I would have to put myself out there. The saving difference was that I was no longer a defenseless boy. I was a grown man who could stand up for himself.

Beleaguered by such thoughts, I groaned as another consideration took hold. Surprisingly, I realized I was worried about Jacques. I knew, even if he did not, that he was as dependent on his role as I had been on mine. If I changed my role, how would that affect his?

Certainly, these were childish thoughts—the thinking derived from childhood typically is—but that did not make them any less potent, but more so, connected as they were to the powerful feelings of that more emotionally charged and splintered age. It took a while, but I worked it out. If I were going to take responsibility for *my* happiness and meaning, I would have to continue evolving. If Jacques came to feel threatened by my growth, which my adult thinking doubted, then he would have to do more maturing as well—nothing wrong with that.

With those concerns laid to rest, the final layer of my resistance came fully to mind with nauseating intensity: What if I failed? The limelight would offer no place to hide. The shame and humiliation, and the ensuing damage to my sense of self would be devastating. Didn't it make more sense for me not to try and, thus, never fail?

In the end, these concerns gave way to a certain knowledge: I would be tormented for the rest of my life, forever disappointed in myself, and always wondering who I might have become if I did not try. I could not bear the idea of the road not traveled, of not exploring where it might have taken me. My choice stood between the risks of moving forward, possibly into a spring-fed life, or dwelling in a growing pool of resignation and stagnation that would eventually hook up with its compatriot despair, as my yesterdays became my tomorrows till the day I died. Then the question, "What's the point?" would become trenchant. I now understood something that had never occurred to me quite this way before: the pursuit of happiness and meaning required the courage to fail.

I began speaking up in team meetings. Using the mindset developed in psychoanalysis, I focused on expressing my thoughts as they pertained to the clinical cases, rather than concerning myself with what others might be thinking about me. I discovered that what I offered was usually taken seriously. One team member remarked, "Charlie, you're making people think." And then, some months later, the miracle of miracles: I was invited to the weekly meetings reserved for psychotherapists.

A day came when Dr. Schulz, who I had hired to supervise my private practice of individual therapy, advised: "Charlie, it's time for you to stop reading and start writing." I was astonished that a highly lauded teaching analyst and author of psychoanalytic books would say this to me. Dr. Schulz planted a seed that would usher in a whole new phase of my life, the likes of which I had never dreamt. In life, as in psychoanalysis, I had discovered that by moving toward rather than away from my fears, I was moving beyond the confines of my childhood and claiming the privilege of living *my* life.

The wonderfully freeing thing was that although I did not know where any of this would lead, I had come to appreciate that that did not matter. What was incredibly valuable was the palpable experience of being more fully engaged in my life. What I did not yet understand was that this more fully invested life would lead to other experiences, the scope of which I could not have imagined, and some of which I wish that I had never come to know. Nevertheless, despite the times to come that would sometimes brim with anguish rather than joy, I am far better for it.

Chapter 22

Anguish and Joy

Psychoanalytically oriented psychotherapy challenges me to the core, not just the ongoing training and education, but the requirement that the therapist attends to his mental and emotional workings as part of assessing the silent, subconscious communication that occurs between patient and therapist.

Self-examination is not always pleasant. It is disquieting to confront one's vulnerabilities—the dark feelings, hypocrisies, and lies that we are all prone to tell ourselves. Nonetheless, a willingness to do so is necessary as part of the implicit contract for any therapist who opts to work in an insight-oriented way.

This challenge can be formidable when treating people suffering from major psychopathology, especially borderline, narcissistic, and paranoid personality disorders. These individuals, gifted in their ability to read the dark undercurrents in others while denying similar feelings within themselves, often lack empathy. As a result, they are prone to launching ruthless attacks on the self of anyone who displeases them.

Working on B-2 was already challenging. On any given day, I could find myself physically restraining a patient as she bolted from my office in a bid to escape; confronting a patient holding a shard of broken lightbulb against her throat, threatening to cut her carotid artery if I did not unlock the door; or, striving to remain calm during a man's agitated rantings while silently praying he did not attack.

Nonetheless, as dramatic as these occurrences were, the worst challenges are in the patient's attack on the self of the therapist, in charges of being sadistic, lustful, greedy, hateful, envious, or jealous. Or to be taunted and called "small-dicked" or "lower than whale shit at the bottom of the ocean." What makes these imputations so unsettling is that if honest with oneself, there is often a smattering of truth. Every human being has within them measures of these elements—lusts, flaws, weaknesses, and feelings of shame and inadequacy. When such elements of the human condition are focused on and amplified under the microscopic intensity of the patient's laser vision while simultaneously being evoked and provoked by the patient's behaviors these flaws are made readily apparent, seemingly more significant than the whole, threatening the capacity for sober reasoning and the ability to retain the light of day.

It is not just the words, but the scorn and disdain with which they are delivered, alongside the provocative behaviors of the patient designed to elicit the very feelings with which I am charged. One patient keeps bumping into me as we walk down the hall while accusing me of not liking her. Another contemptuously mocks me for lusting after her, while crossing and uncrossing her legs, flashing her underwear, and leaning forward so that her blouse falls open, exposing her breasts. A recently discharged patient assures me he has a gun and taunts me: "Don't you believe me? Do you want me to show it to you? Are you afraid? Are you a coward?"

Such a barrage of personal challenges, endured week-in and week-out, forge a mélange of fact and fantasy, fueling self-questioning and self-doubt, threatening to wrest my sense of reality. You see, I was annoyed with the girl who kept bumping into me as we walked down the hall. Did that mean I did not like her? I was titillated by the woman who repeatedly flashed me. Did that mean I lusted after her? I felt frightened by the guy that threatened me with the idea of a gun. Did that make me a coward?

Yet, as personally challenging as these interactions were, the most unsettling experiences of all occur when an entire family choruses such sentiments. On one occasion, a delusionally paranoid family, rife with fears of persecution, would accuse me of saying things I did not think I had said. When I attempted to explore their assertions, they would claim to quote me from a discussion that had occurred minutes earlier, challenging my capacity to recall specifics under the emotionally charged, mind-fogging barrage of their accusations. Often, they would change one or two keywords, use words out of context, or actively interpret what I did say in persecutory ways. Under the pressure of this inquisitional force, it became problematic for me to keep an open mind and maintain perspective while trying to sort the real from the delusional.

The father, in his fifties, six-foot-tall and remarkably fit, dressed in boots, flannel shirt and jeans creased with military precision, and possessing a narrow hawkish face seemingly chiseled from granite, stared at me accusingly with unblinking eyes of blue dots painted on white stone. With his hair pulled so tightly back into a ponytail that it removed all lines from his forehead, he gave the impression of being a predator, ready to pounce on whatever threat he imagined was on its way.

His waif of a wife, dull brown hair hanging lankly above her shoulders, dressed in formless, colorless clothes, seemed beaten down and aquiver with anxiety. She repeatedly snuck peeks at her husband as if trying to predict the timing of a coming storm. Their two sons, large-bodied men with round, puffy faces, took their cues from their father's aggressive leaning into the world and, along with their full-figured wives, provided a chorus of vocal support to the father's every utterance.

Although a family of few words, a conversation was in constant flow; their intense faces, alert postures, and furtive glances giving meanings to which I was not privy. I was the outsider, and somehow, from the beginning, the enemy. My every attempt to connect with this family only spurred their sense of endangerment as if I were trying to invade rather than to relate.

One of my supposed misquotes occurred in the following fashion. As I took a family history, the father pugnaciously announced, as if daring me to take issue, "I didn't grieve the death of my mother. I was glad she was gone." Later, referring to this comment, I said, "You were glad your mom was dead." As if poked with a hot iron, the father took furious exception to my words, spitting out, "I didn't say that! Those aren't my words! You are putting words in my mouth!" The sons and daughters-in-law added their chorus of outrage, the abrupt intensity of it all nearly sweeping me away. All the while, the mother sat silently, her worried eyes flicking here and there, like a terrified mouse trying to find a hiding hole. I now knew the feeling.

Overwhelmed by this unexpected upsurge of virulent protest, I struggled to recover the father's exact wording, all the while fearing, given the absolute certainty of their convictions, that I had invented my interpretation from whole cloth. Fortunately, I was able to recall his words. "I believe you said, 'I was glad she was gone.' I'm sorry if I misinterpreted this to mean you were glad she was dead. Tell me, how should I have understood it?" At this, the father paused, face rigid, and entered a brooding and reproachful silence as if recognizing, for the first time, the meaning of his words and convinced that my intent all along had been to stab him with them.

This family drama was one of many reality undermining interactions with the families of some patients. With them, I always strove to remain open to the family's perceptions, working hard to create a culture in which all things could be considered, including the limitations of the therapist. While an important goal, this striving required I tolerate uncertainty, a state of mind I call "Not-Knowing," necessary for examining things from all perspectives. Conversely, the families, ensconced in the protective battlements of absolutist, all or nothing thinking and feeling, and armored in the unquestioning certainty of their beliefs, were free to spout their righteous indignation. Thus, mine was the fate of a flickering flame in a tornado.

What was real? What was not? Repeatedly caught in such Byzantine considerations, I felt growing dread in anticipation of meeting with these families and knew that this would not do. I fell upon a common-sense solution. I needed someone in the room that was not caught up in the emotional fray. Someone who, free from the need to interact, could more easily maintain perspective: I needed an objective observer. I invited a mental health worker, Rob, to join me in the sessions. Slight of build, solicitous and non-threatening, Rob was well-liked by patients and staff. I told him his job was to listen so that, when needed, I could ask, "Did I say that?" or "Did I misrepresent that?" What amazed me was that the families readily accepted what Rob said, his role as The Observer, seemingly lending him objectivity and authority. Thus, freed, we moved forward in the family work.

The work of the psychotherapist is difficult because all human beings are rife with a panoply of emotions, from the darkest to the brightest. Additionally, mental health does not result from the elimination of less than socially acceptable emotions, which would lend a veneer of welcome invincibility, but their integration. Thus, I *can* be greedy, and I *can* be generous. So, which am I? Reconciling these polarities leads to the understanding that I can be both and all the combinations that lie between them.

When I accept my darker, more socially unacceptable thoughts and feelings, along with my kinder ones, I can think about them and learn from them. Conversely, if I deny the existence of my negative feelings, I cannot. These feelings then become dark passengers, banished from view, but affecting one even more powerfully from the shadows. Accepting one's dark side fosters inclusion rather than exclusion, tolerance rather than intolerance, acceptance rather than rejection, and allows one to relate more fully to self and others.

When an individual's early attachments are fractured by abuse or neglect, their development becomes truncated, curbing their capacity to tolerate ambiguity. Impaired in their ability to reconcile conflicting feelings, they are left literal-minded and given to all-or-nothing thinking and feeling, resolving the conflict by denying one or the other of its poles. However, the denied feelings do not simply disappear; they remain active and are dealt with aggressively via repression and the projecting of the denied aspect onto others. Thus, the girl bumping me as we walked down the hallway, accusing me of disliking her, may have been angry with me, self-hating or both. The contemptuously flirtatious woman might have hated herself for feeling her value as being limited to that of a sexual object or thing. The man who threatened me with the idea of a gun was concerned about his manliness and related in ways to cause me to question my own. Via such methods, individuals substitute intrapsychic conflict for less troubling interpersonal conflict, wherein the denied pole of the conflict is projected onto others — this pattern of coping results in a life characterized by tumultuous relationships.

Primitive mental states are also ahistorical: The experience of the moment overwrites the past and is projected into the future. Thus, when one's need is being satisfied, the other is perceived as *good,* and when one's needs are being frustrated, the other is perceived as *bad.* The disordered individual jumps effortlessly from one absolutist judgment to the other with no sense of disingenuousness.

In similar ways, the disordered individual may idealize some people, while devaluing others. When this occurs with staff members, the preferred staff may come to feel that they have a unique understanding of and relationship with the patient. This dynamic can create another challenge for the therapist and the treatment team. Indeed, it, along with my hubris, led me to take a patient and myself into harm's way.

Within the first few months of joining B-2, the treating psychologist and I decided that a home visit for a patient, Joan, was necessitated. On Friday, Joan reported a phone call from her aged mother, who was said to be in poor health and rapidly declining: Joan exclaimed that she needed to visit her mother before it was too late. The next team meeting wasn't until Monday, and time felt to be of the essence. Neither Joan, the psychologist, or I felt we could wait. Besides, both the psychologist and I were frustrated with the lack of action on the part of the treatment team and, given this opportunity, decided to act on our own. That is how I came to be driving Joan to see her mother.

On the way, an alarming indicator that this decision was not well thought out arose when I began asking myself, *What will I do if Joan tries to open the door and jump out? How would I stop her when I'm driving?* Fortunately, nothing happened, and we arrived without incident at her mother's senior high-rise apartment.

As I sat quietly to the side in the well-ordered living room, listening with half an ear as Joan spoke with her mother, I noticed additional indicators that this plan had not been well-conceived; in fact, I was feeling played and strangely betrayed. I hadn't thought that given our connection that Joan would have done this to me. Joan's mother did not appear to be near death's door, nor anywhere in its vicinity. She was well dressed and groomed, and there were no nurses or medical devices in view. Moreover, she was sharp as a tack and just as biting. Cold and scornful, she showed no sign of affection, recoiling from Joan's every attempt at connection like a Queen from the repulsive touch of a lice-ridden beggar. After some minutes of this thorny reception, Joan, a look of resignation painting her face, announced she had to go to the bathroom. I was uncomfortable allowing her out of my sight but had no choice.

While Joan was in the bathroom, I tried to converse with her mother. But she remained aloof, impervious to my every effort to relate. Now, I just wanted to escape and began wondering what was taking Joan so long. As the seconds crept by, my concern rose. I asked Joan's mother, "Do you think she's okay?" Smiling, as if she had just bitten into lime, the mother dismissively waved aside any need to worry. That is when a thought slammed into my mind—*She wants Joan dead. Joan is going to be a good daughter and comply.* I sprang to my feet and hurried to the bathroom door.

I knocked gently, calling Joan's name. There was no response. I hoped she had not heard me, then prayed that her silence was due to embarrassment over doing her business with me just outside the door. I called again, this time louder, and still, there was no answer. Alarm growing, I called out a third time, only to be met with that intractable silence, stoking the flames of my concern into a bonfire of fear.

At just this moment, Joan hesitantly responded, "Just a minute." Something wet and ugly twisted in my belly. *Why had Joan failed to respond for so long? Why was her speech, hesitant?* That is when I knew the unthinkable was about to happen. I commanded, "Joan, open the door right now!" …Silence.

I turned the knob, but it was locked. Terrified, fully committed, I rammed the door with my shoulder, splintering the lock and swinging the door open. Within, Joan stood two feet away, bent over the sink, her focus entirely on her wrist, razor blade poised.

Shouting, "No!" I lunged. In that nanosecond, everything slowed. I took in the razor, cleaving its way across Joan's wrist, flesh unzipping, yawning open in a scarlet scream. Frightened, angry, panicked, and betrayed, I grabbed the hand holding the blade and banged it against the sink, shouting, "Drop the razor! Drop the razor!" until she did. Freed from that threat, I clutched her injured arm above the gash, fighting to stem the flow of blood while wrestling her to the floor yelling sharply to her bitch of a mother, "Call 911. Do it now!"

The EMTs arrived minutes later to find me on the floor, holding Joan in place as I clutched her injured wrist. I followed the ambulance to the emergency room, knowing two things with certainty: "I'll be fired," and "I should be." Joan suffered a partly severed tendon. Fortunately, she later regained the full functioning of her hand.

The following Monday, *I* was the focus of the team meeting in a way I had never imagined. The entire episode reviewed step by agonizing step, as staff members asked their questions, some reprimanding me. I sat and listened, saying not a single word in defense. I had no defense; I was guilty.

All the while, Dr. Klement listened, exhibiting her enduring quest for understanding. She seemed aware that I was unforgiving of myself and resigned to my fate. Near the end of the meeting, her cultured Austrian accent and bearing lending its usual thoughtful formality, she softly spoke, "Charles, perhaps in the future, you should reconsider when you feel an urge to operate outside the auspices of the treatment team." Nothing more was ever said.

With those words, Dr. Klement informed me that I still had a future on B-2. I am forever grateful. While I had been castigating myself, Dr. Klement had been integrating the conflicting aspects of the situation. I *had* made a serious error in judgment, but it was

not a malicious one. I was also genuinely remorseful. She knew
me to be an earnest person and refused to allow this singular, if
epic, mistake to define me. Thus, she helped forge me into a
humbler, wiser, more compassionate version of myself.

Thankfully, most of my clinical adventures ended more
positively. The story of Sarah comes to mind. In her early thirties,
round of face, brown hair hanging lifelessly to her shoulders, she
was plain in grooming and appearance, perfectly fitting the
prototype of a person with a deeply conservative and religious
upbringing. She carried herself with feminine strength and grace.
I liked her immediately.

Sarah entered the hospital in a state of voluntary mutism.
For nearly a year, she had refused to speak while secluding
herself in her room in the parental home. A previous inpatient
effort had proved futile; the family was desperate. She talked to
no one and did her best to avoid all human contact.

Faced with this challenge, I decided to begin meeting with
Sarah and her parents in family sessions, thinking maybe she
would not talk, but her parents would. The parents, slightly built
and carrying the gray hair of their late sixties, were soft-spoken
with intelligent eyes. Of deep faith, they were not given to
excesses of any kind, dressing and carrying themselves modestly.

They were willing to try anything to be of help. So, one late morning, the sun streaming through the window, we all gathered in Sarah's room, given her refusal to leave it.

Sarah lay unmoving on her bed, feigning sleep. Without paying her the slightest mind, I moved chairs in, and once everyone was seated, began talking with her parents about family life: History, how they met, and what life was like with Sarah growing up, all while Sarah ignored our presence.

About twenty minutes into this pleasant conversation, I noticed Sarah starting to move about in mild agitation: Something was brewing. A few minutes later, my suspicion was confirmed when Sarah began making guttural noises. Encouraged, we all looked at her in askance, but her face remained hidden, facing the wall away from us. Sarah's mother asked, "What is that you're saying, Dear? We can't hear you?" Sarah then spoke, "Shut up! I hate you! Liars." These were the first words Sarah had spoken in over a year.

Confusion and embarrassment worked their way across the mother's face, while the father displayed puzzled concern. Such words did not reconcile easily with their view of themselves. The mother leaned forward, her face hopeful, and said, "What do you mean, Dear?" Sarah fell back into silence. Then, minutes later, as the family meeting continued, Sarah repeated: "I hate you!

Liars!" When I asked to what she was referring, I was ignored, left feeling like a rude interloper rather than a helping professional.

Several weeks passed with twice-weekly family sessions in which Sarah would repeat her words. But, there had been other changes as well. She was now sitting up in bed, scowling at her parents. Then, Sarah upped the ante. She climbed out of bed and began pacing, as far from her parents and me as she could. After some minutes of this disturbed meditation, she halted, stood still, and tilted her head to one side, as if in silent conversation with herself.

Coming to a decision, Sarah began moving toward her parents in a bizarre, slow-motion, stutter-step kind of way, like a person tentatively testing the strength of the ice upon a pond. In this cautious fashion, she slowly approached her parents and then began swatting at them. It bordered on the slapstick, for she had arrived several inches short, resulting in her hands flailing ineffectually in the air. After several failed tries, Sarah readjusted her position and began slapping her parents on their arms and legs, her assault so feminine and restrained that I felt little apprehension.

Sarah's father, spine stiffening, raised his arms to fend off the hits. Her mother seemed torn between a desire to move towards

Sarah to comfort her and the wish to pull self-protectively away. After thirty seconds of observing this puzzling interaction, I intervened, physically wedging myself between Sarah and her parents without touching her. Gently, almost apologetically, I told her I could not allow her to keep hitting her parents. Sarah, briefly looked at me, quickly dismissed what she saw, and immediately went for them again. As I once more put myself between them, one thing became clear: Sarah wanted no physical contact with me. Thus, as I repeatedly countered each of Sarah's efforts to go around me, we came to dance a silent samba of approach and avoidance.

Over the following sessions, Sarah's attacks on her parents continued, yet she would slap at them rather than use her fists—not the actions of a person who wanted to do serious harm. What also stood out for me was that her parents did little to defend themselves. They would turn toward her and hold their arms up in the attempt to ward off her slaps but did nothing to pull away or restrain her. They did not even ask her to stop, perhaps fearful of losing this hard-won contact. Still, the intensity of Sarah's attacks was escalating, and my role as a bodyguard was wearing thin, so I again recruited Rob to join me. His assignment? To protect Sarah's parents when I asked him to but never to cause Sarah to feel subjugated or overpowered in any way.

Behavior communicates. It has intentionality that may reveal underlying motivations. My challenge was to figure out what Sarah's intention was. What was she trying to express? What was she trying to initiate? For reasons that eluded me, I intuited that it was essential to Sarah for her parents to protect themselves and thereby to more fully engage with her. I wondered if the harder slaps arose out of frustration that they had not done so. To this end, I suggested they restrain Sarah by wrapping their arms around her and holding tight. I asked Rob only to intervene if Sarah got the upper hand.

As a result, Sarah and her parents were now having lots of physical contacts. The parents would push Sarah back onto the bed, where they would wrap themselves around her arms and legs and hold on tight. By the end of each session, Sarah would lay panting and exhausted, held in the arms of her parents. Sarah's mother would usually wrap herself around Sarah's upper torso with her front to Sarah's back while her father took Sarah's legs. In this position, Sarah lay exhausted, head lolling onto the chest of her mother, who used each such opportunity to gently stroke her hair: The picture of a loving mother comforting her child.

Over the weeks that followed, Sarah became less physical and more vocal. She was now speaking, sometimes in sentences.

Consequently, I began meeting with her individually several times weekly—in addition to the family sessions—in service of developing our relationship. Slowly, Sarah revealed she had worked for the Peace Corps and became pregnant out of wedlock while in a remote area of Brazil. Hers was a strict religious family, and her parents and her church had responded to her pregnancy by avoiding the topic (i.e., not fully engaging): Sarah felt silently judged. When she later miscarried, she also felt condemned by God. That is when, feeling shunned by the world, she, in turn, began shunning the world: An act of defiance in service of the survival of the self to which I could relate.

Sarah and I talked about her pregnancy, the father of the child, what had happened to that relationship, the feelings she had about her miscarriage, and the difficult weeks of fear and isolation before returning home from Brazil. What was changing now? Why was Sarah coming out of her burrow? I had my ideas. To me, the caring and touch of her parents, their unwavering willingness to participate week-in and week-out in these challenging sessions, and the purity of their desire to hold and comfort her were all felt by Sarah. As Sarah's rage ebbed, she began accepting their care and rewarded them by haltingly putting her feelings into words, words her parents were now willing to hear. They had lost their daughter for a time and now understood why. They were not going to make that mistake again.

Three months later, Sarah was discharged from the hospital and, after a short outpatient stint, moved to California. Many months later, I received a letter from Sarah thanking me for "not giving up" on her and relating that she had completed a master's degree in bilingual education and worked with the Hispanic community. She had gone from being without spoken language to speaking two and helping others learn to speak them as well.

Just as each failure takes something out of the psychotherapist, each success, the fulfillment of being able to help, gives something back, making the therapist's calling worth following and worth suffering. Of both, there has been much, and for you to understand the dimensions of my life and any meaning I attribute to it, you must hear it all. So please forgive me, for I have darker tales to tell.

Chapter 23

Suicide

I once read that the words love, care, and cure share the same Latin root. I have cause to doubt the veracity of this, but I like the idea. Caring for someone is an essential part of the therapist's ability to be of help. Care is necessary, conveying love and acceptance, two experiences of which the patient is usually bereft. Its presence or absence, even if never spoken, is felt in the care-full interactions of psychotherapy.

While it is true that most people are their own worst enemy, this is exponentially the case for individuals suffering significant psychopathology. Suicide is often on the menu of options and can be motivated by many things: self-hate, hatred of others, a psychotic episode, a need to escape, a need for revenge, a desire to protect others from oneself, or oneself from others.

Given that the relationship between therapist and patient is the bedrock of the treatment effort, the loss of a patient to suicide is extraordinarily disturbing. I am left wondering, *Why did she do it? Why didn't he talk to me about it? What was going through her mind? Why didn't I see it coming? How could I have prevented it?* Such questions can never be entirely laid to rest.

I have lost three patients to suicide while they were in my care. For me, each death was a surprise even though I had known suicide was a possibility. It's surprising because while the potential is always there, the action is what makes it real. The suicide of a patient is the sudden rending of the intimate relationship of psychotherapy, sometimes of years' duration. It is also an indictment, revealing the presence of unspoken thoughts, feelings, and motivations that point to a fatal flaw in that relationship. I can run from such considerations, but the truth always follows me, specters hot on my trail.

At a point in my career, I gave a series of talks at Charter Hospital in Charlottesville, VA, on the treatment of difficult to treat patients. After one such speech, a young therapist came up to me with a group of others and confessed that she had recently lost a patient to suicide. She was struggling with guilt and feelings of failed responsibility. Seeing her heart-rending vulnerability, her colleagues quickly moved in, making cooing noises, while asserting that this was a professional risk and expressing confidence she had done everything she could.

To her credit, this young woman was not comforted by these platitudes. She bore them quietly, and when they subsided, again looked to me. I knew then that she was not looking for solace, she was looking for answers, and so I gave her mine: "Accept the possibility that you are guilty: That you could have done something different, something better, something less, something more. Think it through. Give it time, lots of time; it takes time. If you have a nagging thought, move toward it. Consider it. Weigh it. Also, assess what is realistic to expect of yourself. Be as honest as you can. Think it all through. Then come to your conclusion. My guess is, it will not be one thing or another, guilt or innocence, but a combination of both. Learn from it. Use it. Honor your patient by becoming a better person and a better therapist."

If the therapist wants to connect with a seriously suicidal patient, he must recognize his powerlessness without forgetting his skills. He must feel humble, vulnerable, and concerned about the real possibility of an unfolding tragedy—one that may be outside his ability to avert. Suicidal people are not gaming, they are not manipulating; they are not seeking attention: They are deadly serious. The only way to influence someone in that psychological state is from the inside out. It is precisely in the therapist's understanding of his relative helplessness and vulnerability vis-a-vis the patient that he is best able to connect with her. In acknowledging his vulnerabilities, the therapist communicates that one can feel helpless and alone, and yet life and relationship can still be worth living.

It is through the therapist's devotion to the patient and understanding her suffering that the therapist may best connect. Often, there are understandable reasons for the patient's wish to die. Only after the therapist has visited the tar pit of the patient's anguish, without any demand for change, may he have a chance to join with the patient as a companion and as a guide, gently considering her situation, while nudging her toward life and away from death.

This process is an affair of the heart, as well as the head, birthed out of the therapist's genuine care for the patient. It is always a fumbling and stumbling effort of the blind leading the blind. What the patient appreciates is not the therapist's omnipotent attempts to fix things, but his willingness to join her in the labyrinth of her mind, and, at times, become as lost as she. Only then can the therapist personally relate to the patient's plight and lend his knowledge and experience in service of helping the patient find a way through when the road is anything but clear.

What the therapist brings to the effort is the capacity to think, feel, persevere, and see things from different perspectives. Given his separateness from the patient, the therapist is not typically as deeply mired in the regressive quicksand of her emotions. Consequently, he can oscillate between entering into the patient's experience with her on the one hand and separating from it on the other, using his internalized experience of her plight to observe and reflect upon the patient's situation when she cannot.

Essential characteristics of a good therapist are intellect, caring, abiding curiosity, and a willingness to grope around in the dark, floundering, yet forever feeling his way. In some ways, therapy is like spelunking a newly found cave-system. The therapist is the experienced guide, but he doesn't know *the way,* he's never been in this cave before. But he has been in many caves and knows something about finding a way through.

Together, the therapist/guide and the patient, lost at the center of the cave system of the patient's psyche, tentatively probe the dark. The guide, free to observe and think about things, notes the water-wear on the rock and senses the flow of air across his skin, both hinting at the existence of an opening to the world beyond. Incessant in his curiosity and questioning mind, the therapist ventures in all directions, at times crawling forward until the tunnel becomes too tight, then retreating, only to look for passage elsewhere. He feels anxiety when the headlamps go out, plunging them both into darkness, but trusts that the light will return. His is not wishful thinking, but an understanding honed over many such journeys, most of which have met with success and fuel his faith and persistence. Typically, sooner or later, a glimmer of sunlight is detected, signaling a way through.

What the patient most appreciates is the therapist's willingness to visit the cave in the first place. Throughout their journey, they talk, share experiences, sometimes laugh, sometimes cry, and bond. The patient comes to realize he is not alone, not forsaken, and that in and of itself can make the difference. The therapist's persistence communicates his belief in and valuing of the patient and that no matter how grim things may seem, life can still be worth living.

All this said, I have been reminded of my vast limitations as a therapist by three suicides. One of these was distressing but not traumatizing. This man, a surgeon, made an error on the operating table leading to the death of an elderly patient. Of Japanese origin, he had only begun seeing me at the insistence of his wife. He faced a lawsuit, and what was for him public shaming. Uncommunicative and uncooperative, he sat wooden-faced, aloof and impassive, responding monosyllabically if at all while staring into the distance. All he would say is that he had failed and lost his honor; no discussion was allowed. Within weeks, his prevailing storyline, rife with themes of failure and dishonor ruled the day. As disturbing as his death was, the relative brevity of the treatment relationship and my inability to form any connection with him protected me from more damaging feelings of failure and loss.

But that was not at all the case with the other two people who took their lives while in my care. My last patient to commit suicide was Stephanie. My history with Stephanie began on B-2 when she was in her early twenties. Strikingly beautiful, she looked out at the world with wide, shining azure eyes, from beneath a cloud of hair, the color of fresh straw. Suffering from bipolar illness with psychotic episodes and personality disorder, she was given to frequent suicide attempts, repeatedly landing in intensive care units. She was a mental health professional's nightmare: high risk and high maintenance.

During those early days, I would sit with her several times a week, yet she never talked about herself. Instead, she would describe her parents' visits to the unit in literal and concrete ways, without any hint of what, if anything, her observations meant to her. For example, during one of the hottest days of the summer, Stephanie reported that her mother wore a fur coat and sunglasses and kept both on throughout the visit, while her father buried his head inside a newspaper from which he did not emerge until it was time to leave. During their visits, they did not converse with each other or Stephanie: Everyone just sat.

After hearing this atonal description of a wooden visit, I waited to see what else Stephanie would say, but nothing followed. Mulling over what I had heard, I looked up at the ceiling and said, "I wonder if your father was uncomfortable?" As gently as I could, I aimed to stir her thinking, rather than pressure for a response. Nevertheless, my wonderings always met with silence, as Stephanie's blue eyes stared vacuously back at me. After a few more moments of thought, I would again look at the ceiling and say, "Your mother's sunglasses hid her eyes. Do you think she needs to wall herself off from the world?" Or I might venture, "Wearing that fur coat could be a protective cover. Is your mother a fearful woman?" I might even ask, "I wonder what you were feeling during your parents' visit?" but never received an answer.

For months, this was the prevailing character of our meetings: Stephanie describing what was going on around her as if a spectator, rather than a participant, and my directing questions to the ceiling. I knew that the early emerging self of such patients had been hijacked in childhood, perhaps genetically, but also by the impinging demands of others in the form of neglect and abuse. In protective response, the tender shoots of the early emerging self curl in upon themselves. I also knew that for them to re-emerge and for development to resume, time, and an environment safe from impingement were essential. Thus, my purpose was to stimulate rather than to obligate. When and if she answered, it would be because she wanted to, not because she felt pressure to. That is why I looked at the ceiling when wondering aloud. I wanted my wonderings just out there in space, available for consideration, but not requiring a response.

Then, one day, months later, Stephanie described another of her parents' visits, but this time, after a short pause, looked up at the ceiling and said, "I wonder why they did that?" Astonished, I first thought she was poking fun at me but soon set aside this possibility as I watched her struggle to squeeze meaning from what she had observed. From this small beginning, seemingly slight but huge in consequences, therapy began. And that is why, upon Stephanie's discharge, I could not turn my back on her, and for the next twenty years, became the only constant in her treatment life.

Over the final two years of her life, Stephanie matured, becoming increasingly sober-minded, thoughtful, and aware. Her improvement might have had as much to do with aging as with therapy, but, whatever the reason, her growing maturity was evident. Any claim to a contribution on my part might be limited to the fact that, as much as possible, I was there for her. Over the years, I had earned her trust, standing with her through repeated relapses and psychiatric hospitalizations, answering suicidal phone calls, and talking her through psychotic episodes in which angels beckoned her to fly outside her seventh story apartment window. Through the years, she brought her ghoulish thoughts to me, and, as best I could, I guided her away from their siren song.

Stephanie's progress, marked by decreases in suicidal ideation and acting out, a growing spontaneity and thoughtfulness in her interactions, and the development of a burgeoning sense of self was something to behold. She had traveled such a long distance from when we first met on B-2, and I was enjoying the increasing richness and substantialness of the woman she was becoming.

Ironically, it is often when the patient is getting better that they are most at risk of suicide. I do not know why this is. Some theorize that as the depression lifts, the patient has more energy to complete the task. Others contend that the patient recognizes the losses that have occurred and grieves the time lost that can never be retrieved. For my part, I think the road toward health is precarious. Indeed, some of the dangers can reside in the growing awareness of lost opportunities and wasted years. Conversely, something lost may be recovered, and something new may be gained. It is a balancing act, hope against the weight of experience, and even experience decoded and understood differently can sometimes be more than a person can bear.

Another consideration is that mental health entails the lowering of psychological defenses: healthy people feel a greater range of feelings. People just developing the capacity to manage their feelings can be more easily overwhelmed by them. Still, as human beings, we tend to take in only what we can stand to take in; we only grow at the pace of our making. Of course, we all are subject to being overwhelmed by emotions from time to time, and for these people, at the wrong time, the experience can be deadly.

I think this is what happened to Stephanie. There was a confluence of events. I was beginning a one-week vacation, and she had refused treatment coverage, insisting she would be okay. My hands were tied. I could arrange for a covering therapist, but

I could not make her keep appointments. And, in truth, given her growing maturity and stability, I was not overly concerned.

She was also talking more about her parents, coming to better understand them as people with psychiatric issues of their own; she was no longer taking full blame for their rejecting ways. She had recently knit a sweater for her mother and within the week, saw her older sister wearing it: Her mother had given her gift away. This was not new behavior on the mother's part, far from it. What was new was Stephanie's ability to recognize her mother's rejecting and callous nature that stood apart from any failing within herself.

Stephanie was also re-examining her relationship with her father. Idealized as the *good* parent, she was now coming to terms with his repeated failures to protect her from her mother's physically and emotionally abusive treatment throughout childhood and the years that followed. When she sought his help, this passive, hollow man, forever hiding behind his newspaper, would tell her, "You must find a way to live with your mother," and return to reading.

Now, in her mid-forties, Stephanie's need for her parents' love, a need on the level of a young child's, was being stripped away. She recognized the unrealistic and unrealizable nature of her wish for a child-like love and her parents' incapacity to fulfill it then and now. She grieved the loss of her childhood aspirations and mourned their passing.

The call from the State Police came at 10 pm on Friday, the first night of my vacation. Stephanie had jumped from the Key Bridge, a massive structure spanning the turbulent gray waters of the Patapsco River in Baltimore. After years of near-lethal overdoses, Stephanie had chosen an irrevocable measure. Even now, nearly twenty years later, I never cross a tall bridge without thinking of her.

I wonder, *What else could I have done?* And the terrible truth is that there is something. That night, she had left me a message to call her. It made me angry. I had worked hard to get her a covering therapist, just so that I wouldn't have to be on call. Given that it was just one of the hundreds of such messages, and she had not sounded distressed, I decided, *The least she can do is wait until tomorrow morning.* With this, I pushed Stephanie from my mind—that is until 10 pm.

If I had returned her call that night, maybe Stephanie would be alive today; perhaps, I could have talked her through it, like so many times before, but I'm not so sure. Her tone had been calm, and her jumping from that bridge was an irrevocable act requiring something of a plan; maybe she had just had enough.

What I do know is that I miss her and regret never meeting the woman she was becoming.

In memory of her, I keep a small metal sculpture she gave me years ago in the window of my office. It is ocean boardwalk tacky and features various sea creatures. One evening, years after her death, the husband of a couple I was treating, a computer programmer, picked it up, studied it, then announced, "It's code." Disbelieving, I said, "What?" He explained, "The sea creatures are shaped to spell out words, the sea horse is an S." Once he pointed it out, it was easy to see. The message was, "Save Our Seas."

I do not know if Stephanie knew there was a message in the sculpture. Maybe it was evident to her, and she thought it would be obvious to me. How ironic that her gift contained a hidden message that would reference her ending. Stephanie always had me wondering.

Eve, my first patient to commit suicide, was a small angular woman in her late forties, with short cut black hair matted to her crown. She was married, the mother of two teenage boys, and had an extensive history of psychiatric hospitalizations, suicidal behaviors, and abusive treatment of her husband and children. What made Eve stand out was the degree to which she somaticized her feelings. It was said that every organ that could be removed from her body had been, yet no physical problems were found.

The early weeks and months of the family sessions were leaden affairs. Eve would hold center stage while George, her husband, would sit stiff-backed and quiet. The two boys sat silently, displaying sullen expressions as teenagers the world over are wont to do while drinking everything in with their big eyes. I treated the family on B-2 for approximately six months and then on an outpatient basis for another year. During this time, Eve's relationship with her husband and kids steadily improved. She was happier, her kids were speaking more easily, and George even smiled upon occasion.

As with Stephanie, I was beginning a one-week vacation, cooking steaks on the grill for family and friends on a sunny, humid Saturday afternoon, the sound of water splashing, and kids' laughter floating over from the swimming pool. The phone rang. It was George, "I'm sorry to disturb you at home and on your vacation, but I have nowhere else to turn." Dread filled my chest, not from any premonition, but because I imagined losing part of this day to work. I asked, "What is it?" Without preamble, George stammered, "Eve shot herself in the head. The ambulance has taken her to shock-trauma. There is blood all over. I cannot handle it. The kids are at the beach, due back this evening. I don't want them to see it. I have no one to help me. Will you help me?"

I struggled to take in what George was saying. It stood in such dark and ugly juxtaposition to the sounds of life and laughter drifting over from the pool. I heard his words, but it was as if they came from a different universe. They did not fit with what I thought I knew. I had had no concerns about Eve killing herself. Indeed, I had been happy with the way things had been going. But then his words and their meaning sank home: What I thought I knew and what I knew were two vastly different things.

I immediately became self-preserving. I did not want to help George; I did not want to rip myself away from this beautiful day to enter the carnage of his life. But it was already too late. Looking at the steaks on the grill, picturing the aftermath of Eve's shooting, I had the moronic thought *Steaks will never look the same again.* My day, with a pull of a trigger several miles away, had just been obliterated. I overrode my selfish urges, recognizing that I could not leave this man alone in the wreckage of his life or allow his kids to return from a day at the beach to a house turned killing ground. With dread, I bade farewell from the party and drove the lifetime away to Eve's home.

George stood on the concrete stoop of his row-house, overlooking a barren postage-stamp yard, with his usual reserved demeanor; the tremble of his chin and his shaking hands the only indications that he was barely holding together. As I approached, he flatly announced, "Eve has been declared dead."

Walking toward him, I noticed dark spots on the crumbling sidewalk, my mind reeling from the omen they portended. I followed George and the trail of drops inside the house, where they staggered up the worn wooden steps to a second-floor bedroom. There, a blood-spattered wall and ceiling, and a small lake of drying scarlet, mottled with liver-colored chunks of brain, spoke the unspeakable. I fought the urge to gag while irrationally fearing that whatever calamity had befallen Eve would snake out from under the bed and grab me by the ankle. I wanted to run. But I had to help George and protect the kids from these appalling images that, if seen, would haunt them the rest of their lives.

George and I gathered mops and rags and began the gruesome task. Laboring in a trance-like state, moving sluggishly from one erratic thought to another, I recognized that I had agreed to join George in this ghastly world in part as an act of penance. I had badly misread the situation and had not prevented it. Indeed, I had not even seen it coming. Did George hold me responsible? Perhaps his call for help was an expression of his anger, forcing me to face the terrible consequences of my failure, although nothing of the sort was said. I did not think to ask why he had not called a professional crew or made up a reason to tell his kids not to come home. My thinking had been simple, *He called. I must answer. It's not only about cleaning up; it's about being with someone, about not being alone.* Moving from one splash of gore to the next, trapped in a bloody world without horizon, I was unable to finish a thought and did not want to feel a thing.

As I scrubbed the ceiling, rubber-gloved hands covered with gore, drops of liquid fell onto my upturned face. I recoiled from its touch, which filled me with unease and hurried to wash. Returning to my work, I rinsed the washcloth in the bucket, dumbly noting the water turning pink.

It was surreal: sweeping Eve's brains into a dustpan and putting them in the trash, the work gory, and the symbolism horrid. Numbly, I moved from the bedroom ceiling to wall, to floor, to stairway, to wooden steps, and out onto the sidewalk. I made repeated trips to the tiny kitchen through the cramped dining room for clean water, sometimes exiting to the backyard for a breath of fresh air. All the while, I imagined Eve in each of these places where she had ruled and lived, and the family life that had unfolded within these dreary confines.

I questioned everything I thought I knew: How could the world have changed so drastically without warning? I had met with Eve just three days earlier, and everything had seemed fine. She had been relaxed and happy, and I had thought we were all enjoying the benefits of our difficult work. Over the months, we had struggled, suffered, and laughed together. Now, incredibly, without warning, we had all been wrenched into another reality, terrible in its finality and indelibly stained with shock and horror.

I wrestled with coming to grips with this new world in which Eve, a living, vibrant human being had been reduced to bits of brain matter and puddles of blood, being tossed out like the trash and, unimaginably, that I was the one doing the tossing.

I had given up smoking, but now, the need gnawed at me like a rat trying to free itself from a cardboard box. Taking a Salem from a pack Eve had left on the kitchen counter, I lit up, all the while wondering, *How can I stand here and smoke one of Eve's cigarettes, in a sense breathe in her air, while she lays dead?* Crazily, I felt both intrusive and impolite, but my urgent hunger for that nicotine fix was irresistible.

George joined me and revealed that Eve had left a suicide note, writing that she loved her family and was enjoying her new-found relationship with them. But increasingly, she was becoming threatened by an emotional pull, which led her to fear that she would abuse them once again—Eve was not going to allow that to happen. She left the note pinned to the lapel of George's best suit, along with the money she had saved to cover the funeral expenses. Alongside his suit, lay a dress she had picked out for her funeral; both dry-cleaned. She explained that she did not want her death to be any more burdensome than necessary. As George spoke, tears coursed my face as the tragedy struck home: Eve's terror had been of herself.

It was evident that Eve had been planning her suicide for some time, suggesting that her more recent emotional stability and contentment had not only risen from treatment efforts but from the relief she had gained from the decision to take control of her life by ending it. Of course, I will never really know. All I know is that I regret Eve did not share her concerns with me and that we never had the opportunity to see if we could have made it through the labyrinth together. Of course, for Eve to do this, she would have had to risk the possibility that I might have taken control and hospitalized her.

Following Eve's death, I was besieged by images that would crop up throughout the day and night: The chunks of brain matter, the blush-colored water turning scarlet, the sensory memory of the blood-tainted drops falling onto my face, had all burned their way into my psyche. Sitting with friends in a restaurant, I would suddenly associate the food with Eve's brain matter or a ruby-colored glass of wine with her blood. A word spoken in conversation would prompt an association to something she had said, hurtling me back in time, lost to the moment. While my friends chatted on in companionable relationship, I would be alive in an alternate universe of blood and despair. I was not remembering; I was reliving: Past was present.

I did not reveal my troubled state. What would be the point—to destroy the mood of my companions? So, I remained alone with it, and it remained alone with me. For several years, the past re-emerged episodically and unpredictably, until finally fading away, like the color going out of an aging photo. Now, I can remember without reliving.

Of course, I questioned myself, *What could I have done?* However, unlike my experience with Stephanie, I could not think of anything. Eve's presentation had been seamless, her suicide entirely unexpected, a humbling and troubling reminder that none of us ever fully knows the mind of another.

These deaths cannot be reversed. No matter how much good I have done as a therapist throughout my career, they represent failures of the therapist-patient relationship that stay with me. Of course, part of the responsibility belongs to the patient, but part belongs to me. The blame can never be apportioned—this much hers, this much mine—because we never fully know why something happens, and death cuts off all inquiry: I can never ask; she can never tell. The possibility that I might have done something different, something better, something more, something less is forever present.

This may sound grim: Indeed, it is a weight. But I would not have it any other way. If I cannot feel deeply about something as important as this, how can I possibly have a meaningful life?

Chapter 24

The Goths Are at The Gates

By the mid-1980s, corporations hired companies to lower health care costs. Shamelessly, these companies referred to themselves as *Managed Care* companies, as if *caring* had anything to do with what they did. In truth, their only concern was the profit motive, lowering costs through the elimination of care, and they did so without mercy or morality.

Their strategy? Make the provision of treatment so burdensome that mental health professionals could not provide it and the making of claims so arduous that many would forego the process. The managed care automatons put providers under siege through near-daily audits of each patient's medical records and ceaseless demands for phone interviews in which they plumbed for any reason to have the patient discharged. In short order, the staff's attention turned to trying to protect the patient via *proving* the need for treatment and away from the treatment itself. The expression, *"Treating the medical record,"* was born.

These agents of managed care companies made life-changing determinations without meeting the patient. They claimed to ascertain all they needed from reading the medical record and questioning staff on the phone like attorneys taking depositions. I can only conclude that it is easier to risk the destruction of someone's life when there is not a face attached to it.

The managed care companies created a catch 22: If progress could be proven, they would argue the patient no longer needed inpatient treatment, and if progress were not demonstrated, that would be construed as evidence that treatment was ineffective rather than treatment takes time.

But that was not the end of it. The amazingly unethical thing was that when these managed care companies succeeded in driving the patient from inpatient care, having touted the viability of outpatient options, they would then assault the patient's need for outpatient treatment.

The utterly absurd aspect of all this is that outpatient sessions were approved like a miser's doling out pennies: on a-once-a-week basis for four weeks at a time, at which point, treatment would be terminated, or the entire charade repeated.

Time, space, and safety are all elements necessary to healing the human psyche. However, these companies managed to undermine any notion of sanctuary or asylum, inpatient or out. This was true even when four weeks of sessions were repeatedly authorized. Why? Because the imminent possibility of treatment ending hung forever heavy in the air, destroying any sense of safety or security and any hope of the patient or therapist being able to relax into treatment; no therapist wanted to open a can of worms that they might not be around to help the patient process. To paraphrase Winnicott, "You can't practice therapy in a burning building."

And, if a patient suicided? Like Pontius Pilot washing his hands, the managed care acolytes would say, "That kind of thing happens. After all, they are psychiatric patients." No how, no way, did the managed care companies hold themselves liable, nor incredibly did the courts. The latter asserted that it was the therapist's responsibility to provide treatment, not the insurance company. Certainly, a patient in crisis would receive treatment, and many therapists offered pro bono counseling, but it was unrealistic to expect therapists to work for free with difficult to treat patients. Resentment would naturally build, and they too had families to feed.

The managed care companies' tawdry tactics were endless. They only recruited therapists who demonstrated a willingness to discharge patients just after a few sessions to participate in their insurance networks. You can imagine how the best and brightest flocked to that less than honorable standard.

I hated the disingenuous bastards. One reviewer stridently insisted that I allow a patient to take a day-pass with his family. When the patient returned unharmed, the reviewer declared this was proof that hospitalization was no longer required. When I asked the reviewer with genuine curiosity, "Off the record, as a clinician, are you okay with this? Does this make any sense to you?"

She stammered, "That's not the point. I'm merely following the rules here."

When I countered, "That sounds dangerously close to Nazi prison guards saying they were only following orders," she hung up the phone. This exchange earned me a rebuke from the office of the president of the hospital; the managed care company had complained. I asked, "What did I get wrong?"

He responded, "Comparing her to a Nazi. She was distraught."

I said, "Again, what part did I get wrong?"

Exasperated, he shouted, "She was upset!" as if her upset was a clinching argument.

I answered, "Good. She should be. Maybe I helped her out."

One day, as the treatment team was again discussing discharging yet another patient due to managed care pressure, I could contain myself no longer. Filled with outrage, I burst out of my chair, shouting, "This is bullshit!" and stormed out of the room.

It was at this point, recognizing my reactivity and the uncontainable nature of my feelings, that I had to wonder, *What's going on with me?* Then I remembered how my fear of confronting the wrong of racism had turned me into a coward in that Montgomery, Alabama movie theater years earlier and how diminished I felt when I failed to bear witness to that mixed-race couple being harassed by the MPs in Heidelberg, Germany. I plunged into the shame and fury I felt when my Dad was slapping me around or demeaning me and the incalculable rage at his audacity of prohibiting me from asking questions or ordering me to keep my hands clasped behind my back while he freely slapped my face. Now, in the here and now, I was being pressed into destroying something I loved, a place where wounded souls might rest and recover, the core need of which I fully understood. That was unbearable; I had found my voice and the wherewithal to do something in the face of wrongdoing, even if the only thing I could do was to name it for what it was and call it out as both ignorant and morally bankrupt.

What got to me when I descended from my moral high horse is that such horrid behavior says something about we human beings in general. We all wax eloquent about the wrongs that are done by others, such as the horrors imposed by Hitler in the concentration camps, by Pol Pot in the killing fields of Cambodia, or by Donald Trump's inhumane separation of children from their parents and failing to reunite hundreds of them. I mean, how does anyone do that? And these people do not act alone, what about all the people who support and carry out such policies.

Similar crimes, albeit on a lesser scale, are occurring all the time. And it is not just one victimizer: it's thousands. In fact, they *are* you and me. We all suffer moments where we lose our moral compass, are overly influenced by the authorities in our lives, or give in to self-interest. Remember the Toyota dealership that did not change the transmission oil? Who was the oil changer? Remember the auto-body shop bogusly selling reclaimed wrecks? Who was trying to weld them together? Many people cheat on their taxes.

The point is, none of us is immune from greed or envy or doing what we're told even if it's wrong. All that is part of the human condition, but the least we can do is struggle with those decisions and acknowledge our guilt. What is important to realize is that grappling with such issues should not be understood as a sacrifice because doing so is in our best interest, for in my view, integrity is the essential ingredient in the journey toward a happy and meaningful life. Ultimately, a positive sense of self depends more on doing the right thing than on personal aggrandizement or material gain. And the ones to be afraid of? Those who claim to do no wrong.

Reluctantly, I began accepting that the era of long-term inpatient care was over and started writing. Career ambition wasn't the motivating force. Indeed, given the primal intensity of my feelings, ambition was nowhere to be found. Instead, I was consumed by a compelling need to get *something out*. At the start, I did not know what that something was; I had no words for it. But, like a glowing ember, it burst into flame as I began to write, and the words came rushing in.

What emerged was an attempt to articulate the lessons learned on B-2. Above all, I wanted to preserve an understanding of the vital necessity of sanctuary and asylum, and how to implement it on an outpatient basis in individual and couples' therapy. Of course, psychoanalytic theory had always addressed the importance of asylum, but I needed to add my voice. In the midst of writing, I became aware that the writing was also my way of grieving, a means of helping me come to terms with the loss of my professional home during the last ten years and cope with watching B-2, the equivalent of a Stradivarius violin, being dismantled piece by piece and turned into a child's toy by ignorant vandals.

It took me a year to write that paper, which underlined the importance of creating a treatment space in which each spouse could think, feel, and voice their more intimate thoughts and feelings without fear of shame, blame, attack, or demand for change. It was titled *The Borderline/Schizoid Marriage: The Holding Environment as an Essential Treatment Construct* and published in the *Journal of Marriage and Family Therapy (1989)*.

What I did not know, had no way of foreseeing, was that this publication would change my life. What I had not understood was that while I was grieving the outgoing tide of inpatient psychiatric treatment, with this writing another tide was coming in—way, way in, and about to take me on a journey I had never imagined.

Chapter 25

Coming Home, Again

1990. Age forty-one.

Ring. Ring. Ring.

My sleep-addled brain struggled to wrap itself around the sound until I realize it is the phone. In the dark, I grope and bobble the handset to my ear, croaking out, "Hello." A man's voice answers into my mouth: I was speaking into the receiver. As I struggle to fumble the phone around, his words keep sliding off my ears. But eventually, after this inauspicious beginning, I piece together that the man is named Bob Winer, a psychoanalyst affiliated with a training program in Washington, D.C. He is saying, "We would like you to present your paper at our annual conference." I wonder, *What paper?* As if reading my mind, he explains that Patricia Alfin, one of my supervisees, had sent a copy of my paper to the Washington School of Psychiatry; She had never mentioned this to me. Then, like the facets of a Rubik's cube falling into place, I understand, *"Jesus, this is The Washington School of Psychiatry. They want me to present my paper on the treatment of the borderline/schizoid marriage at their annual conference."*

The Washington School of Psychiatry is one of the premier schools of psychoanalytically informed psychotherapy in the country. I had taken a workshop there years earlier and been extremely impressed. Flattered to be invited to speak at their conference, I responded, "Sure, be glad to," trying far too late for an air of nonchalance.

These were heady times, and recognition was not something to which I was accustomed. Occasionally, feeling full of myself, I would allow displays of conceit to seep out. Thus far, my major accomplishment was being named Senior Social Worker of Adult Long-Term Inpatient Services at Sheppard-Pratt in 1988. I was now the top master sergeant I had aspired to be, but that promotion had occurred without fanfare.

As I began to appreciate the depth of the leap I was making, a galaxy apart from anything I had known, a growing panic took hold. When Bob had invited me to *read* my paper, it had sounded straightforward: *I'd read my paper. How hard could that be?* But now, presented with more details, it had assumed daunting proportions. I learned I would have thirty minutes to present my paper, followed by a question-and-answer period. The audience would include over 400 psychoanalysts, psychiatrists, psychologists, and social workers, most from the U.S., but several handfuls from around the world. I would be asked unscripted questions from a knowledgeable audience, many trained at Harvard, Yale, Oxford, London's Tavistock Clinic, and the University of Edinburgh, all far better educated than me. I also learned that what I had written fell into a theoretical orientation called the Psychoanalytic Object Relations Theory of the British School. That was a mouthful and I had had no idea I had become a part of it. Unlike me, most of the attendees had heard of the British School of Object Relations, and many had written books and papers on the subject. I knew because I had read their work. Mostly self-taught, I felt utterly out classed. Finally, there was my lack of public speaking experience: one sparsely attended talk at Sheppard-Pratt, which I nervously read through, sounding like a chipmunk on steroids. With the conference looming, the real possibility of public embarrassment took hold, and sleep became an elusive companion.

On the first morning of the four-day conference, I met Dr. Winer, along with Drs. David and Jill Scharff. Each of the first two had degrees from both Harvard and Yale, and Jill had graduated from the University of Aberdeen, Scotland. The Scharffs had trained at the world-famous Tavistock clinic in London and were the director and co-director of the school. Each had written a handful of books on psychoanalytic theory and practice. I was a child among adults.

That morning, I was asked to co-lead a small group of attendees with David Scharff. The purpose of the group was to help the participants process the presentations of the day. Having little group experience, no formal education in object relations couples and family theory, and no experience in training others, I had little to offer.

That afternoon, my discomfort only grew as I co-led a group with Jill Scharff—now realizing they were evaluating me. Though I would later come to know Jill as a caring and supportive person, on this day, she was aggressive with both the group and me: In front of the group, she criticized me for being too passive. I felt like a man without clothes. That evening, I left the conference, feeling fraudulent for being there in the role of faculty and worried about what was to come.

The following morning, the small group leaders reported that the attendees were dissatisfied with the conference, finding it neither illuminating nor engaging. At the end of their reporting in, David Scharff solemnly asserted, "It's up to the presenters this morning to save the conference." My spine turned to goo. By my accounting, there were only two speakers that morning: Jill and *me*. Dismayed, I replayed the words "save the conference" in my head and wondered, *Who are they kidding? I have already demonstrated the vast limits of my knowledge.* I imagined the upcoming debacle, and fought to calm myself, reasoning that Dr. Scharff could not be talking to me; he must be talking to Jill. After all, she was the one that was internationally recognized and respected; I had one small journal article to my name. I looked over at Jill, who appeared calm and unruffled, exuding steadfast confidence. Buoyed by this perception, I happily imagined myself being pulled along in the wake of her stellar presentation.

After the faculty meeting, battling an anxiety that threatened to overwhelm me, I could not sit still. Accordingly, I elected to observe Jill's presentation from the empty balcony, where I would be free to exit to the upstairs hallway and pace to my heart's content when I felt the need. That was a good decision. I alternated between listening to Jill's presentation and pacing in the outer hallway. Gradually, my jitters bled off, and I became more confident that I could get through this with some modicum of self-respect left intact.

That is, until I returned from a trip to the hall mid-way through Jill's talk, just in time to capture an acerbic interchange between her and the audience. In wide-eyed horror, I watched the fractious interaction, having no idea what had happened. Later, I learned that Jill had chided the audience to "put down your pens and listen." My anxiety soared, like a kite whose string had been cut. I thought, *Oh my god! I will be such a lightning rod for all the ill-contained furor of the audience. They will pick me apart as an embodiment of the inadequacies of the conference.*

Minutes before I was due to speak, I considered fleeing, but instead, forced my feet down the stairs and scurried to join the faculty. As I took a chair, a fellow faculty member leaned over and whispered, "I thought you had run for it." Having my assessment of the situation so concisely confirmed, including that the thought of fleeing was not beyond the pale, made me laugh. Animosity was indeed loose in the room; it wasn't a construction of my anxiety-ridden mind. I was then pulled from my musings by someone calling my name.

After months, the moment I had anticipated with dread and excitement was upon me. It felt surreal. I felt strangely removed, unknowingly dissociating from the calamity that was coming. I rose on wet-noodle legs and wobbled up the stairs to the stage, my head feeling like a bowling ball stuck on a stick of over-ripe celery.

There, I confronted a mind-boggling apparatus: the podium. It was a technological marvel worthy of the Starship Enterprise. There were buttons for lights and volume dials, pin microphones for lapels, standard microphones attached to the podium, handheld microphones for walking around, dimmer switches to adjust the lights for reading, buttons for slides and videos and for moving the entire apparatus up and down, and buttons and switches the functions of which I couldn't begin to fathom. I stared at it uncomprehendingly, not having a clue as to what to do.

That is when I made my first mistake. I looked up and into the unblinking eyes of the tripod-mounted cameras dotting the auditorium, their muzzles sighting in on me, ready to capture my every utterance for posterity. Then I took in the audience and realized it had grown quiet: They were waiting for *me* as I just stood there, feeling inanely proud that I could stand at all.

Finally, an assistant, recognizing my bewilderment, joined me on the stage. Mics went on my lapel, microphones adjusted, the podium raised, and the lights amplified. He also poured me a glass of water from a pitcher atop the podium, a kindness for which I was absurdly grateful given my trembling hands. If left to myself, I imagined spilling water over the rostrum, shorting out the whole apparatus and thereby, the entire conference. Dumbly I thought, *Wouldn't that be a moment in the sun?*

At this time, I slowly became aware that the audience had grown eerily silent, holding their collective breath as they sensed the precariousness of my mental state. The hum of social noise now completely absent, I looked out at them, as they looked in at me. I was unmistakably the sole focus of all four hundred and twenty sets of piercing eyes and unsmiling faces.

That is when I realized my mouth was chalk dry, and that I needed a sip of water to begin speaking. I slowly extended my trembling hand toward the glass situated at the far reaches of the podium, my arm feeling robotic and no longer a part of me. My hand completed its journey an eternity later. Breathing a sigh of relief, I prayed that I would not knock the glass over and instructed my fingers, one by one, to wrap themselves around it. This feat accomplished, I thought, *I'm halfway there,* then cautioned myself: *Don't hurry. Take your time. Grip the glass but not so hard as to break it.*

When my hand finally completed its trembling return voyage from the podium to my mouth, the water was sloshing about, threatening to spill over the sides of the cup. But this was not the worst of it; I had not even imagined the worst of it. As I put the glass to my mouth, it ticked against my teeth—that is when all those microphones came into play. "Tick, tick, tick," "Tick, tick, tick," the rapping of the glass against my teeth faithfully amplified throughout the auditorium for all to hear; "Tick, tick, tick."

At this juncture, I had an out of body experience, watching the entire auditorium, including myself from on high. That is when I noticed that I had unwittingly accomplished the most amazing thing: I had rendered an audience of over four hundred people not only silent but mesmerized: entirely still, not a movement, a cough, a sniffle, or the clearing of a throat. Entranced by what they sensed was the beginning of a ten-car pileup of a presentation, the audience, like rubberneckers the world over, could not tear their eyes away.

After tick, tick, ticking myself through several sips of water, I managed to affect the lumbering return journey of the glass to the podium. Then, I could delay no longer: *No climbing back down the ladder,* and so I leaped.

I began speaking, but instead of seeking the illusion of safety in the written word and launching like that Chipmunk of old into reading my paper as fast as I could to get the whole thing over with, I felt a need to stave off the agonizing isolation I felt. I spoke extemporaneously, referring both to the crosscurrents of tensions that had been rippling through the auditorium that morning and to my manifest anxiety. My first words were, "I guess this is what's called a pisser."

It took a moment for my words to register—such vocabulary is not a standard part of highbrow conferences. Scattered laughter broke out, slowly gaining momentum as more people realized what I had said. It was a warm laugh, a laugh of recognition; the audience could relate to what I was going through, and I could relate to the anger in the room. I then said, "For some reason, the words 'I guess we're not in Kansas anymore, Toto' keep running through my mind." The audience at large broke out into laughter, and, thankfully, it was not at me, but with me, both heartfelt and welcoming.

After waiting for the laughter to subside, I began reading in a conversational tone. I had written the paper with this aim in mind, with a reminder to speak slowly written in the margins. I also interrupted my reading several times, to look out at the sea of faces, and ask, "Are you with me?" wanting to maintain that connection and invite questions if there was any confusion. The response was a resounding, "Yes." When I finished reading, the audience began applauding, the sound gaining as it went, forming a series of sonic waves that washed over me again and again. It went on and on and became the closest thing to a standing ovation in a professional setting I was ever to receive: It was glorious.

I think it was precisely the tension-filled context in which the audience and I found ourselves that paved the way. I had not talked down to them or up to them. I had shown human vulnerability without pretense or apology and soldiered on giving a good paper and an accessible story.

After my talk, I went to the restroom. A guy came up to the adjacent urinal, began his business, then looked over at me, saying, "Man, that was great. Really good job." Throughout the day, others offered similar praise. Treated like a celebrity, I tried to contain how puffed up I felt. And then, as the day wore on, I reached my social threshold. My face hurt from smiling, and my brain hurt from the effort of making small talk: I just wanted to go home.

Following that talk, the leaders of the Washington School of Psychiatry invited me to join the faculty. Not wanting to drive to the many meetings that would require, and given the needs of my family, I opted to become Guest Faculty. In the years to follow, I grew to love these people, who were so unstinting in their willingness to share their time and expertise. They did not do this for money; there was no money. They did it for the love of their profession and analytically informed psychotherapy.

In the years to come, Bob Winer and his wife, Bo, welcomed me into their home and provided support during one of the most trying times of my life that was just beginning to break upon me.

Part V

Swallow the Shadow

It was here, that monster that had been chasing me all my life. What I now understood is that it had not been chasing me at all: I had been carrying it the whole time.

Chapter 26

Love Stories

As a couple's therapist, I enjoy talking about relationships; that is everyones' but my own. Not only are my relationships personal, and sometimes embarrassing, but I cannot hide the identity of the people involved. Even so, I must talk about what I can.

I have found and lost several loves. I have been addicted to love. I had learned how a relationship could seem to change suddenly when the seeds of its demise had been there all along. I have discovered how needs change over time and that what attracts in one era can deter or even repel in another. I have learned how you can be with someone for years and never really know them and how time or events can seem to flip a switch and change people in unanticipated ways.

I must also confess a problem of listening. Most of us do not listen well, and I can be as guilty as the next, hearing what I want to hear and minimizing or misinterpreting the rest. Like most people, I pay selective attention and have a selective memory that tends to support my view of myself and the world around me.

Yet, despite these impediments, I have learned from my relationships. Remarkably, what I have learned always boils down to the same lesson, just given in different ways. The teaching is akin to a multi-faceted diamond spotlighted on the black velvet of a slowly turning pedestal. I stare at a facet of the problem, then just when I think *I've got it*, the pedestal turns, revealing the same problem but from a different perspective. What's uncanny is that each lesson always points back to me: I am the one responsible, my happiness and fulfillment are up to me. I now understand that when I hold others accountable, it is I, not they, who is guilty of wrongdoing.

Accepting responsibility for one's happiness fosters independence and lessens the burden we place on others. The result is that when two relatively independent people get together, they do so because they *want* to, not because they *need* to.

I have come to understand that my over-romanticized notion of love, the blinding kind so eulogized in movies and songs, is not loving at all. When *blinded by love,* I am foisting my internally fabricated fantasy of the Other upon the other. How can that be *love*? Of course, my mental creation of the Other *is* incredibly enticing. Why wouldn't it be? Created by me, my Other is formed by my deepest needs and can easily fulfill them with one caveat, "If only She would."

When my construction of the Other is burning hot, the experience intoxicates with promise. Of course, if my needs are frustrated, *She must* also be the cause: rejecting rather than nurturing. Thus, my *Imaginary Other* shape-changes between a woman who excites my every yearning to a woman who holds my needs in contempt and delights in frustrating them. All the while, needing to preserve my idealized image of her, I secretly feel that I deserve it.

Let me put flesh on the bones of how one's imagination can turn an ordinary person into an *Imaginary Other*. I was age eleven and just learned that I was to leave home with my father to accompany him to Heidelberg, Germany. This announcement correlated in time with my sudden obsession with a girl named Mary. Though we had been in the same class all year, only then did she explode into my consciousness. For the first time, I noticed her entering the classroom, books clutched demurely to her petite frame, auburn hair shining, nickel-colored eyes serene.

As she floated across the room to her desk, I hoped she would favor me with a smile, but that did not happen. As if everyone could read my heart, I shrank with embarrassment.

Every morning after that, I ran to school in anticipation of stealing glimpses of Mary: Something both titillating and torturing had taken me over; I had no idea what it was, never having felt such a thing before. But here, I found myself increasingly self-conscious, knowing that for her, I did not exist. Where I had not noticed Mary before, she had somehow become the center of my existence. Her cream-colored skin, her movements, the slope of her neck, the tilt of her head, her smile, her serenity, all sent my heart trilling. Curiously, as she became increasingly infused with color and light, I felt proportionally drained and pallid. I envied the bounty of life that emanated from her and wondered, *Would she give some of that to me?*

I wanted her attention, but I was at a loss for words. I could only imagine inanely intoning, "I love you; I love you; I love you, …forever." But, I could not even do this, knowing that the incendiary intensity of my feelings, fanned by her attention, would burst into flame and engulf me. I fantasized other options: I could save her life, push her out of the way of an oncoming car—but no such heroic opportunities arose. Or, maybe, I could garner her favor by performing breathtaking acrobatic feats—but no such talent was at hand. Possibly, I could defend her honor, declaring my love in a chivalric manner—but no infraction occurred. My impotent musings only rendered me increasingly anemic, undeserving of a word, much less a smile, as Mary's aura grew ever brighter.

All I wanted was to serve her in some way, knowing her approval would fill the emptiness that had taken root within me. My desperation mounted as the gulf between dream and reality grew, the window for fulfillment closing with the passing of each day, and the approaching end of the school year looming larger. Finally, I thought of an answer: I would buy Mary a gift.

Marshaling my courage, I told Mom about my wish to buy a girl a present. Her blue eyes looked back at me, a whirlpool of tenderness with sparks of amusement flickering within. Thankfully, she did not delve. We went to a store to look for jewelry. She asked, "Charlie, what do you think Mary might like?" As I perused the bracelets, I spied a silver chain threaded through tiny gray-blue stones, the color of Mary's eyes. It was lovely and delicate; it was Mary. I pointed the piece out and paid for it; Mom gift-wrapped the box. The rest was up to me.

How was I to give it to Mary? A public display was out of the question, the risk of humiliation too great. I decided to wait until she was walking home alone from school. Staying well behind to avoid detection, I followed day after day. But, to my growing chagrin, she was always accompanied by friends, leaving me pitched between the recurring rise of anticipation and the repeated fall of disappointment.

Then, as fate would have it, the last day of class, Mary walked alone. Just like that, the moment was upon me. Needing to end my ordeal, I fought down my trepidation and ran up to Mary. Face flushed, heart in danger of collapsing, it was at this moment I realized I had not thought about what to say. I also discovered that I could not bring myself to look directly into her eyes, knowing that if I did, I would shatter like a porcelain cup falling on a granite floor. Like a blind man groping about in a burning room, the rising heat forced me to say something, anything that would get me out of the growing pressure cooker intensity of that impasse. At a complete loss, I finally blurted out, "I want to give you this," thrusting the gift unceremoniously toward her.

Overcome by my sudden and intense arrival, Mary reacted as if mildly concussed; her eyes unfocused, and her delicate features contorted by the effort to make sense of what was happening. Responding instinctively, she held out her hand for the proffered box. For my part, I waited for several thunderous heartbeats then, unable to bear a scintilla more of the exquisite agony of what I was feeling, turned, and ran.

I did not realize until later that my hit and run tactic had prevented Mary from saying anything more in line with my fears of rejection than my hopes of love found. Now, I would never know what she might have said or had the opportunity to receive that long-dreamt-of smile. But I had paid homage, and that seemed enough for I was relieved of my obsession. I never saw Mary again. It was only years later that I considered the idea that my infatuation with Mary might have been spurred by my intense need to get away from the loss I was feeling about having to leave my family to live with Dad in Heidelberg.

Was this love? Certainly. But how could it be of Mary? I did not know Mary. Until I gave her my gift, I *had* never spoken to her, nor she to me. It was a fantastical love woven by *my* mental rendering of Mary that promised to rescue me from my dysphoria. With this imaginative act, I had transformed Mary into the wellspring of my every longing and imbued *Her* with the power to fill every void. I had turned Mary into my *Imaginary Other, My Healing Amulet.*

Now, I must apply the lessons of this story to the one I am about to tell. Not that it gives me great comfort or puts me in a shining light—far from it on both counts. I tell the story in the hope that it might help some readers better understand their troubles with love and loss for my story captures some of the issues with which many relationships contend—albeit certainly in more pathologic form than some. Nonetheless, any understanding derived from illuminating how people who were once in love can fall out of love makes the telling worthwhile.

You have met my first wife, Jane. She was much like Mary: gentle, sweet, and kind. Jane and I journeyed together for twenty years, the early ones relatively happy. We had made our trip around the country, returned to school, and weathered the car accident. Jane had become a teacher and a good one, receiving high ratings. I was proud of her, more than she was of herself, given her need to be perfect in whatever she did. Though highly regarded, Jane left teaching, too burdened by the stress of trying to meet her perfectionistic standards. She took less demanding secretarial jobs with a temp agency. Ironically, in this capacity, her intelligence still shone through. Within two years of temping with Meals on Wheels of Maryland, she became its Acting Director.

Our home life was good. We laughed at the antics of our Pomeranians and the toddling achievements of our children. We took thousands of photos and hours of videos, made love with some regularity, and argued upon occasion. However, with the arrival of kids, all this started to change. With the birth of our second child, we agreed she should be a stay-at-home mom. As time passed, Jane grew ever-more child-centric, preparing a different meal for each of the kids to avoid their complaints and insisting on going to Disney World every day for a week without taking any time to enjoy the beach. To me, this spoke to her need to provide her children with what she thought would give them the happy childhood she had never known and, importantly, to lessen any childhood complaints that might stimulate the negative feelings that linked her to her ever-critical and abusive mother. Jane, thus fell victim to parenting for *the good feel*—the approval of her children—to avoid feeling like a *bad* mother, to avoid *being* her mother.

After the kids were in school, I felt Jane should return to work. What I did not grasp was the level of her discontent with this change. She wanted to be a full-time homemaker and was surprised by my insistence, thinking that we were happy. Indeed, mostly we were, but increasingly, I was feeling displaced by her child-centric focus, her catering to each kid's every want, along with the financial pressures of being the only bread earner. I did not see having a part-time job and taking care of the kids as mutually exclusive, particularly when the kids were in school. I was wrong. Believing that Jane's return to work meant she had accepted my position; I did not realize that inwardly she simmered with resentment. Even though words were spoken, I was deaf to their meaning.

It was around 1989, following her help in editing my first paper, that the worm started to turn. But, in truth, the seeds of the demise of our relationship were there from the beginning. Unconsciously, I had chosen someone who was the opposite of my father and did not threaten me with domination. The problem was that in doing so, I chose someone who had difficulty asserting her own needs and would come to feel dominated by me. Where I thought conflict did not exist in any meaningful way, it was there aplenty, just kept quiet in the tribunal of Jane's mind. There, I was repeatedly accused and found guilty. Unaware of these proceedings because of Jane's difficulty in asserting herself, I could not plead my case; I did not know there was a case to plead. Accordingly, over the years, I was convicted of crime after crime in the sealed courtroom of Jane's mind, therein assuming many of the characteristics of her critical and rejecting mother and the hated attributes of my father. Where I did not want to be dominated, Jane perceived me as dominating.

But even if we had been able to talk about it, I doubt that much would have changed: We were too different, each moving in a direction, not to the other's liking. Jane had passively gone along with most of my wishes, such as the trip to Mexico and then to Baltimore. She also went along with my working and going to school full-time, even though this shifted the burden of childcare almost entirely to her. She had yet to find her voice, at least, one strong enough for me to hear.

Reciprocally, I think I met her need to have someone lead the way who could maintain the illusion of knowing what he was doing. I was the verbal and outgoing one at parties; she was shy and uncomfortable. She was the one who wanted to leave early while I wanted to stay late. Over time, I felt burdened by her insistent need to leave and embarrassed by her passivity and falling asleep in the coat-room if we did not, as she must have felt equally controlled by my desire to stay. We began taking two cars. It seemed like a brilliant solution; I did not appreciate the symbolism at the time. Even if I had, I doubt I would have changed it. And thus, we went, each in our direction, so slowly that it was not apparent, but, as steady rain, ever leaching nutrients from the soil of our relationship.

Where our respective needs had meshed in our early years, our needs of the middle years were pushing us apart. Jane expressed hers in the uncomplicated metaphor of wanting a small brick home with a white fence and more children, her version of the TV series, *Little House on the Prairie*. Jane had a real and vital need for a quiet, non-complicated life, her sanctuary, and asylum, a safe space in which she could emerge in her soft-spoken way to be herself. My need was more aggressive, to explore new worlds, and to expand my bounds.

I kept thinking we would adjust to one another, that we could breach the divide. I kept telling myself, "All we need to do is hang in. We will find a way." But even with couple's therapy, that was not to be: our needs were in fatal competition with one another.

Things went bad, really bad. Unbeknownst to me, Jane's discontent, forever feeding upon itself, only festered. One evening, as I was trying to talk through the unhappiness between us, Jane burst out of her shell, vehemently reciting a catalog of my complaints from a piece of paper. This inventory included every criticism I had ever made during our twenty-year relationship. Recited all together and all at once, they formed a damning refrain and a punch to my heart that woke me to her primal, red-eyed rage.

I was completely taken aback. I had not known Jane had been listening, much less taking my criticisms like stabs to the heart. But there they were, like bodies frozen in a cryogenic tank, only to be brought back to life en masse, imbued with a zombie-like horror. In Jane's mind, I was selfish, self-absorbed, self-centered, over-controlling, attacking, belittling, and incessantly pushing her to live her life *my* way. I could not imagine a more damning portrayal, encompassing every personality trait I hated in my father and leaving me feeling ugly and repellent to my core.

She tried, and I tried, but in hindsight, there was never a possibility of repair. When relationships become so de-illusioned, there never is. In the meantime, Jane was in torment, unable to recapture her love of me, leading her to question her capacity for love. All this was made worse by her remorseless self-damnation: the voice of her mother calling from the grave.

Caught in an unrelenting web of conflicting desires and strictures, Jane tried all means to escape her self-loathing, as well as to communicate her rage to me in non-verbal ways. She binge-drank and went for long runs, to be brought home by strangers upon whose yards she had passed out. She agreed to go into therapy. But then, her psychiatrist would call: She had arrived intoxicated with our kids in tow.

Jane tried gaining a feeling of control through bouts of anorexia with purging and by soothing herself through delicate self-cutting so extensive that the scabs appeared to form leather bands on her arms. Then the suicide attempts began. Gestures

really, but ones that could have easily led to her demise:
overdoses of prescribed medications combined with alcohol.
Numerous intensive care visits and psychiatric hospitalizations
followed.

I was in constant torment, continually worrying about Jane,
the kids, and myself. The kids were calling me daily at work,
anxiously noting bloodstains on the cuffs of Jane's blouse or her
carrying a brown paper bag they feared contained alcohol into
the house.

For a long while, my primary feeling had been of empathy
for Jane, alongside fear and helplessness. But after several years, I
was wearing down and grew angry as Jane continued her slide
and to subject the kids and me to terrible fear and anxiety.
Finally, I drew a line, telling Jane that I would support her going
to the hospital, but would leave her if she continued to seek
hospitalization via self-destructive acts.

All the while, as frightening and dangerous as these years
were, there was a part of me that admired Jane. I recognized she
was running with the wolves and fighting an epic battle. I just
did not know if she would win or what shape winning would
take. From meager and abusive beginnings, Jane, now in early
middle age, was fighting to claim her life and find that voice she
had been missing. She was breaking out of her timidity and the

shadow of her mother, that now over-shadowed me. This life-giving need was so compelling that it erupted with the ferocity of someone clawing her way from the cold depths of a mountain lake to the sun-lit surface for air.

There is nothing more heartbreaking than to ever so slowly, over months and years, come to understand that you are toxic to a person for whom you care. It is a slow roast over an open fire, skin bubbling as you rotate on the turning spit. Through Jane's behavior, she communicated her feelings in the most direct and over-powering ways. As a result, she was becoming ever more toxic to the kids and me.

I had come to dislike many things about Jane's way, as she had come to despise many about mine. We were each changing, ever more on the road to becoming ourselves. What had been a good fit in the past, now was corrosive. What we had not understood then was how different we were, a difference that became increasingly apparent over time, and one so great that all marvel that we had ever been together, including Jane and me.

Jane continued suicidal acting out. Later, she told me that once I drew a line, she felt compelled to cross it. Enough was more than enough. I met with Jane in the psych ward and told her I was separating. We wept together, the rending one of the most painful experiences in each of our lives that had already known their measure of pain. So many years traveled together, and now it was coming to an end — something neither of us had anticipated or would have scripted.

I grieved for Jane and for the children we loved. We would no longer have an intact family. We would, never again, celebrate a Christmas morning together nor a Thanksgiving dinner. Jane and I would not watch our children grow up in the same house, nor would we grow old in each other's company. Instead, a future that had once seemed well-established, now lay wide open, a vast wind-swept tundra on a grey winter's day, its frigid barrenness stretching farther than my heart could bear.

In this way, I became a single parent, staggering under the loss of my wife, the challenge of trying to run a household and meet the needs of my kids, themselves angry and heartbroken. Add the complete absence of family support in the area, the financial pressures of maintaining a household on a social worker's pay, the cost of various therapies for family members including inpatient stays for Jane, and the continuing needs of my patients and my hospital responsibilities, and you begin to appreciate the spirit-sapping pressure I felt. Depression, anxiety, and exhaustion became my companions, suicide a considered option: I lost forty pounds.

Having always fended for myself, I often did not realize when I needed help. Reality broke through the walls of my ignorance, for no matter how hard I tried, I could not find a way to be in different places at the same time. I marveled at how people I barely knew were so ready to help, often offering what I had not recognized I needed: Help with the kids, a place for them to stay after school, and the occasional cooked meal, to name but a few. It was humbling and heartwarming, reminding me that I was not completely alone unless I made myself so.

Outside of work, after grocery shopping, cleaning the house, cooking dinner, intervening between bickering children, and nurturing them to the best of my compromised ability, I would retreat to my room and collapse on the bed, alone and forlorn. The feelings associated with Collège St. Etienne had returned with a vengeance; the nightmare made worse in that my children were sharing in it. As I had lost my mother, they had lost theirs. I walked in a world of broken shadows.

All the while, I was treating patients and going about my business as if everything were fine, aside from crying between appointments. To my surprise, I found myself more, rather than less, emotionally attuned to my patients; my empathy and my work were deepening. As my patients were struggling with their impossible situations, I was struggling with mine. My treatment skills were developing. I could hear more, listen better, and relate more fully. As Jane was discovering new dimensions of herself, I was uncovering new dimensions of mine.

All the while, as I ran errands to the grocery store or the mall, I would notice people walking by, excitedly chattering away, seemingly happy and untroubled. All of which only highlighted my aloneness and led me to wonder why such devastation permeated my life? I returned to therapy.

I had left psychoanalysis in the middle of my marital troubles because it did not provide the active support and advice I needed. A colleague referred me to Len Press, LCSW-C, whom I had been distantly aware of as a grandfather of clinical social work in the Baltimore area. Therapy with Len was not psychoanalysis but psychoanalytically informed. We sat facing each other, and he was interactive, providing a constant, empathetic presence that helped me contain and make sense of my emotions.

He explained that the loss of Jane reawakened the feeling of abandonment I felt at Collège St. Etienne at ages eleven and twelve. I already knew this, but he expanded my understanding, pointing out that the developmental task of the typical ten to twelve-year-old is to begin separating from home, moving incrementally away from the family toward a peer group and the wider world. For me, there had been no choice, it had not been a self-directed movement, and there had been nothing incremental about it. There had been no known culture, language, or peer group to hold me. I had been torn from my family and set adrift in an alien world.

The resulting feeling of abandonment and aloneness took root within me and, to some extent, remains to this day. Bunkered in the ashes of the years gone by, it still bursts into flame given an ill wind. With the loss of Jane, that wind was blowing with tornadic force, returning me to that barren and bereft time, that all alone, all alone feeling without end. Thus, as Jane was struggling with her demons, I was grappling with mine.

Upon discharge from the hospital, Jane lived alone for many months, continuing a course of life-threatening acts and hospitalizations. She only stabilized when I advised my daughters not to attend a discharge planning meeting during her last hospitalization. I had seen my girls assume a parental and caretaking role with Jane that was supplanting their own lives and knew that continuing to participate in discharge planning meetings would only foster that pathologic role-reversal. Their failure to appear at this meeting was a wake-up call for Jane: She did not want to lose her daughters. That was Jane's last hospitalization.

Over time, Jane settled into her new life, and after months of stability, I invited her to move back into the house; I would move out. Jane could again become a full-time mother and the long journey of healing between her, and the kids could begin.

Months later, I received a letter from Jane, asking for a divorce. In it, she expressed concern I would be angry and feared I would want to hurt her in some unspecified way. That was an eye-opener, so *not-me* when it came to Jane that it cut the final strands of my attachment to her, revealing far more about her childhood history than having any relationship to who I was and what I was about. Contrary to her fears, I did not feel a trace of anger; I had gotten by that. Rather, I felt relief. By initiating the divorce, Jane freed me from my abiding concern that if I left, I would be abandoning her. Something I could not do given my own searing experience with abandonment.

Over the years to follow, Jane attended AA meetings and continued individual therapy. She also took yoga classes and attended a Buddhist ashram.

Amazingly, despite the intensity of the marital conflicts, the undercurrent of care we had for one another was always apparent. The divorce went smoothly, and through the ensuing years, we have shared grand-parenting and concern for one another and the kids. A genuinely moving conversation occurred at the wedding of our son. When alone together at the dinner table, Jane expressed her regrets about how she had been and all that she had done. She spoke with wisdom and compassion and a hard-earned maturity that I admired, and that moved me to tears.

Through the years, we have continued to celebrate our kids' milestone events together, inclusive of current spouses and extended family. These are wonderful occasions, forever healing across time. Just the other day, we were both at Keeley's house, Jane rocking Caitlin's two-year-old son, Ryan, in a chair, while I paced holding Quincy, Keeley's three-month-old in my arms. Jane gently called my name. I turned to see Ryan in her arms raising his right arm straight up alongside his head, then flipping his hand like a periscope, giving me his signature wave: He was starting to warm to me. Jane smiled her tender smile, and I smiled back.

Jane returned to work, formed many valuable friendships, and upon retirement, devoted herself to the care of her seven grandchildren. Where once she had been absent from her children, she is now fully present and an integral part of their lives. She lives with her husband in a small brick home he grew up in, happier than she has ever been, and a living tribute to the power of resiliency and the human spirit.

Chapter 27

Post-Divorce

*A*fter the divorce, I raced to escape the agony of loneliness and made many of the mistakes people make to fend off feeling their losses. I entered a rebound relationship with Lynn, a much younger, flirtatious, and titillating woman whose smile and light gray eyes sparkled in delight whenever she saw me. This was captivatingly refreshing; for Lynn, I was an elixir, not a poison. That was heady stuff, compounded by my readiness to interpret youth for renewal and lust for love. Thus, I became a cliché.

I turned Lynn into my *Healing Amulet* and gave her one to seal the deal. I designed a wedding ring woven with seven strands of gold, each representing a member of the newly formed family: her two kids, my three kids, her and me. That was my formula: ta-da, instant family.

I would soon realize what I should have known from the beginning. Lynn was not only pretty and vivacious but also unabashedly flirtatious. I had known she had no close female friends but had not fully recognized that the tributaries to her sense of self flowed from male attention. Although never unfaithful, Lynn was a great fisher of men, continually luring them in, then pushing them away in her catch and release program. I filed for divorce within three years of first meeting her.

After Lynn, there was another petite, quiet, and sweet woman with doe eyes who was also named Jane. My friends referred to her as Jane-2. Over time, Jane-2's quiet took its customary toll. In response to my growing unhappiness with the absence of connection, she announced that she thought we should live apart but continue the relationship. I had no interest in this, but curious, asked, "Would we be monogamous?" Off-handily, she responded, "I guess so"—that sounded like a "No" to me.

Before we separated, I received an anonymous email accusing Jane-2 of having an affair. I wasn't surprised; Jane had a history of affairs when exiting relationships. She denied the affair in her soft-spoken way, but I had tripped over her lies before when she was embarrassed by the truth. It did not matter. I felt no jealousy. The relationship had been over for some time even though I, true to form, had refused to accept it.

What surprised me was the depth and breadth of my feelings of eviscerating loss, seemingly entirely out of proportion to the event. Thinking about this over the years, led me to recognize that not only was I grieving Jane-2 but also what she represented: My belief in an *Imaginary Other* and the possibility of *Healing Amulets*. Hope had gone from me. For the first time, I was acknowledging that the root of my continued unhappiness both when alone and in relationships resided within me and always had: there was no external fix. The broken attachments and abandonment suffered during my childhood had become the prototypical structure of my relationships in adulthood.

My belief in the *Imaginary Other* and the possibility of a *Healing Amulet* had provided hope that cushioned the jagged edges of loss and betrayal and the ensuing void that had comprised my early years. My wishful believes had blanketed me somewhat from the cold winds of a cratered childhood. But now, I recognized that my fantastical renderings of romantic love invariably promised much but delivered little, aside from the recurrent bouts of loss and despair.

Now that I had turned to face my demons and the terrible feeling of aloneness from which my fantasies had protected me, I could fully understand why I had needed them. Barely capable of enduring these losses revisited in adulthood, how could the child-me have possibly managed, I would have been completely swept away in the torrent of my despair. My challenge was clear: The problem wasn't other people, it was me. To find a woman I could love securely, I had to grow myself up. I had to evolve this part of me frozen in childhood in order to learn how to love and be by myself in adulthood.

That was easier said than done. I felt utterly orphaned. But I was now willing to pay that price because I understood that if I continued to deny my grief, I would be destined to repeatedly re-live it.

Perhaps you have guessed it by now, but for me—weathered by time and the rack of experience—so-called great love stories hold little allure. For me, a *real-love* story no longer entails the white-hot, spectacularly short life of a shooting star as in the relationship between Romeo and Juliet. Nor does it involve the epic endurance of separation and loss conveyed in the movie, *Cold Mountain,* in which the hero spends years overcoming great perils to reunite with his love, copulate once and die—Essentially the life of a cicada.

Have you ever wondered why classic love stories speak of great suffering and pull the heartstrings of most of us? My thought is that it is because they resonate with the losses that are an inevitable part of childhood. Great or small, these are felt intensely in childhood, and become etched in the early rings of our psyches, even when unremembered.

Have you noticed that the people in these love stories are almost always struggling with impending separation or loss, and often, the couple does not spend much time together, except in their minds? Take the hit movie, *The Bridges of Madison County*. Here, the passions of the characters portrayed by Meryl Streep (Francesca) and Clint Eastwood (Robert) are fueled by frustrated longings for soul-mate connection (the *Healing Amulet*), which harkens back to the symbiosis of the early mother-child relationship. Throw in the emotional rending of impending separation or loss, and voila, we have the requisite sense of dramatic tension.

Francesca and Robert's relationship only lasts a handful of days, thereby avoiding the day-in and day-out grindstone of life and preserving their idealization of one another. Great story, but no less crazy than mine. Francesca is the more mature of the two.

She decides to go on with her life, accepts her relationship with her husband, has her friends, raises her children, and enjoys her grandchildren. All the while, Robert remains smitten with Francesca as his *one-and-only* for the rest of his life, a state made apparent when years later, Francesca receives a cardboard box containing his earthly remains.

Can the symbolism be any clearer? Robert's life reduced to a few trinkets in a cardboard box left in homage to a woman he barely knew. If the symbolism of that over-romanticized, frozen in time, love relationship does not tell it all, what does? Think about Robert and his life. Was there no one else on the entire planet with a warm beating heart whom Robert could love during *all* the ensuing years? Had he spent his whole life shorn of a loving relationship in homage to the one he could not have? Had an affair with Francesca impoverished his ability to form meaningful relationships with other women? Had he ever had this ability? After all, he had spent his entire adult life alone, traveling to all parts of the world. Were ordinary women, tainted by the yellowing stains of reality, simply unable to compete with his fantastical renderings of Francesca?

And how could a real woman compete? You know, the kind that farts, snores, has morning breath, wakes up grumpy, bitches at you, orders you around and complains, but also loves you, hugs you, and creates a home, until you laughingly or otherwise say, "Stop it." Then the two of you hug, apologize if necessary, smile sheepishly at your foolishness, and sooner or later, do it all over again. Now, that to my mind is a *love* story!

I was an expert at unknowingly reliving the love story of my childhood, enduring its epic losses, only to climb blissful heights in each new relationship, and then do it all over again. Of course, this cycle of ecstasy and enmity had taken its toll. With each turn of the screw, I would feel the feelings of that frightened eleven-year-old boy standing in that chilly cobblestone courtyard as his mother pulled away, and the frigid air of reality had rushed in where warmth had once been. Yet, curiously, throughout it all, I would be in the known and the knowable, the stably unstable familiar feel of my childhood, albeit a childhood I could no longer endure.

I finally understood I'm doomed, my yesterdays will be my todays, and my todays will be my tomorrows until the day I die. That life-sapping realization spawned another—unless *I* do something about it. At that moment, I threw away my notion of the mythical *Healing (m)Other* and turned to embrace that lonely and frightened child part of myself. The only question: *How?*

Chapter 28

Meeting Myself

ow? That question transported me to the time of my separation from Jane when I had lost forty pounds without trying and just wanted to stay in bed. Ron-Z called, suggesting we go rock climbing at a place called Wolf's Head in the Catoctin Mountain Park, near Camp David. Lethargy lay upon me, but I knew I had to do something. "A day in nature," says Ron, "just the thing."

It was a warm, humid, sun-soaked day, the hike laborious, up and down hills and through the forest until the cliff rose before us like the curved bow of a ship. Fifty yards wide and thirty feet high, rounded boulders littered its base impersonating ocean waves. The western part of the cliff fell off gradually, but eastward transitioned to true vertical.

Ron and I clambered up the western side, taking in the arboreal view of the valley below, and the range of luminescent blue hills cascading to the horizon. What had seemed a steep climb from afar, swallowed whole by the eye, was easily managed up close, taken step by step. Consequently, this tame experience did nothing to get me out of my self and away from my depression. I gradually shifted east along the base of the cliff, trying increasingly difficult climbs. Then, skin shining with sweat, I stood at the Wolf's Head: the true vertical.

I thought, "I think I can do it," and must have spoken aloud for Ron asked, "Are you sure?" I smiled, thinking I'm no longer sure of anything, "I have no idea, but it will be interesting to try." Thankfully, the fog of my depression was already lifting as I considered the challenge. *Thirty feet is not all that high, and if I can clear the first ten, I can make the rest. The only problem is the boulder-strewn ground at the base of the cliff; there is no safe place to fall.* Ron opted to walk around and meet me at the top.

I began climbing, quickly entering a rhythm, reminding myself to maintain at least three points of contact while moving the fourth limb, be it arm or leg, to the next point of purchase. Plastered against the cliff wall, cheek to mottled stone, my perspective reduced to the grain of the rock in front of my eyes, I tilted my head upward, looking for signs of another quarter-inch fissure to hook with my fingers and groping blindly below with my foot for any outcropping upon which to wedge the sole of my boot, first one, then another, and on I went.

A moment arrived when the next handhold was not readily apparent. I used this break to take in my surroundings: *Oh shit. I'm twenty feet up!* After pausing for breath, I resumed my search for another handhold only to discover that the rock was smooth. What had begun as a trivial concern was growing more acute as the cliff face refused to give up its secrets.

I considered climbing down but ruled that out, imagining that lowering myself up and down with one leg to blindly feel around with the other would soon drain the support leg of strength. Heart sinking, I re-examined the cliff face, soon acknowledging that desperately wishing for something does not make it appear. With mounting apprehension, I readjusted the parameters of my search, now looking for any blemish on the rock's skin. I finally saw a shadow that might or might not be a small outcropping. The bad news was that this imperfection, transformed to beauty mark by my increasingly desperate situation, was four inches beyond my out-stretched hand.

I realized; *I must jump for it.* That is when my imagination began tormenting me. It was an insane idea. *It could be a ledge, but maybe it is only a shadow. If it is a ledge, it might be too narrow or covered with sand-like pebbles that acting like ball bearings could cause my fingers to slip.* The idea of initiating such a leap, small in inches but large in consequences, hit home. Serious injury, if not death, was in the offing. Fear constricted my chest, making it harder to breathe, and my legs began to tremble with the strain of clinging to the cliff's face—I feared cramps would soon follow. That is when the indisputable fact drove home: I could not keep this position forever and certainly not long enough for help to arrive.

At this point, Ron, curious about the silence, peered over the cliff's edge ten feet above, anxiously calling out, "Charlie, are you all right?" Given the precariousness of my situation and the all the worried ruminating I was in the midst of, that question struck me as oddly hilarious. A full-body laugh erupted from within me, accompanied by a burst of words I had not known were there, "I think I just met myself!" It was then the revelation struck home all those years ago that resonated with my situation today. Stripped of all fantasy and denial: I had gotten myself into this situation, no one else, and no one else was going to get me out.

At this moment an understanding arrived, that bordered on the profound: What felt like the safest position, the most familiar, secure, and stable, was the only position that guaranteed I would fall. Continuing to cling to that cliff had become a metaphor for my life: The songs of my childhood danced in my adulthood could be the death of me.

Another leg tremor brought me back to the present, warning that not only did I have to leap for that shadow of a ledge, but I had to do it now. Chattering thoughts and fear would only weaken me. With this understanding, I pushed aside doubt and uncertainty, as luxuries I could ill afford. In their wake lay the resolute calm of acceptance. I took a deep breath, gathered my strength, readied my legs, then leaped, my fingers scrabbling blindly up the rock wall, clawing their way to the shadow of a ledge and me to my fate.

Moments later, I made it to the clifftop. Ron pulled me over, asking with a quizzical look, "What were you laughing about? And what was that about meeting yourself?"

I smiled, answering, "I have no idea." It was all too much for me to process at the time.

Now, all these years later, I realized I was on another cliff, securely ensconced in the familiar self-limiting and self-destructive patterns of my life. I would have to face that which I feared most, harkening as it did to a time of unremitting loneliness and dread. I would have to confront that bereft feeling of childhood, the fear of which had hijacked my life, to have any hope of coming out on the other side.

In the months to come, I abandoned dating and devoted myself to being alone, committing to that state rather than running from it. As I did, I recognized my loneliness for the old companion it was. I studied it, rather than ran from it and, over time, discovered that being alone meant that I was with me and that self-relationship was like any other. As with any companion, I could become tired or bored of me, or catch the blues, but eventually, these feelings would pass, giving way to other times when I thoroughly enjoyed my own company and sang without restraint in my cracking off-key voice as I relished cooking a special meal for myself and drinking a good glass of wine.

I discovered as I passed through the obscuring veils of my fears that I was never alone, for better and worse, I always had *me.* Remembering the pain of my past relationships, I knew that no matter how lonely, lonely might be, there is nothing lonelier than feeling lonely in a relationship.

I had learned the problem was *me.* I was instinctively attracted to women upon whom I could project my *Imaginary Other.* Modifying the word radar, I began using the word Gal-dar to describe that acutely attuned, complex, and unconscious system of attraction that went off with all the fanfare of a video arcade machine whenever I was around a woman that would meet my pathologic need. I knew something about this part of the brain: It was in the deepest recesses, before words, and impervious to reason and logic.

What was I to do? How does one talk themselves out of an instinctive attraction? Then an idea occurred to me: I did not need to. What I could do was re-interpret their meaning. In the past, I had understood these magnetic pulls as go-signals, prompting pedal-to-the-metal pursuits.

The challenge now was how to deal with my romantic attractions constructively? First, I needed to avoid being *blinded by love,* to appreciate that what I was feeling was not love at all. Rather, it was my childhood yearnings forming an infatuation that over-rode reason, logic, and analytic abilities. I needed feeling and thinking to work together if I had any hope of taking control of my life.

I began re-interpreting my electric attractions. No longer did they represent a go-signal, but instead a flashing yellow light warning of possible danger, the equivalent of the Sirens in Greek mythology standing on rocky shoals, luring sailors to their deaths. That awareness, along with the memory of the pain these relationships inevitably wrought, took the steam out of any desire of headlong pursuit. Now, whenever the siren songs of my attractions sounded, they clanged like a claxon in my head with much the same urgency one hears in old submarine warfare movies as the captain shouts into the com, "Dive! Dive! Dive!"

Over the months to follow, as I turned away from my magic attractions, they dissipated, though never entirely disappeared. I had learned the obvious: Because I desired something did not mean it was good for me or that I had to act on that desire. A choice now existed where previously none had been apparent. I was opting to maintain my sense of self by choosing not to lose myself in my *Imaginary Others*.

I now appreciated that to connect with another securely, I had to raise up the childish parts of me. Instead of feeding their wishful needs, I worked to embrace the loss that had birthed them. In accepting my loss, I was accepting my separateness from others and of others from me, and the existential loneliness that such awareness includes.

I came to understand that feeling without thinking is as crazy as thinking without feeling; to row the boat of life successfully, you must use both oars. I understood that a healthy relationship would consist of two relatively autonomous individuals, each enjoying their separateness. Indeed, each would have a need to stand up for it thereby not succumbing to the unfounded projections of the other. Finally, each would have a willingness to work on improving the relationship, but not stay in it no matter what.

Much of the pain I have been through in my adult life has been self-inflicted. In this, I am not the exception, but the rule. Of course, things happen to all of us that we cannot foresee. Even so, if you can accept that you are the author of your life, it may help you avoid some of the mistakes I have made. But, frankly, I doubt it. I think we human beings are driven to make whatever mistakes we *need* to make until we resolve the underlying issues that birthed those needs. Some few may be able to do that alone, while others make use of psychotherapy.

The most challenging part of understanding any recurring pattern of suffering in relationships is recognizing the centrality of one's own contribution to it and that this contribution is likely powered by one's often earliest unmet and ungrieved needs of attachment.

Like most people, I am far happier sharing my life than alone. Having a real and substantial feminine energy in my world adds to it immensely, and helps complete me, but that is different than needing someone like a choking man needs air.

I alone am responsible for my happiness and fulfillment; no one else. Although things have and will be done to me that are outside my control, it is I who is responsible for how I deal with them and the lessons I draw. After all, it is *my* life we are talking about; I alone must write my story and its meaning.

Of course, making such changes may sound daunting and in some ways it is. However, the most daunting aspect is simply recognizing what is needed, that is what takes the time. Once one accepts what is needed, change often follows quickly. And, to understand what is needed often only takes a well-chosen or well-timed word or the slightest of shifts in perspective.

Chapter 29

You Can't Get There From Here

1994. Age forty-five.

I was in my office when the phone rang. The caller introduced herself then launched into a question that caught me entirely by surprise, so much so that I asked her to repeat it. She said, "Would you be willing to accept the nomination as the 1994 Clinician of the Year by the Maryland Society of Clinical Social Workers?"

A relative social isolate, and not given to active participation in any organizations outside of the Washington School of Psychiatry, I had no idea what she was saying. My first thought was that a friend was putting me on. But, as she continued, I realized she was serious. Even so, I wondered: *Why would any organization reach out to me, a virtual stranger, to honor in such a way? It made no sense.*

Nonetheless, seeing no downside, I assured the caller I would accept the nomination. Thinking about the call afterward, I realized that I had been a member of the Maryland Society of Clinical Social Workers for years but had confined my involvement to writing the annual dues check while never attending a meeting.

That week, I mentioned this incident to my therapist, Len Press. In a curiously guarded fashion, he asked, "You don't know this group?" I told him I had figured that out but that it was hard to imagine them selecting a non-participating member. Len asked, "Do you know that that award began a year ago and who the first honoree was?" I assured him I did not. He responded, "It was me."

Despite my vetting the validity of the award, I assumed it would be some small, dry, short ceremony, and reasoned that I should not take the kids out of school for it. That was until I arrived at the venue and took in the linen-covered tables set for fine dining, formally dressed wait staff, and many people milling about. Introducing myself to the receptionist, I was warmly welcomed and escorted to the head table. There, I met the honorees for two other awards who had their families with them, and instantly regretted not having mine.

As I sat there listening to the other honorees accepting their awards, I thought about what a circuitous journey it had been from my flitting among the shadows in that Alabama woods, to the abandonment at Collège St. Etienne, through my many failures, acts of delinquency, and nomadic wanderings on to the present day. I wondered, *What had made that difference in my life?* It wasn't any great intellect or profound wisdom, but rather an abiding curiosity and a dogged need to make sense of things. When my turn came to accept my award, I decided to tell a true story that seemed loosely relevant to these thoughts. It did not have a title, but I will give it one now: "You Can't Get There from Here," which also speaks to how can feel when first setting out to find greater happiness or fulfillment in their lives.

I had finished giving Grand Rounds at the Maine Medical Center, Portland, Maine, and a talk at the state hospital and was on my way back to the airport. As I drove, thinking about the presentations I had given, I became aware of a niggling concern: A lot of time had passed, and I had not seen any signs for the airport. At first, I shrugged off my worry as travel anxiety, but as the miles mounted, so did evidence that this was not the case. Finally, I decided to break the cardinal rule of every male: Thou shall never ask for directions. The wisdom of this injunction soon became apparent as I grew more rather than less lost after each stop for assistance. The people were friendly and accommodating, but the multi-step directions and the New England accents made it hard for me to take in what they were saying.

I was now percolating with anxiety as my flight was due to depart in twenty minutes. I did not know how missing a flight would affect me; I had never missed one. My mind cavorted with possibilities: Would I be put on standby for later flights? Could I be stranded in Portland over-night? Would I have to pay for a new ticket?

Amidst my cacophony of worries, I registered flags waving in the distance, as if beckoning me to a carnival. It was a gas station. Now, with fifteen minutes left until my flight, a last burst of hope bloomed within me. I pulled into the station, leaped from the car, and ran into the office. There, I beheld a dough-faced, stout young man, in grease-stained overalls, with an orange baseball cap embossed with a truck logo planted crookedly on his head. With arresting intensity, I shouted: "How do I get to the airport from here?"

Curiously, despite the electric charge of my arrival, the young man did not seem to register my presence. Rather, he stood unmoving, glassy eyed, as if in a trace, so devoid of animation that I wondered if he was aware of me at all. I considered repeating my question but worried that he might be processing, and that any interruption could trigger a reboot, costing valuable time.

Just as I was accepting that all was lost, I thought I noticed the slightest of movements. *Was desperation prompting me to see things that were not there? Had the young man's eyes exhibited some deep spark of awareness?* I could not tell. Enthralled, I carefully studied him. *Yes! There it was again.* His right hand, with the ponderous speed of maple syrup on a cold late winter's day, was starting to move, making its tortoise like way toward his forehead. Once there, ever so slowly, he pushed his hat back and began rubbing his forehead, effecting a posture that most would associate with ponderous deliberation. As profound meditations tend to do, this process was also taking its fair measure of time, and the last dregs of hope of catching my flight were draining from me.

Then, suddenly, his eyes focused, and, for the first time, he looked directly into mine. With that, I understood the young man was about to speak. So ready was I for any pearl of utterance that I felt something akin to what I imagine I would feel sitting at the feet of the Dalai Lama. The gas station attendant, now Dalai

Lama, then slowly and emphatically pronounced the following words: "You… can't… get… there… from… here."

Wow! That sentence instantaneously extinguished the last embers of hope of catching my flight and with it all my angst. Just like that, I was no longer in a hurry; there was no place I *had* to be. I now had the unfettered mind, time, and space to consider his words, "You can't get there from here." They were the equivalent of a Zen Buddhist Koan or the words of a great philosopher or wise man. I do not think I had ever heard a more Zen-like statement or existential thought. The total is-ness of those words: pure, concrete, absolute, certain, blew my mind. I strived to make sense of them. *What was he saying? What could he possibly mean? Was I in a twilight zone of experience? Were we on another planet devoid of means of transportation? Were we in another dimension of reality where there was no Portland airport?* My questioning mind churned. *How was this possible?*

Although he had unequivocally stated that I could not get *there* from *here*, I was reasonably sure I could. He and I were in competing universes: He could be right, or I could be right, but both of us couldn't be right, could we? I did not want to challenge the young man's thinking and risk giving insult. Indeed, being right was less important to me now than satisfying my curiosity about the meaning of his words. To test them further, I needed to introduce a third possibility, an alternative to the all-or-nothingness of it being either his way or mine so we could think about things together. Looking him squarely in the eye, I said, "Okay, I get that, but what if I was standing over there?" pointing to the floor three feet to my left.

The young man somberly considered my question, then, his pale face illuminated from within as if beholding a rising sun. Emanating newfound energy, he energetically stated, "Oh! You pull right out on the road, take a left, go down one block to the stoplight, take a right, go two blocks till you come to a T at Airport Way, take a left, and it'll take you there."

Hope flared within me, but still cautious, I asked, "And how long might that take?"

He responded, "Five minutes."

Instantly, I became a Road Runner, lost in that legendary cloud of dust, the only sign of my passage the echo of my shouted: "Thank You!" I made the flight.

That story came to mind because those words, "You can't get there from here," had once applied to my thinking about myself. Nowhere, no how, could I have ever scripted the jumble of paths that took me from that young boy getting his fortune told in those shadowed Alabaman woods some thirty-five years earlier to a man being honored by his peers as a psychotherapist. Nor would I have imagined that much of my success would derive from the worse times in my life. Such as my need to convey the lessons learned in inpatient work as it was being suffocated by managed care or my intimate understanding of primitive mental states because of suffering my own at Collège St. Etienne.

What was the key to my transformations? The will to persevere and to explore alternative perspectives, such as in psychotherapy and when my analyst had asked, "Why just a master sergeant?" I had learned something important: Life-changing shifts do not have to be epic. They can occur with a slight shift in perspective, a mere five words or three feet away.

Chapter 30

Writing Myself

*I*n my late thirties, I developed a love-hate relationship with writing. It began when I authored my first published article. The thinking and feeling entailed in writing helped me discover thoughts I had not known I had and understand what was going on within me. It helped me come to terms with the ending of long-term inpatient treatment. It also led to the unforeseen outcome of speaking engagements. These, in turn, stimulated more writing. In this way, writing became an important part of my life, and the more I wrote, the more I discovered and the more personally rewarding it became.

The love part of writing occurs when scrawling words across the computer screen leads to a better understanding of myself and what it I am trying to articulate. The hate part is that writing is a struggle for me, a mentally laborious effort comparable to plowing a rocky West Virginia field with a cantankerous flea-bitten mule, the mule being the lugubrious workings of my mind.

When I start, I usually have a topic, but never know what will develop. Only as I stare into the unblinking phosphorous eye of the computer monitor and it stares into me, do words finally begin scrolling across the screen. That's when I discover what is at play in the depths of my mind. At first, the words confuse me; I do not like what the words say or how they say it, but I have learned to trust that they point toward where I need to get. It is my job to form this inchoate jumble into furrows of understanding. The crop blooms when I am finally able to put together a sentence and then a paragraph that expresses something I was thinking or feeling but had not fully recognized. It's then, like a photograph coming into focus, that I've made sense of something and the satisfaction arrives.

Most of my professional writing emanated from talks delivered at the Washington School of Psychiatry. In 1991, David Scharff, building a library of psychoanalytic books on Object Relations Theory, asked me to write one. I was shocked; I had never considered such a monumental undertaking. Also, I was suffering from the collapse of my marriage with Jane and possessed neither the focus, confidence, nor energy for such a daunting task. David persisted, noting that when he was going through a similar personal trial, writing a book had helped. He ended his pitch by remarking that it only took him a year. *My God*, I thought, *a year isn't much.*

What I discovered was that I was no David Scharff. I did not have his intellect or fluid mastery of writing; I also did not have the emotional reserves. But he had planted a seed, and it took root. One day, months later, I sat down and started writing in an on and off kind of way, tossed between the excitement of the challenge and recurring bouts of suffocating loneliness.

The one thing I knew was that I wanted to write a book that would help my patients and others suffering from mental illness or their families to better understand themselves and what they were going through.

My writing entailed re-visiting many difficult clinical cases and reliving them through a lens deepened by my personal experience struggling with mental illness in my family. I toiled to write the book in a way that would induce in the reader some measure of the experience of treating, living with, or being a person who has a personality disorder. To convey the desire, the hope, the despair, the anxiety, the confusion, the doubt, the frustration, and the golden moments of intimate connection encountered by any therapist aspiring to work with a patient population suffering from major psychopathology. It was not an easy book to write, nor is it an easy book to read, but, as my editor, Margaret Diehl, who loves the psychological, exclaimed, "But, oh so worthwhile!"

The near experience nature of the writing was emotionally draining. Finishing a chapter, I would take a break from writing, from thinking, from feeling, from remembering. Once recovered, I would return to the task, each time pushing further ahead. In this way, *The Book* became a constant companion, forever on my mind. It took on many characteristics, ranging from a dark cloud of obligation to a source of deepening understanding and gratification. It became my Mount Everest, a grueling climb with moments of satisfaction whenever a higher plateau, the end of a paragraph or chapter, was reached. It was the ultimate challenge, but I refused to be that guy that talked about writing a book but never did. A mere seven years later, I finished.

As a boy who stole that ninth-grade English exam, I would never have guessed that writing would become an essential part of my life. But *something* takes me over; then I must get that *something* out. Writing is the midwife. It is in writing that I find out what that something is. That is how my love of writing is reborn again and again.

It was a great ride, one rife with accomplishment and satisfaction. But what I was learning is that all that mattered on one level, but on another, not so much. By now, I had slain my share of dragons, but this had not brought me the lasting fulfillment I had sought. I knew I was not as happy as I should be, that something within me was amiss, but I did not know what that something was. So, I started writing once again and thus, Hatching Charlie was born and led me to the following realization

Chapter 31

The Only Dance There Is

The function of grief and mourning is to free the mourner to move on with her life. Counter-intuitively, I believe grieving the loss of a genuinely connected relationship is easier than mourning a conflicted one. Like good milk, a fulfilling relationship is metabolized and internalized and thus never lost. Conversely, a conflicted relationship is like sour milk: indigestible, remaining a foreign body making mourning difficult to complete. After all, how do you let go of someone important to you but never yours?

In my case, I erroneously believed that I had separated from my father after confronting him on two different occasions, both in my early thirties. In the first, I had risen from the dinner table to get seconds when he barked at me in a voice one uses to call a dog to heel, "Charlie! Bring me more roast beef!" He had often referred to us disparagingly in our earlier years as his "little n**gers," and his tone triggered within me those deep-seated feelings of humiliation. Also, talking to me in this debasing way in front of my kids was unacceptable. I would not give them the idea that I would tolerate such treatment.

While a primordial fear grazed my spine, echoing painful memories of his abuse of me during childhood, I sharply responded, "No! I'll be happy to bring you more roast beef when you can ask politely." Silence filled the gulf following my rebuke, as would any narcissist, Dad refused to, apologize, or ask politely. And, like any narcissist, he never got up to get roast beef for himself.

The second instance occurred when the family gathered around the dinner table in animated conversation. I began to insert myself into the flow, when Dad, sitting catty-corner to me, slapped me sharply on the forehead. I instantly recognized that he felt stymied, given his speech impediment, in getting a word in edgewise and that I had been the handiest outlet for his frustration. But I would not be his whipping boy anymore. I immediately struck him back on his forehead with equal force, and in a low, tight voice, my eyes fixed like a bayonet upon his, said: "Dad, don't *ever* hit me again."

He looked straight at me, then for a weapon, his eyes falling upon his steak knife. He looked from the knife to me, then back to the knife and started moving his hand. With genuine disdain, words dripping with the acid of my contempt, I challenged him: "Really? You're going to kill me?" After a long pause of consideration, the tension left his body. He never hit me again.

These events signaled my willingness to end my relationship with my father, and if necessary, by extension with my mother. I *wanted* my parents in my life, but not at any cost.

What I did not recognize was that putting Dad in his place in the physical world had not gotten rid of his ubiquitous presence in my internal one. I could swallow, but not digest. How could it be otherwise? We had never reconciled. He had never taken responsibility for any wrongdoings nor made amends. I knew I did not hold a special place in his heart. I do not think anyone did, at least, any more so than a rich man values his possessions.

When Dad passed away, I was troubled by his loss but felt nothing like the acute pain of grief I had felt with the death of my mother, which though searing, passed quickly. With Dad, there was only the background hum of a general disquiet. Although gone from my life, he was a remorseless persecutory presence in my psyche.

Years later, while touring Florence, Italy, with my wife, Janet, we visited the US military cemetery located there, its thousands of pearl-white gravestones gracing the rolling hillsides. The cemetery reminded me of one I had visited with Dad when touring Italy as a boy; perhaps it was even the same one. As I walked alone among the monuments and those thousands upon thousands of graves, I wondered who these men and women had been, what their stories were, the lives they lived, the families they left behind, their parents long dead. These men and women, in their twenties and thirties, had died seventy or more years earlier; I doubted many were alive that remembered them. I wondered if the meaning of their lives had been reduced to standing eternal guard as one of these gravestones, awesome to behold in their regimented multitude, but their individual stories lost forever.

I meandered among the graves for half an hour, musing upon such questions, when a daub of color caught my eye. In the distance, among all those thousands of graves, I spied a single bouquet as if in answer to my unvoiced questions. Intrigued, I made my way to that grave and the fresh flowers carefully arranged by the headstone. It was the grave of a young man, a private, killed in his early twenties.

Captured by the unknown story behind the flowers, I became lost in reverie. *Someone had recently visited this man and lovingly paid homage. Who could that have been, given that this man would have been at least ninety years old if he were alive today? Was it a girlfriend or a wife, nearing the end of her own life, still carrying the flame of her love? Was it a brother or sister, who missed him terribly and still held him alive in memory? Was it a child, now near seventy years old herself, paying tribute to a father she had barely known — or not known at all?*

Those flowers, resting on that grave, were made even more poignant by the likelihood that whoever had left them, the holder of the memories, in a few short years would be gone herself. Then there would be no flowers nor anyone to hold his story.

My musings kindled within me memories of times I'd lived with my parents. That's when the nostalgia, after all these years, finally slipped in, both sad and gently caressing, not for my mother but my father. I thought of stories lived and of stories told that, under the erosion of time, will be lost forever with no one left to leave a bouquet of memory. At first, my thoughts and feelings emerged as insubstantial as mirages, best seen from the corner of my eye. As I had discharged the effluvia of my anger toward Dad over the years, I now understood it had interfered with my ability to acknowledge the good he had also brought into my life. As these memories slowly came into focus, I realized why I had needed to keep them as ghosts: Despite all that was said and done, I missed those wild and wondrous moments that arose unexpectedly from time to time when in Dad's company.

It was morning. Dad called out: "Charlie, come with me; I want you to see something." We descended to the lakeshore, Dad carrying a tin can half-full of dried kernels of corn. A low-hanging fog cloaked the surface of the lake, its uppermost wisps cast in a golden halo by the early morning sun. As we stood on the shore, Dad began shaking the can, creating a sound like hard rain on a tin roof. Curiosity aroused, I waited silently, and soon detected a faint whisper in the distance which became increasingly recognized as a rhythmic whooshing of air growing ever louder, its source, coming fast. A primal chill traversed my spine, giving a warning my mind had yet to grasp. Then, almost upon us, a wedge of geese, cawing like pre-historic beasts, burst from the fog. Just as I thought they had no time to stop, they, as one, broke their careening flight and splashed onto the water, turning it to a froth by the furor of their pulsating wings. Dad, grinning, cast the corn upon the shore.

Of course, neither the neighbors nor my mother appreciated Dad's luring of these poop factories into their yards, but, as usual, the feelings of others were like the writings of the Rosetta Stone to Dad: They did not translate. Nonetheless, I could understand his motivation. The pure primitive power and wonder of that moment had called to my deepest nature.

Dad did one fatherly task extremely well: He introduced his kids to the excitement of the world. It was Dad who carried us into various parts of Europe: Paris, Versailles, the Eiffel Tower, and the Louvre, where I saw the Mona Lisa for the first time. With him, we toured the Netherlands, visited the Madurodam, where we walked like giants about the miniaturized city and later drove by vast fields abloom with tulips as charming windmills slowly churned the air.

With him, we awoke to continental breakfasts of meats and cheeses, butter and jellies and bread of all kinds and traversed the snow-capped Alps, our car laboring up steep inclines while we looked out at villages, miniaturized by the enormity of the mountains, that dotted shadowed valleys, and sun-lit mountainsides alike.

With him, we camped at Lake Garda, Italy, ensconced in a family-sized tent that Dad taught us how to erect out of a confusing mélange of canvas and aluminum rods. There, he took us on a powerboat ride, skimming across the swells, as our eyes blazed with excitement and our hearts filled with exhilaration as the spray of wind-blown water anointed our faces.

It was Dad, a history buff, who led us on a fantastic tour of Italy, bringing the ancient buildings and cities to life with his stories, taking us hundreds and thousands of years back in time as we crossed the remnants of old Roman roads and crumbling viaducts plunging down steep mountainsides.

Dad fought WW-II in Italy. He told us of Mussolini and how he got the trains to run on time, and he showed us the balcony from which an angry mob hung Mussolini at the end of the war. As we traversed the route of his military campaign, from one end of Italy to the other, Dad recounted his stories as a young artillery officer. Upon a curving mountain road, a sniper's bullet just missed him as he drove in a jeep. On a hilltop, Dad fell into a trench latrine when a German artillery round exploded nearby. And, from a hillside overlooking an open field bracketed by dense woods, he recreated the tension and disbelief he felt when a German infantry battalion, oblivious to the danger, emerged from the forest below. As the Germans approached the center of the field, farthest from the safety of the woods, his canon opened fire and obliterated them.

Amazingly, we also stopped at a hilltop manor that Dad said was the home of a girlfriend of that time. He knocked on the door, and an attractive, dignified middle-aged woman answered. Dad introduced himself, and with surprised delight, she gave him a warm hug and a kiss on the cheek.

I marveled at Dad's capacity to navigate across Europe and through the narrow streets of the Italian cities with a map alone, respect that grew more profound as I repeatedly lost my way, even with the benefit of GPS, some forty-five years later. We drove into Venice, where we watched Murano glassmakers work their art and rode in a Gondola. Then we moved to the wonders of Rome: the Vatican and the Colosseum, as Dad spun his tales and wove new worlds into our imaginings.

He explained the symbolism of the sculptures found in various squares and within the many fountains dotting the city and purchased indulgences for each of us that guaranteed we could bypass the trials of Purgatory and gain direct access to heaven upon our deaths.

With Dad, we toured the United States, going to many of the places I would return to years later in my trip with Jane and to which I would subsequently take my kids: The Grand Canyon, the Painted Desert, the Petrified Forest. We also rode ponies in Colorado and had our picture taken near bison. All this we owed to Dad, and now, I could find my way to thank him, as tears flood my eyes.

It was in passing through and beyond my anger, which
allowed me to remember the good times with Dad and to find
compassion for him that I was finally free to mourn. In
reconciling myself with him in this more complete way, I was
able to let go of his oppressive hold upon me and become more
open to moving on more freely with my life.

Mom was the yin to Dad's yang. Her domain was that of
thoughtful conversations, evening walks, and nightly
meditations called prayer. When visiting, I would join her on her
walks along the hard-packed dirt streets that crisscrossed Lake
Monticello as the sun gave way to the moon, and bright stars
competed with the glow of fireflies. As we walked, we talked
about God, my siblings, and what was going on in our lives, as
the song of crickets and the chorus of bullfrogs vied for
dominance, threatening to drown out our conversation.

Throughout the years, Mom had grown while maintaining
an active, caring presence, and when she had done what she
could, she left the rest in the hands of her God. This had not
always been the case. As the mother of twenty-somethings, she
would stand firm against anything that broke her sense of
righteousness. I remember her sputtering with indignation over
what she saw as the impropriety of Jacques' wife, Christine,

going out one night with her girlfriends while Jacques was in Vietnam. On another occasion, she took issue with how Christine was raising her children, prompting Christine to order Mutti from her home. Mutti was equally dogmatic when confronting Jane about pre-marital sex, essentially driving her away. And, when Ed told them he was marrying Ellen, of Philippine descent, mother along with Dad cautioned against, warning that Ed's life would be ruined.

However, in the years to follow, Mom mended these relationships, turning them into ones of mutual love and respect. Rather than remaining rigid, she flexed and became a more rounded and wiser person.

As with many mothers, Mom created the ground upon which the family rested and was the glue that held it together. She worried about the kids and took care of them. She did most of the cooking and the cleaning and railed at us boys to clean our rooms and make our beds, then followed behind to straighten up to her exacting standards. She was also quite the character, donning a cowboy skirt and hat, corncob pipe in her mouth as she hammed it up in the kitchen and cut a comical figure when trying to drive the geese from her yard by shooting them in the butt with a pellet gun from the upper deck.

Mom had grown more spiritual over the years, no longer governed by dogma but having her own thinking and beliefs on issues that troubled her vis-à-vis the church. Although she no longer marched in lockstep with church doctrine, she attended Mass every Sunday and knelt beside her bed every night for prayer. Her developing spirituality served her well in her living and her dying. She had become a whole person, no longer burdened by despair or regrets as her life was nearing its end.

During her last two years, diagnosed with terminal cancer, Mutti lived her dying in a way beyond compare: With grace and unflinchingly, made strong by her faith and a soul-full conviction that she was returning to her God. Indeed, she made the process magnificent. I marveled, *How was that possible?* as she became ever more emaciated by radiation and chemotherapy treatments, lost all her hair, and endured frequent bouts of nausea. Yet, it was unmistakably true: She was ever more becoming herself and at her most beautiful.

On two separate occasions, she did the most astonishing thing. She struggled out of bed in the late evening while I was sitting with my siblings and their spouses around the dining room table. Teetering over, she placed her palms on the table for support, and ignoring everyone else, leaned forward, looked me fiercely in the eye, and emphatically demanded, "Charlie, have a *good* life! Charlie, have a *good* life!" She then waited, unmoving, until, looking directly back into her eyes, I responded, choking back tears, "I will, Mom. I will." Without another word, she turned and tottered her frail, bent body back to bed.

Several months later, Mutti, even more sapped of energy, again made that arduous trek from her bed and repeated the very same words in the very same way. It seemed all-important to her to drive the point home, to drive the point *into* me, "Charlie, have a *good* life! Charlie, have a *good* life!"

I think she could see the dark ampule of my abandonment planted all those years ago and refused to leave me a second time. She was telling me that she *knew* with absolute conviction that it was within *my* power to move beyond it—if only I would. It was her blessing and her dying wish for me; I took it to heart. Like a radioactive pellet inserted in the middle of a cancerous tumor, the whole notion of "Have a good life," became my goal.

My mother's love was not the perfect love I had wished for, and it was not always in a love language I could appreciate, but it was really honest to God love, only conveyed with increasing conviction by her emphatically challenging me to have a good life. By the time of her death, I knew that regardless of what had happened or why, she had always loved me. With that certain knowledge, she is forever with me.

My mother's peace with herself and with her dying allowed
her to keep her sense of humor and her spirituality. Indeed, not
only did these never flag, they burned ever brighter as cancer
ravaged her body but never grazed her spirit. Near the end, I
took a picture of her and my daughter, Keeley, sitting together.
Mutti's head bare, bald crown held erect, as both she and Keeley
stared resolutely into the lens of the camera with their steady
blue eyes. Two strong women, the younger channeling the older.
I wondered if they knew how alike they were.

It was soon after this picture that Mutti laughingly showed me a note she had received from her best friend, Dot. In beautiful flowing cursive, Dot wished her farewell and "Bon Voyage." *Christ!* I thought. *Now that's courage and class on the part of both these good and strong women.* Each of them faced death head-on. Mom's death would be within weeks, Dot's years later, but neither was afraid to meet it. For them, death was an accepted part of life, not separate from it.

Madeleine Marie Alberta McCormack (nee Turgeon) passed away on February 20th, 1997, at age seventy-eight and was buried at Arlington National Cemetery, the funeral services conducted in North Post Chapel, Fort Myer, Virginia, the very chapel where she and my father had married more than fifty years earlier.

Many years ago, the philosopher, Ram Dass, wrote a book entitled: *The Only Dance There Is.* In it, he offered that people have a signature way of going through life that is only danced harder as life nears its end. I took this to heart as both a blessing and a warning. As Ram Dass had foretold, my mother lived her dying the way she had lived her living, only doing it better and better as the years went on. I cannot think of any greater gift a parent can give her children than the opportunity to witness an individual, a soul, continue to evolve until death do them part.

Dad also danced his dance and to a predictably different outcome: He withered. His dying years, marked by increasing ugliness: strokes, dementia, and Alzheimer's, alcoholism, hardening of the arteries, paranoia, fearfulness, and isolation, all mirroring his lifetime of self-devouring self-absorption. My parents' separate paths were not coincidental; each reflected the cumulative outcome of *how* they lived their living.

The last time I saw Dad, he was sitting in the community room of his nursing home in South Carolina, which bristled with the faint, acrid scent of urine. Jane-2 and I had spent several hours visiting, showing him family photographs to stimulate his memory. Occasionally a look, which I took to be of recognition, would fleetingly cross his face only to disappear. This process mirrored his attempts to talk: He would begin a sentence only to lose the thread before completing it.

Patients lined the walls of the room in chairs and wheelchairs, some dressed in suits or frilly dresses from a bygone era, as music from the forties played on a boom box. Occasionally, a resident would join us on the couch, mistaking me for a son, brother, father, or friend, devouring me with their eyes as they hungered for contact with whichever partially remembered person my presence evoked within them.

At one point, a little boy ran into the room, chasing a large yellow balloon that he kept bouncing in the air. I worried that his mad-dash presence might result in a damaging collision, but amazingly, he avoided this. As he darted about, none of the wizened patients seemed to notice; their heads continued to hang, and they remained slack-jawed, as their parchment textured hands rested unmoving upon their laps.

Then magic. The boy lost control of the balloon, and just before it landed on the head of one of the patients, her hand shot up and knocked it back into the air. This event repeated itself five or six times as different residents reacted to the balloon. Before I knew it, the room was alive with active, smiling people. To my delight, my father was one of them, having returned for a moment, from wherever he had been, as his instincts had taken over where his mind could not and brought him into the present.

The boy's father then entered the room and retrieved him, and, as suddenly as it had begun, it stopped. Like a ballerina atop a music box that had wound down, the residents slumped back into their chairs as if nothing had occurred. Perhaps, as far as they knew, nothing had.

Several months later, the call came. My father was dead. Although we had not been close, I missed those random moments when our time together would suddenly sing with manic aliveness before disappearing again, so like the yellow balloon.

My father did not learn or grow from his mistakes, leading him into an ever-weakening position. His fate and his Karma had been to die frightened and alone, trapped in the ever-diminishing, depopulated world of his mind as the walls closed in.

For years, he had inhabited my psyche as a dark passenger and an indigestible presence until I was able to grieve him more fully by also acknowledging the good he had done. Wherever he is, whatever form he is in, I only wish him well.

John Crisler McCormack died on September 4th, 2003, at the age of eighty-five. He was buried on a rainy day at Arlington National Cemetery with full military honors, casket pulled on a caisson, followed by the honor guard led by a riderless horse, empty boot facing backward in the stirrup. At the gravesite, a bagpiper played "Amazing Grace," followed by a bugler sounding out the hauntingly beautiful last twenty-four notes of taps. The sharp clap of three rifle volleys rang out in final salute and farewell; silence flooded into the ensuing void.

Part VI

Reconciliation

Typically, when I think of reconciliation, I think of a couple reconciling. But this time, the couple is within me. In fact, it is not even a couple; it's an amalgamation of life experiences and relationships, each vying for attention, pulling and pushing me in different ways.

Included among these are the voices of my children. They have been with me through the last forty-five years of my journey, and each has played an important role in influencing in I am today, reminding me to live beyond myself. As time has passed, they continue to prod me to grow, introducing new people into my life, including in-laws and especially my grandkids. I have learned that it is not the control of events that matters, but the openness to being in the mix.

Chapter 32

The Family Crucible

A crucible is a situation or severe trial, in which different elements interact, leading to the creation of something new. Such is the nature of life and family. Not only does each parent help mold the child, but each child also shapes its siblings and parents.

At first, my kids' power over me was an epiphany. Holding Chandler for the first time, I was dumb-struck by the ferocity of my protective feelings. Never more clearly, was someone more important to me than me.

Each in their turn, my children have taught me that love is not a simple thing. It goes well beyond kisses and hugs, often requiring sacrifices and losses, all of which pushes me to continue growing. As I struggled to get out of bed in the middle of the night to comfort one or another of them as young children,

I still remember vividly my grumpiness evaporating under the warmth of their innocent greeting smiles.

In their teen years, I discovered that it is one thing to be a young person struggling to separate from his parents, and another to be the parent from whom the young person is striving to separate. I learned that not only did I need to let go, but that I had to support the process.

Being the father of young children, though demanding, was great, full of cuddling and kisses, and relatively straightforward. There were values I wanted to impart and did, usually unchallenged. But, as they grew into teenagers and young adults, ever more invested in growing into their own lives, they became more forceful in moving out of mine. Thus, they pushed me to pause and think and to consider their diverging interests and needs.

Adding to the parental challenge is that one parent does not fit all. Each child has his or personality, gifts, and vulnerabilities. The parent must become attuned to the different needs of each child, each needs a father and mother of their own.

With single parenthood these challenges only deepened. Here, I was forced out of my singular role of Father to become both Father and Mother, responsible for setting limits and nurturing. Single parenthood was by far the most difficult yet rewarding challenge of my life, pushing me into a depth of relationship with my children that I otherwise would have never known.

Then there is the fact that children function as time machines, stimulating recollections that transport me back to my childhood. Like archaeologists, they sweep aside the dust of years, exposing memories of my relationship with my parents, but this time with me on the other side of the parent-child divide.

Now, years have passed, and where once my children's lives had rotated around mine, we are now in separate over-lapping orbits. Caught in the complex needs of their families, they sail into their respective futures, ever so slowly leaving me in their wake. Now I play a peripheral yet, still important, role.

As my kids have developed lives of their own, they have brought new people into mine. Becoming a father-in-law was something to which I had given little consideration. I had not thought about fully-grown adults, each having different loyalties and family cultures, being inserted into and altering mine.

Now, all three of my children are married with kids of their own. These three in-laws are a surprising addition to my family and one I would never have thought to script. Finding a more diverse group would be difficult.

Just imagine a 6'1" tall, straight-talking blond German businesswoman, the vice-president and chief financial officer of her company; a 6'3" African-American male who read the Bible each morning before two children took over this time; and a short, stocky, bald Caucasian Muslim, tattoos adorning his torso and arms, who at first spoke so little that he earned the nickname, *Justin-Two-Words*. It is a surreal cast, and I am stunned with amazement at the ease with which they come together, and I respect them all.

All this makes me wonder: Is the success of this family in growing authentic and resiliemynt relationships despite or because of the trials and tribulations we have navigated together? I am reasonably certain it is the latter. Through all, we have faced reality, including ugly parts, not just me with the kids, but over time with the kids and Jane, fostering healing and a secure reconnection.

Sure, we are all have our flaws, subject as any family to disappointments, misbehaving, or getting angry, but we never pretend otherwise. We talk, laugh, and cry together and feel our way through messy moments, all the while taking genuine pleasure in each other's successes. From a hidden corner of my mind I ask, "How does it get any better than this?" I have scoured the universe for the answer and found it: It does not.

All the same, I am not inoculated from sometimes wanting to stop time. But just when I am feeling nostalgic, my newest instructors arrive on the scene: A villainous crew of grandkids: Benjamin, Stella, Cormac, Alexandra, Johnathan, Ryan, Quincy, Asher, and Marin.

I had never realized how having these young people in my life could rejuvenate my own and help lead to a greater appreciation of all that I have. I love not having parental responsibilities and the freedom to do what I like when I am with them, which is *Being Bad*. And I love being *Very Bad* when it comes to them, advocating rebellion and revolution as we play pirates sailing a timeless sea.

Not surprisingly, my grandkids enjoy being *Very Bad Kids* with me, rejoicing in the power of over-throwing at least one of the authorities in their lives. Repeatedly attacking me en-masse, like iron filings attracted to a magnet, is one of their favorite pass-times. In truth, we are all so *Very Bad* together we have the *Goodest of Times*. Yet, despite their gleefully rowdy assault, they are rendered instantaneously sweet when they incur a booboo and look to me for soothing.

The grandkids are a force of nature, their innocent, shining eyes breathing new life into this aging man. They do not allow me to rest on my laurels. Indeed, they do not recognize that I have laurels upon which to rest. Instead, one must earn one's stripes in the moment. It is all about the moment from moment to moment as they weave their curative powers. This is clear to me when Alexandra, age 4, yells from another room, "Opa, help me find the TV channel," or "Opa, be good," or "Opa go outside" if she deems I have not been. Unfortunately, I cannot go into episodes with each of my grandchildren, that would make a much longer read. So, I will use one episode to capture the feel of it all.

I am in the living room as Janet helps three-year-old Macaroni, Keeley's son Comac, nicknamed for his hair, don his bright red Spiderman outfit for the first time. Dark ringlets frame his small, handsome brown face before his helmet mask is donned, leaving two startling blue eyes peering out at me, alight with mischievousness. I feel like prey.

Fully uniformed, this three-year-old turned Spiderman Superhero struts forward, then stops, freezing into a Superhero pose for fifteen seconds, seeming to derive some magical power from it. Then, he marches forward and clocks me upside the head with his tiny fist. Dramatically, I yell, "Ouch!" and fall wounded to the floor, cursing him as a *Bad Boy* in my play voice. His joy over his power soars, and he giggles delightedly as I slowly pick myself up with awkward difficulty, grumbling all the while.

Macaroni watches cautiously. Baring my teeth, I growl, then strike my own admittedly pathetic ninja pose, readying for combat.

I signal an end to all this displaying with a battle cry that causes Mac to turn in desperation and attempt to run, his excited laughter robbing him of breath as his face flashes from panic to glee in his frantic effort to get away. Round we go, chasing one another, or me, once out of sight, hiding behind the dining room table as I watch him cautiously look about, his body abuzz with suspense. With perfect timing, I jump out with a blood-curdling scream, only matched by his terrified one, before he remembers we are just playing and breathlessly runs off. Then the chase is on again, and again until I crumple with exhaustion as Janet shakes her head in bemusement. The cramps hit that night. With this cast of characters, ingrates all, you can appreciate my fate. Multiply this experience by nine, and you understand my joy and my plight.

I have discovered that Grandkids bring the cycle of life full circle, returning me to that time of joy and innocence that is found only in dogs and young children. They push me to seize the moment and to let the moment occupy me. When I give myself over to their world, everything is as it should be, for I am in the timelessness of the right now: Play Time!

And so, it goes, new lives, new loves, new worries, new joys, and new memories. And it just keeps on going, spiraling outward, round and round, reminding me that just like my parents, my time is coming to an end, not necessarily soon, but inevitably on the way, as each generation gives way to the next. As I leave the company of my grandchildren, I hope I will be around to meet the adults they will become, and perhaps, their children as well.

I cannot help wondering, *When I am gone, will they leave a bouquet of memory for me?*

Chapter 33

A Second Chance for a Happy Childhood

*I*n the last quarter of my life, I'm in another love story. This one has a distinctly different quality, somewhat like the atmospheric change one experiences in moving from the glare and heat of an unremitting sun to the shade of an oak tree under which stands two chairs, a table, and a cold pitcher of Sangria. Unlike my previous romantic relationships, this story is not dramatic or eventful, and I love it that way.

Janet and I met on a social website. What attracted me, besides her appearance, was her plain-spoken profile. She had a good job, owned her home, and raised two boys, all while obtaining a master's degree. These characteristics suggested a strong work ethic, strength of character, courage, the capacity to persevere, independence, intelligence, and well-established personhood.

I email her, then gulp when she immediately suggests we talk on the phone. I call and swallow hard again when she proposes we meet in person. Already being Friday night, I suggest the following weekend. She demurs; she has plans. I suggest the weekend following that. Again, she balks, noting that is a long time off. I am confused, *What's left?* The only time I can think of is the next night. Without hesitation, she chirps, "That works fine," as if it had been my idea.

I knock on the door of her split-level brick and aluminum sided house situated in a middle-class neighborhood. The door opens, revealing Janet, bent over, struggling to keep her cat from escaping. She tilts her head up and struck by the humor of that awkward greeting, smiles a smile that threatens to give way to laughter. Along with the warmth of her humor resides the radiance of her frankly appraising eyes: one brown, the other green, both offering the warm welcome of a winter's fire.

We close-down an Italian restaurant that evening, not dancing the fandango but in animated conversation. Throughout, I keep watching, looking for pretense, or a vain woman's use of her wiles. But with Janet, what you see is what you get. I was not dumbstruck or infatuated, just relaxed, with an unexpected feeling of being at home. Given the mind-frying electric overloads of previous relationships, this is a welcome relief. Subsequently, we spend nearly every weekend together: talking, cooking, slow dancing, and eventually making love.

Some might say that Janet sounds like the safe choice of someone who now finds passion too risky. Perhaps they are right; I do not know how to gauge that. What I do *know* is that, with Janet, I experience lasting contentment that is well beyond any I have known. While other relationships offered intermittent spikes of ecstasy, they also included stomach tightening troughs of enmity, and none has come close to raising the floor of secure connection and contentment that I experience daily with Janet.

Janet's ability to be herself, her strength of character, her personhood, her unwillingness to be pushed from a point of view if the shift is not genuine, thrills me. Her straightforwardness, her willingness to confront me when unhappy with what I am doing, and to genuinely take to heart what I have to say when I am concerned by something, fills me with an exquisite feeling of love and being loved that has a tensile strength unlike any other that I have known.

Janet also brings to the relationship her phenomenal capacity to enjoy ordinary things: seasonal decorating, cooking, and spontaneous hugs and kisses.

I am astonished by her generosity of spirit and personal integrity, as well as her capacity to speak her mind, but rarely nastily. She never talks the talk; she only, without fanfare or self-promotion, walks the walk. She inhabits herself, her world, and her relationships, providing a secure and loving relationship that I have always wanted. She gives me that special place called home.

Importantly, Janet is game for going on my occasional adventures. Before we were married, she went with me, along with my daughters and son-in-law, Jason, for a ten-day sailing vacation around the Greek Isles. I hired a boat and captain, so on the cheap that I had concerns about the seaworthiness of both. The trip was wonderful. We laugh when remembering Captain George loudly announcing at 9 am each morning that it was, "Beer-O'clock!" as he cracked his first beer of the day and how he would hoot while telling the tale of an English gentleman who, when the cocktail hour arrived, would announce, "It's time for a stiffy." We smile when remembering Jason's newly discovered love of goat meat, warranting the nickname: The Goat Hunter. And sympathize, as we recall Cait bursting into tears when at a shack of a restaurant on an isolated Greek island, we so entertained the owner that he plopped a liver, dripping with its jellies, upon the table as a gift, proudly proclaiming he had just cut it from a baby goat.

But the most treasured memory occurred on the trip over. Janet and I had a seven-hour layover in Athens and caught a cab to what I promised was a renowned restaurant. The taxi dropped us off in a narrow, crowded alleyway of a street, humming with commerce, where merchants hung colorful garments and adorned makeshift shelves with items for sale. There was no restaurant to be found at the address, only a jewelry store. Janet asked, "Where's the restaurant?" Professing confusion, I commented, "It must be around here somewhere," while watching Janet's eyes being inexorably drawn to the sparkling store window. After a few minutes, her eyes alight looking at the bright objects, the restaurant momentarily forgotten, I whisper in her ear, "While you're looking, why don't you pick out a wedding ring?" Her radiant smile was all for me.

On a more recent adventure, Janet overcame her trepidation to go along with my desire to rent a trawler in Sarasota, Florida. I wanted to see if I liked cruising the intercoastal waterway; I was considering cruising the Great Loop. Several days into our excursion, we were hammered by a sudden squall, which brought rain and wind so hard that visibility dropped to near zero. As the boat rocked and swung about in the storm, life sprung one of its little surprises: The windlass (the automatic anchor release mechanism) failed. We watched helplessly as the anchor and 1500 feet of chain were lost overboard. Without the stabilizing powers of the anchor, our 25,000-pound trawler whipped around like a miniature toy before running aground.

As the storm passed, we discovered ourselves some distance from where we had been, facing 180 degrees in the opposite direction, grounded on a sandbar, and beginning to roll, not knowing if or when it would stop. Finally, it settled on a twenty-degree angle, spilling gallons of diesel fuel into the cabin. Driven out by fumes and worried about fire, we spent the night on deck, feet propped against railings to prevent us from sliding overboard. That was enough for Janet to nix any idea of traveling the Great Loop.

In my relationship with Janet, now twelve years and nine grandchildren long, our willingness to be intimate meets with consistently good results, and our connection grows, not with all the fire of Halley's comet but in a slow, steady climb. Rather than having *fallen in love*, we continue to *ascend to love*, talking, laughing, and occasionally crying, mostly in joy, sometimes, in sorrow.

Recently, Janet looked over at me, eyes welling with tears, and said, "Charlie, I'm so happy with my life, and that mainly

has to do with you. Thank you. I love you." At that, she was not
the only person with tears in her eyes.

Chapter 34

Au Revoir

Now, all these years later, as I gaze out upon the incomparable beauty of the Bush River, I imagine each of you with my mind's eye. Many of you, grown, have left home and created lives and families of your own; while others are new to the fold, your lives just beginning. I also see the many patients, my fellow travelers, who have honored me over the years by allowing me into their lives, thereby adding immeasurably to my own. And I see others still, strangers who are not strangers at all, who have stumbled upon this work and recognize some of themselves in my story and some of me in theirs.

For my part, clearing seventy, I try to pare the "to do" list of daily life and obligations to essentials, enjoying the oscillating interplay of being with others and the luxury of being with myself. Janet is about, but we each do our own thing during the day, coming together for cards, TV, and dinner in the evening, and for boat rides or the occasional trip. Over the years, I have come to appreciate how much love and the acceptance of separateness and difference go together.

Now, partially retired, I am generally able to do what I want when I want, an oddly discombobulating experience after years of maintaining stimulating identities as friend, father, therapist, author, lecturer, and mate. Although it may seem somewhat inane, I continue to ask myself, *Who am I now? Who am I becoming? Who do I want to become?*

I am not one of those people who want to *kill time* by going through the motions or by staying busy for busy's sake. I call on myself to be patient, to take one step at a time, to *be* with myself then to *go on being* with myself until I figure out where my being is going. In this way, I try to make space for whatever might emerge from within me.

Now, through the course of a day, I move from seeing a few patients to reading, to picking a guitar, to writing, swimming, or boating with Janet, finding joy in the swooping seagulls that follow our wake in shallow flight. I sit in the sunroom listening to the river lapping against the beach as the leaves of the ancient oaks whisper secrets, squirrels irreverently chatter, and scramble up tree trunks, as birds chirp and squawk. I watch geese moving along the sandy beach below my house and smile in memory at the shenanigans of Mom and Dad, now fully appreciating the problem of poop. I listen to the wind and, on those rainy days, the thrumming of the raindrops on the windowpane. All these sounds intone in the deep background of my consciousness, quieting the ghosts of decades past in a language that, like the sound of ocean waves breaking upon the beach or the rhythmic beating of a mother's heart, soothes the soul.

I look forward to visiting with my grandkids, watching the joy that lights their faces when they see me, only equaled, if not surpassed, by my delight in seeing and playing with them. But soon, tired, body aching, and mind restless with the need for adult stimulation, I am glad to get back to my more solitary pursuits.

I question myself from time to time, *Am I in the most secure position, or one from which I am guaranteed to fall? Am I in mid-leap, letting go of over-used and obsolete senses of self in search of emerging ones?* Sometimes, I know the answer; sometimes, I do not.

I think about how far I have come from those early traumas and failures. I remember in trying to understand myself that I use to ask one question at each psychoanalytic conference, hoping that these world-class thinkers could light the way, "What makes the difference between those who fall and can't get up, and those who do get up and go on to live meaningful lives?" I never did receive a satisfying answer. Then one night, while paging through a book of art, I happened upon a picture of a seventeenth-century American Indian shaman with the following caption:

"What I am trying to say is hard to tell and hard to understand...
unless, unless...
you have been yourself at the edge of the Deep Canyon and have come
back unharmed.
Maybe it all depends on something within yourself—
whether you are trying to see the Watersnake or the sacred Cornflower,
whether you go out to meet death or to Seek Life."

Shaman: The Paintings of Susan Seddon Boulet (1989)

Those words resonated within me: It depends on what you are looking for. Are *you* looking for life or death? Are *you* looking for love or hate? Are *you* engaged in a continual re-working of the unworkable past or striving to create a fresh day and future? Are *you* looking to play the music of your life like yourself, composing new melodies, or like that of your childhood, marching lockstep with your parents and their parents, and the generations that came before? The Indian shaman and the Bible agree, "Seek, and ye shall find."

Now, it is time for me to embark on my solo trip to Norfolk, Virginia, on my 25' deck boat: *Enchanted.* Norfolk is 180 nautical miles away, a 360-mile roundtrip: I feel a need to push myself again, to return to the edge of my comfort zone. To get out of my head and into the moment. I have never done anything like *this* before, but I need to clear the cobwebs that are beginning to bind, and there is nothing like a Great Adventure to do that.

I could not find anyone crazy enough to go along with me, so I am going alone. I think that turned out for the best; I hunger to be alone with myself. My main worry is that there are parts of the journey where land is not visible and where radio and cell phone reception is not available. I ask myself, "What happens if the engine throws a belt or if one of the Chesapeake Bay's infamous thunderstorms catches me?" I know what a squall can do to a twenty-five-thousand-pound trawler, what would it do to my thirty-five-hundred-pound deck boat?

Ah! These worries, these risks, they are not to be avoided; they *are* the point. The challenge they represent sharpens my thinking. Depending upon sea and weather conditions, the trip could take anywhere from eight to eighteen hours or not completed at all. I buy a spotlight in case I end up traveling after dark, double-check the safety equipment, scour marine weather forecasts, wave heights and frequency, currents, wind speed, and direction predictions, for mine is not a suicidal wish. What better way to clear a mind than dancing with Mother Nature? It all looks good, but marine forecasts can be as wrong as any other and given to sudden change.

The night before my trip, I stand alone at the end of the pier. A quarter moon graces the black-felt sky, framed by five glimmering stars rendering jeweled elegance as Rosetta color slivers the skyline. The sun had set long ago, its rays now traveling so far around the world they barely blush the edge of the night. Pilings stand tall, casting dark shadows upon the shadowed water—itself eerily still as if waiting to draw a breath. Canadian Geese caw, unseen in the distance, as they prepare for their winter migration. The pre-historic black profile of a blue heron soundlessly cuts the night in front of my eyes. I fill with gratitude.

At 6:15 am. the next morning, Janet walks me to the boat. We hug goodbye, tears in our eyes, and my heart in my throat. I start the engine, put the boat in gear, and cruise slowly away from Janet, from home, wondering if *this* will be a *last of things* as I travel toward the rising sun.

I feel so alive!

I hear my mother calling—

"Charlie, have a good life! Charlie, have a good life!"

And I hear Aunt Dot's voice echoing down through the years—

"Bon Voyage!"

A Short Course on Human Psychology

The psyche is both friend and foe developing habituated ways of thinking and feeling, and its foundational classroom is early family life. It is here that the *sense* of self and our relationship to the world begins. We absorb the early atmospheres and tensions of family life and learn lessons, not only about who we are and our place in the world, but how to get through as safely as possible. The training is often subliminal and immersive, supported by hundreds of thousands of interactions, micro-gestures, and micro-expressions that impress themselves upon the child's body and mind, influencing his *sense of self* and his place in the world.

If you doubt the power of the environment to shape you, consider how people are affected by something as ubiquitous as the climate in the part of the country in which they grew up. For the most part, Southerners enjoy the heat, and Northerners, the cold. They absorbed their surroundings, as unconsciously as they acquired their accents, and it becomes a fiercely held part of their identity.

In similar ways, we absorb the emotions, tensions, and atmospheres of family life, beginning in utero. These become foundational to the sense of self, to the sense of *Me*. Oddly, in adulthood, when this sense of self is challenged, even when for the better, it can unsettle the individual, somewhat like a sailboat begins to wobble if it loses its keel.

A patient of mine, a successful businessman, started feeling strange when driving. Unable to identify what he was feeling, he became frightened and pulled to the side of the road. There he sat. In the space thus created, he thought about what might be going on. He had grown up in a depressed and fearful family in which acknowledging, much less talking about feelings, had been completely discouraged. Now, he had just ended a toxic marriage and was on his way to celebrate this occasion and his birthday with life-long friends. As he sat observing his feeling, noticing the lifting of the weight of the marriage, and relief over the end of the fractious process of divorce, he was finally able to give his feeling a name. It was called Happy."

Another patient, a wife in couple's therapy, who had been the responsible one in her highly dysfunctional family of origin, complained bitterly about her husband's uncaring and couch potatoe ways. After months of couple's therapy, she happily began reporting positive changes: Her husband was doing more around the yard and house without having to be asked. For weeks she was excited and happy as she continued to report new gains.

Then, her tone began to change. She started questioning her husband's motivations. She would exclaim, "I know he's not doing this for me," or "He won't keep this up." But he did, and each week, her anxiety grew. I referred her for individual therapy, but that did not take. Several weeks later, she quit marital therapy in a highly agitated state. I could only imagine that in the months to come, her husband would return to his couch potatoe ways, thus allowing her to return to her familiar identity as the responsible, yet unloved, one in the relationship.

The psyche can be incredibly close-minded. It travels well-worn neuronal pathways, churning out the same familiar thoughts and feelings, and maintaining the same old storylines. The trouble sets in when we encounter the unfamiliar or unpredictable that cannot be easily shoehorned into our familiar narrative, the foundational paradigm of old. Our brains do not like uncertainty, for it challenges predictive capacities, upon which we relye to keep us safe. In this way, the lessons of childhood become the quicksand of adulthood.

Humans have a proclivity for self-deception. Indeed, it might be one of humanity's most defining traits. Contrary to what we like to think, we are often unaware of why we do what we do. Cat Scans of the brain show that often the initial mental activity that precedes an action occurs in areas of the brain outside of access to consciousness.

There is also a story of Freud who, interested in post-hypnotic suggestion, visited a clinic researching the topic. The subjects were told to open an umbrella over their head two minutes after they awakened from their trance and to forget this instruction. Each subject performed the task. The interesting thing was that when questioned about it, each immediately came up with an explanation for doing so, such as "I wanted to see how the mechanism worked," or "I wanted to see if there was a design on it." None referenced the hypnotic suggestion. Rather, each stubbornly maintained their explanation until repeatedly confronted by its inconsistencies. Moreover, when they acknowledged they did not know why they had held the umbrella over their head, and this answer was also not accepted, each subject finally recalled the post-hypnotic suggestion.

Everyone is guilty of almost instantaneously making up reasons for why they do what they do, and yet none of us is intentionally lying. It is merely our psychological defenses unconsciously at work, protecting us from vulnerability and uncertainty.

Facing the unknown is often frightening or distressing, and triggers the Generals (our defenses), as well as our familial and familiar habituated feeling states. The good news is that we are *not* the Generals; they are just one part of a multi-faceted psyche. Importantly, a different part of the unconscious mind houses the unmet yearnings and desires of childhood. The Generals, antagonistic to needfulness because it makes us vulnerable (the risk of emotional injury or loss), attack such feelings, often before they become conscious, before they can lure us into harm's way. Although this may keep us safe from acute disappointment or emotional distress, it does so at the expense of not being in touch with our feelings and our needs. Every human being is faced with this quandary: Balancing the drive for security with the pursuit of fulfillment. For my part, I had grown bone-weary of The Generals and their oppressive effects. I was no longer willing to stifle joy to avoid the return of the repressed and the distress carried with it.

Unfortunately, expanding one's capacity for happiness is not a one-and-done deal. It is an ongoing process of progress and regress, as our wants for safety and security vie with our drive for fulfillment. You may well ask, "What does this struggle look like, and how might one engage in it?"

I love the idea of unexpected, life-changing epiphanies and spiritual awakenings. But, regretfully, there is no magic way to happiness and a meaningful life; the truth is, we have to *live* our lives and confront the way we are living them. Even the most actualized individuals are not fully at peace all the time. Jesus purportedly sweated blood as he anticipated his crucifixion, and The Dalai Lama unashamedly acknowledges not always being at peace with himself.

I believe that happiness and meaning are states gained, lost, and gained again. Fortunately, we can evolve, gradually raising the floor of our contentment while continuing to shape and re-shape our ongoing *sense of self*. The price? Accepting responsibility for our lives as active agents not victims, confronting what we think, how we feel, and how we behave. It also involves overcoming the mind's tendency to automatically return to those foundational feeling states, often riven with fear or unease, but with which we so identify.

To do this, we must become aware of our prevailing feeling states, conflicts, and concerns, swapping the short-term comfort of denial or avoidance for the long-term prospect of being better able to put these recurrent issues behind us, remembered but no longer acted out. Fortunately, a small understanding of psychology can help. For example, although psychological defenses operate unconsciously, their functioning is detected whenever there is an inconsistency between our words, feelings, thoughts, or actions or when we become burdened by feelings we don't understand.

The thing to appreciate is that psychological defenses serve to minimize or negate our awareness of that which troubles us, thereby distancing us from emotional pain or distress. Here the psychoanalytic injunction to say (or think about) whatever comes to mind is helpful. This free-associative process bypasses the suppressive power of the defenses and opens us up to the subconscious.

For example, when I am feeling troubled, but cannot identify the cause, I will take a walk and think about what is going on in my life. Appreciating the minimizing effects of psychological defenses, I over-ride my tendency to edit, giving equal weight to thoughts or feelings large or small.

During one such walk, I noted that I had been ruminating about several home maintenance issues: A drip below the kitchen sink that was rotting out the floorboard; mortar coming loose between bricks on the house; and a shrub that was not faring well in the yard. Yet, none of these issues was compelling. So, I kept walking. I thought, *These thoughts don't seem to warrant my worry, so let me think about the themes. These are of things dying, breaking down or falling apart.* That is when understanding arrived. My fiftieth birthday was fast approaching, and this milestone was working me over more than I had allowed myself to know. Accepting this knowledge served to alleviate my angst for now I had identified its source and thus could begin to come to terms with it.

One reason that happiness is not a one-and-done effort is that life itself is a struggle and can be frightening. The passage of time and inevitably changing circumstances are forever creating new challenges and presenting new threats. We human beings are in constant flux, from childhood through the middle years and beyond. As we age, we face an ongoing river of necessary and unnecessary losses. In each phase of life, a whole host of new challenges arises. This is true for every age, but for the aged, time is ruthless, offering no quarter, and taking no captives. Hormonal changes, the ravages of menopause, increased risk of cancer, erectile dysfunction, the loss of lubrication and elasticity, arthritis, knee, hip, joint and foot problems, lessening stamina, and a litany of other physical issues afflict aging people, combining to create a warren of issues that foster anxiety and depression.

Add to this, that we are aware of our mortality, that our time is coming to an end, if not today, then tomorrow, and if not tomorrow later still, but that the end *is* on its way, and we have a powerful brew for unease, which, with advancing years becomes increasingly trenchant as family and friends pass away. Denial of these certainties inhibits our capacity to deal with them and leads to an evergrowing fear-ridden life. Remember the difference between the way each of my parents dealt with their lives and relationships, and how they lived their dying.

Perhaps the most difficult challenge of all in pursuing happiness and meaning is dealing with those foundational feelings, which we began experiencing in the womb, during infancy, and in early childhood that rule at the core of us, comprising default feeling states that we readily fall back into as our first organizing structures, equating these deeply rooted sensory and feeling states with "me," erroneously believing that we are finished products, incapable of changing. We say to ourselves, "That's the way I am," or "That's the way she is," as if there is no alternative.

In my view, these core feeling states reside beyond the reach of verbal therapies alone. Yet, their abiding presence can be mitigated with targeted mindfulness techniques, which help us feed the Good Wolf rather than the Evil One. Mindfulness techniques get us out of our heads and back into our body, and where life is lived: in the unself-conscious moment of the here and now as experienced in the moment-to-moment play time with young children. A list of useful techniques would include (but not be limited to) martial arts, deep breathing, meditation, yoga, painting, dance, rock climbing or merely becoming conscious of the pressure of our feet on the floor or the flow of air upon our skin, all of which help disrupt the habituated early feeling states of anxiety or depression and help raise the floor of our happiness.

Let me tell you a story to illustrate how it can work. A man is on his morning walk, takes a right turn at the next block, and continues until he unexpectedly falls into a sinkhole he did not see (the sinkhole of foundational memory). He cries out for help, someone lends assistance, and the man keeps on his way. The next day, the man repeats his journey, again on autopilot, and falls into the hole he does not see. Once more, he calls for help. Day after day, week after week, the man continues to take that right turn and fall into that hole to which he is blind. At first, he forgets about what happens each day; after all, though quite familiar, it is not a pleasant feeling. Nonetheless, as the number of falls increases and becomes an increasingly disturbing part of his life, he becomes aware of a growing weight without knowing its cause. He does not dwell on this unhappy state, choosing instead to discount his growing dysphoria.

However, eventually, he can no longer ignore his growing dread or dysphoria and begins to try to make sense of them. In this state of readiness, he finally sees the hole but, to his dismay, falls in any way; he could not stop himself. It was as if he knew no other way of being and that his feet had a mind of their own. This process, of seeing the hole and still falling in, repeats itself time and again.

Growing ever more miserable about his seeming inability to change anything, the man becomes increasingly determined to take charge of his life and his prevailing feeling states: that is his *sense of self*. One day, as he sees the hole, he adamantly forces himself to stop, recognizing that there is no external world reason to keep falling in. There, teetering on the edge, arms windmilling, he finally regains his balance. Feeling awkward with this new-found position, he takes a deep breath, looks around at his surroundings, sees everything is fine in the here and now of the moment, and then forces himself to walk around the hole, thereby rejecting the false comfort of "Better the Devil you know than the Devil you don't." Each day, the man continues his efforts to see the hole and take the route around. Sometimes he still falls in but for the most part either gets himself out quickly or walks around.

A day finally arrives in which the man becomes confident of not falling into the old and familiar trap of the hole and discovers that in some ways, the new route does not have the appeal of the old. It is like losing an old, tattered coat he has been wearing forever. He misses that familiar feeling but also remembers the cold that continually seeped in, thereby putting the attractions of the old way of being into a realistic perspective.

Then, as the man is taking his usual walk, he reaches the point of the right-hand turn and stops. He is tired of the same old route, the known and predictable, and, having gained confidence in his ability to handle new experiences, feels excited by the possibility of discovery. He ignores the right-hand turn and continues, unexpectedly feeling freer, not only more open to the world but also feeling that the world is more open to him. He feels alive.

I was working to see the sinkholes in my life. It was not enough to stop feeding the Evil Wolf, to limit the ruminations that made me anxious or depressed; it was equally important to feed the Good Wolf, to recognize the good things going on around me to which I was often impervious. Understanding that life and death dance together hand-in-hand, I recognized that if I perversely chose to focus on death to the relative exclusion of life, then that morbid view of the world would inevitably continue to color my reality.

Accordingly, I began thinking of specific things I am grateful for each day and actively returning to the here and now whenever I catch my mind returning to its darker moods. Sometimes, I think of that fisherman of long ago who told me that ninety-eight percent of what he spent his time worrying about never came to pass. Then I laugh and move on with my day.

Just yesterday, I was taking an afternoon walk, the sun warming my back and casting my shadow long when a butterfly shadow appeared in dancing flight above my right shoulder. Our shadows walked together for quite a while, my heart soaring on the wings of the butterfly's dance before its shadow flitted away.

Over the last several weeks, I noticed a praying mantis had taken up residence on the side of my hummingbird feeder. I get such a kick out of it as it just sits there, even allowing me to touch it without fleeing.

Then, there are the hummingbirds who, if I stand very still, come within inches of my face, hovering there, staring at me as the thrumming of their wings fills my ears, and their beautiful colors and darting movements delight my eyes.

There is also the huge Grasshopper, undoubtedly a grandfather to his kind. I was on a ladder, drilling holes in the brick-and-mortar wall of my house to put up a shutter when I noticed him painstakingly trundling along the many feet of wall to join me. I was incredulous as he lumbered ever nearer across that expanse, totally ignoring the clamor of the drill, and the dust and bits of brick erupting volcanically from the hole. One slow, ponderous step at a time, he kept coming. In homage and respect, I turned off the drill and removed the bit from the hole. The Grasshopper, thoroughly unimpressed by my consideration, seemingly assured that this was the only possible course of action I could take, continued relentlessly forward, finally sidled-up to the hole, and then placed his body astride it, as if in protection.

Perched on my ladder, my face mere inches from him, I could only marvel. Whatever happened to this Granddaddy Grasshopper's survival instinct? Why had it dared to approach this human being and all the sound and fury in such unconcerned fashion? I watched him for a while and then reached out with my finger and played with his whiskers. Unperturbed, he continued to sit like a grasshopper Buddha. So, there we sat together, two grandfathers communing in the warmth of the sun. I did not know how long he planned to stay, but that did not matter; I would wait as necessary: I knew holiness when I saw it. Eventually, for reasons unclear to me, Grasshopper decided it was time to move on. He lifted himself and, in his signature movement, trundled away, back across the expanse of the brick wall, around the corner of the house, and out of my life. I felt blessed by his visit, which I suspect was of no surprise to him at all.

Earlier this summer, driving home from dinner, the last of the light leaching from the sky, Janet and I passed a farmer's field. There, a sight filled our field of vision and claimed our hearts. Lifting from the tall grass were hundreds of thousands of fireflies, twinkling into the night like sparks from a giant bonfire. Overcome, I pulled to the side of the road, turned the engine off, and sat silently, absorbing the sparkling spectacle and allowing myself to become one with it. A few minutes later, another car pulled over in the distance, as drawn to the incredible display as we.

During each of these events, dark feelings were nowhere to be found. Instead, they reminded me that the drama and ugliness we humans create in our minds stand as nothing against the timeless beauty of nature and, if spiritual, God's touch if only we will allow it.

These days, I work to actively recognize the large and small bounties that fill my life daily. Each morning my cat, Emma, rushes to the top of the steps as I descend. She then pokes her head through the balustrades, so we can rub our heads together before we each go on with our day.

Similar moments of joyful connection result from getting together with family and friends, and those superheroes called my grandchildren, each a tributary to what is increasingly becoming the spring-fed pond of my life.

Recently, Chandler emailed me, asking to make a father-son trip together; my heart swelled with a feeling of fulfillment. Then Keeley calls telling me Cormac has recently become a Baltimore Ravens fan and would like to watch the game with me. How does it get any better than that?

And, every day, if something happens that pulls on a thread of anxious or depressive thought, I consider it but also ask, *Am I being lazy, running on autopilot, resurrecting old familial and familiar ways of feeling and being? Am I falling back into timeworn internal narratives in defense against a future unknown?* When I suspect that is the case, I gently chastise myself, *How boring and uncreative can I be, recurrently re-enacting that colorless, dull one-act play?* Then I return to the moment in my day.

In such ways, I strive to walk my talk, sometimes failing, but always returning to trying again. Over the years, this has become ever easier and rewarding.

Many people tell themselves or others they are happy, but I am dubious. I often find such people rather shallow, not because they claim happiness, but because of their steadfast focus on having a good time or whooping it up while sharing little of their interior lives. I suspect that what they are talking about is not the kind of deep-rooted happiness that is important to me, but the brittle *happiness* derived from psychological defenses that avoid, deny or minimize one's concerns. Nor am I talking about a feeling of supposed fulfillment derived from constant fine dining or five-star travel, the accumulation of things, or the idea that if everything looks good, it is good. I am also not talking about people-pleasing or the maintaining of the illusion of harmony via the avoidance of conflict, or about those people who consider themselves happy only because they have never entertained a suicidal thought. You know, people who repeatedly say when asked how they're doing, "Okay. Can't complain," but never say, "The most astonishing thing happened yesterday…"

What *I am* talking about is a kind of happiness that derives exactly from having confronted that which ails us, that which has kept us up in the middle of the night or had us harbor grievances or led to a disconnect from our others. The happiness and contentment I am talking about includes acknowledging the finiteness of all things, including ourselves, and thereby being fully aware that there is *a last of things*. There will inevitably be that last kiss, that final hug, the permanent leaving of a place called home. I'm talking about a sense of appreciation that springs from the watercolors of the sunset, vivified precisely because of your awareness that this may be the last sunset shared with another or the final sunset beheld by oneself.

Paradoxically, I believe it is in embracing our finiteness, our mortality, the temporariness of all things that gives life its meaning and value. This striving to be a sentient being is life itself, by its nature fluid, in near-constant movement, replete with gains and losses, joys and sadness, moments of falling off track and getting back on. What is essential is not controlling the experience but the process itself, of stringing as many such moments of meaning and aliveness together as possible, then, when the string breaks, beginning anew.

I think if there is any final test of how well we have lived our lives, it will be in the way we live our dying. Choose aliveness. Leap while you have the strength.

THE END

Note to the reader: Thank you for reading, *As Happy as I can Stand.*
please take a moment to share your experience with others by
submitting a review. The stigmatization of mental/emotional
difficulties is ongoing. The only way to lessen it is by an increasing
public dialogue. If you wish to contact me directly:
charlesmccormack81@gmail.com.
With heartfelt thanks,

Charles McCormack

Charles McCormack, MA, MSW, LCSW-C, with his grandson, Benjamin, a first grader and a winner of the MLK Jr. World Peace Rose Garden contest in Atlanta, GA, for the following poem commemorated with a plaque at the MLK National Historic site.

Peace is love

Peace is calm and kind

Peace is not grumpy or sad

Or anger or yelling

It's nice and happy

And helpful too

Peace is caring

Charles McCormack holds master's degrees in Psychology and Clinical Social Work. Over his forty-five-year career, he has worked in drug treatment, psychiatric day and evening hospitals, inner-city family violence, and sexual abuse treatment programs. In 1982 McCormack began working in long-term inpatient treatment and in 1988 became the Senior Social Worker of Adult Long-term Inpatient Services of Sheppard-Pratt Hospital.

In 1989, McCormack authored the paper *The Borderline/Schizoid Marriage: The Holding Environment as an Essential Treatment Construct,* translating lessons learned in inpatient care to outpatient practice. In 1990, the Washington School of Psychiatry invited McCormack to speak at their annual conference and subsequently to join the faculty. In 1994, McCormack was named the Clinician of the Year by the Maryland Society of Clinical Social Workers. In 2000 he published the book *Treating Borderline States in Marriage: Dealing with Oppositionalism, Ruthless Aggression, and Severe Resistance.*

In 2006 McCormack graduated from The New Directions Writing from a Psychoanalytic Perspective program of the Washington Center for Psychoanalysis and in 2016 began writing the first edition of Hatching Charlie, using the story of his life to illustrate the effects of childhood emotional and physical abuse and abandonment on the child and later adult. Finally, McCormack illuminates the benefits of psychotherapy, and mindfulness practices, to, if not completely

transcend the past, make significant strides beyond it.